Power and Law in International Society

When studying international law, there is often a risk of focusing entirely on the content of international rules (i.e. regimes), and ignoring why these regimes exist and to what extent the rules affect state behavior. Similarly, international relations studies can focus so much on theories based on the distribution of power among states that it overlooks the existence and relevance of the rules of international law. Both approaches hold their dangers. The overlooking of international relations risks assuming that states actually follow international law, and discounting the specific rules of international law makes it difficult for readers to understand the impact of the rules in more than a superficial manner.

This book unifies international law and international relations by exploring how international law and its institutions may be relevant and how it influences the course of international relations in international trade, protection of the environment, human rights, international criminal justice and the use of force.

As a study on the intersection of power and law, this book will be of great interest and use to scholars and students of international law, international relations, political science, international trade, and conflict resolution.

Mark Klamberg is an Associate Professor in International Law at Uppsala University, Sweden.

Routledge Research in International Law

Available:

International Law and the Third World
Reshaping Justice
Edited by Richard Falk, Balakrishnan Rajagopal and Jacqueline Stevens

International Legal Theory
Essays and Engagements, 1966–2006
Nicholas Onuf

The Problem of Enforcement in International Law
Countermeasures, the Non-Injured State and the Idea of International Community
Elena Katselli Proukaki

International Economic Actors and Human Rights
Adam McBeth

The Law of Consular Access
A Documentary Guide
John Quigley, William J. Aceves and S. Adele Shank

State Accountability under International Law
Holding States Accountable for a Breach of Jus Cogens Norms
Lisa Yarwood

International Organizations and the Idea of Autonomy
Institutional Independence in the International Legal Order
Edited by Richard Collins and Nigel D. White

Self-Determination in the Post-9/11 Era
Elizabeth Chadwick

Participants in the International Legal System
Multiple Perspectives on Non-State Actors in International Law
Jean d'Aspremont

Sovereignty and Jurisdiction in the Airspace and Outer Space
Legal Criteria for Spatial Delimitation
Gbenga Oduntan

International Law in a Multipolar World
Edited by Matthew Happold

The Law on the Use of Force
A Feminist Analysis
Gina Heathcote

The ICJ and the Development of International Law
The Lasting Impact of the Corfu Channel Case
Edited by Karine Bannelier, Théodore Christakis and Sarah Heathcote

UNHCR and International Refugee Law
From Treaties to Innovation
Corinne Lewis

Asian Approaches to International Law and the Legacy of Colonialism
The Law of the Sea, Territorial Disputes and International Dispute Settlement
Edited by Jin-Hyun Paik, Seok-Woo Lee, Kevin Y L Tan

The Right to Self-determination Under International Law
"Selfistans," Secession, and the Rule of the Great Powers
Milena Sterio

Reforming the UN Security Council Membership
The Illusion of Representativeness
Sabine Hassler

Threats of Force
International Law and Strategy
Francis Grimal

The Changing Role of Nationality in International Law
Edited by Alessandra Annoni and Serena Forlati

Criminal Responsibility for the Crime of Aggression
Patrycja Grzebyk

Regional Maintenance of Peace and Security under International Law
The Distorted Mirror
Dace Winther

International Law-Making
Essays in Honour of Jan Klabbers
Edited by Rain Liivoja and Jarna Petman

Resolving Claims to Self-Determination
Is There a Role of the International Court of Justice?
Andrew Coleman

The Rise of Tamil Separatism in Sri Lanka
From Communalism to Secession
Gnanapala Welhengama and Nirmala Pillay

The United Nations and Collective Security
Gary Wilson

Justice for Victims before the International Criminal Court
Luke Moffett

Public-Private Partnerships and Responsibility under International Law
A Global Health Perspective
Lisa Clarke

Cultural Diversity in International Law
The Effectiveness of the UNESCO Convention on the Protection and Promotion of the Diversity of Cultural Expressions
Edited by Lilian Hanania

Incitement in International Law
Wibke K. Timmermann

The Cuban Embargo under International Law
El Bloqueo
Nigel D. White

Resisting United Nations Security Council Resolutions
Sufyan Droubi

The Changing Nature of Customary International Law
Methods of Interpreting the Concept of Custom in International Criminal Tribunals
Noora Arajärvi

Power and Law in International Society
International Relations as the Sociology of International Law
Mark Klamberg

Forthcoming titles in this series include:

Technology and the Law on the Use of Force
New Security Challenges in the Twenty First Century
Jackson Maogoto

International Law and Boundary Disputes in Africa
Gbenga Oduntan

Justice in International Law
The Legal, Political, and Moral Dimensions of Indigenous Peoples' Rights
Mauro Barelli

Means of Transportation and Registration of Nationality
Transportation Register by International Organizations
Vincent P. Cogliati-Bantz

The International Criminal Court in Search of its Purpose and Identity
Edited by Triestino Mariniello

The Responsibility to Protect in International Law
An Emerging Paradigm Shift
Susan Breau

Legal Accountability and Britain's Wars 2000-2014
Peter Rowe

Power and Law in International Society

International Relations as the Sociology of International Law

Mark Klamberg

Routledge
Taylor & Francis Group
LONDON AND NEW YORK

First published 2015
by Routledge
2 Park Square, Milton Park, Abingdon, Oxfordshire, OX14 4RN

and by Routledge
711 Third Avenue, New York, NY 10017

First issued in paperback 2016

Routledge is an imprint of the Taylor & Francis Group, an informa business

British Library Cataloguing in Publication Data
A catalogue record for this book is available from the British Library

Library of Congress Cataloging-in-Publication Data
A catalogue record has been requested for this book

ISBN: 978-1-138-70195-3 (pbk)
ISBN: 978-1-138-80460-9 (hbk)

Typeset in 11/12 Garamond 3 LT Std by
Servis Filmsetting Ltd, Stockport, Cheshire

Contents

Preface

What legal scholarship is or should be is a question that may arise in different contexts. The student aspiring to attain a law degree or a practitioner may be content with identifying the relevant legal rules and the means to interpret these rules, while studies and research at the more advanced level require a greater sophistication in their methods and perspectives. In legal research, there is often a challenge to go beyond the merely descriptive, to include more analytical and critical approaches. There are arguably different suitable ways of meeting this challenge. We can, for example, make use of comparative studies, discuss the virtues of different schools and approaches to legal sources, examine the coherence and consistency of legal frameworks and even make suggestions on how the law should be changed. What is striking is the fact that although legal scholars deal with societal matters that are the concern of other academic fields, we use methodologies quite different from social sciences. Consider how universities and academic faculties are organized – law is placed in a separate realm, outside the social sciences. Why?

The separation of law faculties and thus also its research from other social sciences can be seen as both a strength and a weakness. By having a distinct methodology, legal scholars add value and create unique insights. However, if we distance ourselves too much from other fields, we may have difficulty in explaining why and how legal scholarship is a discipline of relevance and what relationship it has to its object of study – societal affairs. Legal scholars tend to focus on the content of legal rules, too often ignoring questions of whether the rules are reasonable and whether they actually have an impact on society. This dilemma becomes even more pertinent within international legal scholarship due to the different nature of the legal sources compared to domestic legal systems. This book seeks to explain the relationship between international legal scholarship and social sciences. Are we offering competitive, mutually exclusive accounts of reality or complementary narratives for the same social phenomena?

The seed for the current book was first planted just before starting university and having to choose between studying law or political science. In the end I did both, but gravitated more towards law. Having zig-zagged between different fields in academia and professional work, this book is an attempt to connect the dots that at first appeared interesting and puzzling in an isolated setting, but now make more sense when different fields and experiences are connected.

I wish to express my gratitude to Idris Ahmedi, Mauro Zamboni, Pål Wrange, Jonas Tallberg, Pål Levin, Niklas Bremberg, Malena Britz, Johan Karlsson Schaffer, David Langlet, Lisa Carlsson and Andrea Feuer who provided helpful comments on the project, the manuscript or parts thereof at various stages in its development. As far as shortcomings are concerned, they are all attributable to the author.

The language of the present study has benefited greatly from the competent editing by Sally Longworth and the funds provided for that purpose by Emil Heijnes Stiftelse.

Lastly, I dedicate the present book to my loving wife, Birgitta, and our daughters Stella and Olivia.

Mark Klamberg
Uppsala, 8 December 2014

Table of cases

Abbreviations

ACHPR	African Charter on Human and Peoples' Rights
ACtHPR	African Court of Human and Peoples' Rights
AmCHR	American Convention on Human Rights
CAR	Central African Republic
CAT	Convention Against Torture
CEDAW	Convention on the Elimination of All Forms of Discrimination against Women
CERD	Convention on the Elimination of All Forms of Racial Discrimination
CITES	Secretariat for the Convention on the International Trade in Endangered Species of Wild Fauna and Flora
COP	Conference of the Parties
DRC	Democratic Republic of the Congo
DSB	Dispute Settlement Body (of the WTO)
DSU	Dispute Settlement Understanding (of the WTO)
ECHR	European Convention for the Protection of Human Rights and Fundamental Freedoms
ECtHR	European Court of Human Rights
EU	European Union
FAO	United Nations Food and Agriculture Organization
GATT	General Agreement on Tariffs and Trade
GSP	Generalized System of Preferences
HRC	Human Rights Council
IACtHR	Inter-American Court of Human Rights
IACmHR	Inter-American Commission on Human Rights
ICC	International Criminal Court
ICCPR	International Covenant on Civil and Political Rights
ICESCR	International Covenant on Economic, Social and Cultural Rights
ICISS	International Commission on Intervention and State Sovereignty
ICJ	International Court of Justice
ICTR	International Criminal Tribunal for Rwanda
ICTY	International Criminal Tribunal for the former Yugoslavia

IGO	Intergovernmental Organization
ILC	International Law Commission
ITLOS	International Tribunal for the Law of the Sea
LDC	Less Developed Country
MDSD	Most Different Systems Design
MFN	Most Favored Nation
MICT	Mechanism for International Criminal Tribunals
MOP	Meeting of the Parties
MSSD	Most Similar Systems Design
NAAEC	North American Agreement on Environmental Cooperation
NATO	North Atlantic Treaty Organization
NGO	Non-governmental organization
OAS	Organization of American States
P-5	Permanent five members of the United Nations Security Council
R2P	Responsibility to Protect
RPE	Rules of Procedure and Evidence
TNC	Transnational Corporations
TRIPS	Agreement on Trade-Related Aspects of Intellectual Property Rights
UK	United Kingdom of Great Britain and Northern Ireland
UN	United Nations
UNCLOS	United Nations Convention on the Law of the Sea
UNFCCC	UN Framework Convention on Climate Change
UNGA	United Nations General Assembly
US	United States of America
VCLT	Vienna Convention on the Law of Treaties
WTO	World Trade Organization

1 International law as a leap of faith?

There is a need for international law scholars to engage in interdisciplinary collaboration. Even though international law scholars often are aware of the fact that law is only one of many factors affecting individual and collective action, we too often restrict our enquiries to the content of the law, with the tacit assumption that the law will be enforced. At the other end of the spectrum, international relations scholars belonging to the realist camp perceive international law as a mere component in the struggle of states for power or security, devoid of non-instrumental significance or prescriptive worth. Little to no consideration is therefore afforded to the content of international law or to facts which challenge this narrow view. As asserted by Henkin, "almost all nations observe almost all principles of international law and almost all of their obligations almost all of the time",[1] but it is difficult to obtain evidence and to evaluate the influence of international law.

Is the supposed relevance of international law therefore a leap of faith? Is international law a religion where we are supposed to treat vital state interests, ultimately the survival of nations, as a matter of belief? International law may at times mandate states to take action or abstain from doing so, which may contradict states' political or economic interests. Should states obey the law in the blind faith that other states will do likewise? Belief in god is sometimes portrayed as an all-or-nothing affair. In a similar way, is the existence of international law a digital choice between utopian idealism and apologetic realism? Fortunately, as this book argues, the study of international law does not need and should not be regarded as a religion. As Gardner argues, "Law is not God and happily lawyers need not, in their professional capacity, be true believers".[2] The question of legal compliance at the international level has over the years been treated as a religious, moral and philosophical question,

1 Piper, Don C., 'Determining State Adherence to International Law', 12 *Journal of Conflict Resolution* (1968) 398–401, p. 399; Henkin, Louis, *How Nations Behave* (2nd edn, New York, NY: Columbia University Press, 1979), pp. 26, 44, 46–47 and 246.

2 Gardner, John, *Law as a Leap of Faith* (Oxford: Oxford University Press, 2012), pp. 6, 7 and 19. On p. 67 Gardner even argues that international law is "a borderline case of a legal system".

and only recently as an empirical question.[3] Consistent with this development, it is argued in this book that international legal scholarship to a larger extent should use empirical techniques and relate to international relations theories.

Klabbers warns against fully-fledged interdisciplinary projects, such as between international law and international relations. His main argument is that "appeals for interdisciplinarity, however laudable in the abstract, carry a serious risk of reproducing, or even strengthening, existing power configurations".[4] In other words, he argues that interdisciplinarity does not necessarily create a better understanding of international law. He also notes that "[i]nterdisciplinarity often presumes a flat, one-dimensional vision of the discipline-to-relate-with, yet such a one-dimensional view will rarely, if ever, be persuasive".[5] The present book attempts to avoid this specific pitfall by discussing several international relations approaches.[6] States accept international regimes—delineated areas of rule-governed activity—in the international system. This is a puzzle insofar as the international system is anarchic (without a ruler). How is it possible to have rules without a central authority to legislate, adjudicate and enforce international law? Why should states consider rules when they balance power and/or threats or pursue ideological aims? Why and when do states accept international legal regimes when their autonomy would be less constrained by avoiding legalization?[7] How do we account for the willingness of major powers to invest resources in regimes, if such regimes are lacking in significance?[8]

As indicated above, the rationale behind this book is that international law literature tends to focus on the content of international rules (or regimes, as referred to in international relations scholarship) but have a tendency to ignore why these rules exist and to what extent they actually affect state behavior. The assumption is that states follow international law when the reality sometimes tells us differently. In its extreme form, legal scholarship operates in a "social, economic and political vacuum".[9] Turning to international relations literature, some scholars focus on theories based on the distribution of power

3 Koh, Harold Hongju, 'Why Do Nations Obey International Law?', 106 *The Yale Law Journal* (1997) 2599–2659, p. 2604.

4 Klabbers, Jan, 'The Relative Autonomy of International Law or The Forgotten Politics of Interdisciplinarity', 1 *Journal of International Law & International Relations* (2004) 35–48, pp. 35–36.

5 Ibid, pp. 37–38.

6 Ibid, pp. 41–42.

7 Abbott, Kenneth W. et al., 'The Concept of Legalization' in Goldstein, Judith L. et al. (eds), *Legalization and World Politics* (Cambridge, MA and London: MIT Press, 2001), pp. 17–35, p. 7.

8 Keohane, Robert O. and Martin, Lisa L., 'The Promise of Institutionalist Theory', 20 *International Security* (1995) 39–51, p. 40 in a rejoinder to Mearsheimer.

9 Smits, Jan M., 'Redfining Normative Legal Science; Towards an Argumentative Discipline' in Coomans, Fons, Grünfeld, Fred and Kamminga, Menno T. (eds), *Methods of Human Rights Research* (Antwerp; Oxford: Intersentia, 2009), pp. 45–58, pp. 46–48.

among states, ignoring or questioning whether international law is of any relevance.[10] International relations scholars who acknowledge the existence and relevance of international law tend to describe the regimes in a cursory manner. This means that it is difficult for readers to understand international law in more than a superficial manner. In other words, there is a lack of precision when they discuss such matters. Thus, existing research often fails to discuss in a unified context the two concepts of power and law, and how they interrelate to each other in more detail. This book covers theories of international relations, international law and formal institutions, as well as an account of empirical research on the relevance of international law on the behavior of states. It does not aim to give a full account of all the details of the regimes surveyed. Rather, it is a snap-shot of some of the critical aspects of international relations and international law.

The aim of this book is to assess how international law and its institutions may be relevant and influence the course of international relations. In this, it is a study on the relationship between power and law. Five regimes are analyzed: international trade, environmental protection, human rights, international criminal justice and the use of force. This book conveys two main arguments. First, it is argued that variations in the degree of legalization between different regimes concern to a lesser extent whether states have consented to legal obligations, but rather on who has the power to interpret and enforce the obligations. States have consented, to varying extents, to general rules and exceptions on the five regimes covered in this book. The question is who decides whether it is the general rules or the exceptions that are applicable in a given situation and how are such decisions enforced? States are, arguably, unwilling to delegate the powers of interpretation and implementation to a third party when their own survival is at issue. Second, it is argued that international relations—to the extent it considers the impact and relevance of legal rules—is the sociology of international law.

To examine whether and how international law influences state behavior does not mean that decision-makers and international judges should ignore the content of law.[11] These are two different perspectives with different purposes.

The present book has a differentiated approach to the sub-components, institutions and regimes of the international system and international law. The differentiated approach is used to analyze the relationship between politics and law in relation to the five abovementioned regimes. This sample is done so as to represent one area of high politics (the use of force), one area which concerns technical matters (trade law) and areas between those two ends of the spectrum (environmental protection, human rights, international criminal justice). This characterization of high politics on the one hand and technical matters on the other is revisited in sections 2.1.1 and 2.3.

10 Henkin, 1979, p. 3.

11 Compare with Thirlway, Hugo, *The Sources of International Law* (Oxford University Press, 2014), p. 203.

Chapter 1 briefly explains why there is a need to discuss the content of international regimes, provides a definition of international regimes and introduces a framework on how different international regimes may be compared, analyzed and understood. Chapter 2 describes different scholarly approaches within the fields of international relations and international law towards regimes, power and law. Chapter 3 discusses trade law with a particular focus on the General Agreement on Tariffs and Trade (GATT). Chapter 4 deals with environmental protection, looking particularly at the obligation of states to ensure that activities within their jurisdiction and control respect the environment of other states. The discussion in Chapter 5 on human rights is primarily be based on the nine "core" international human treaties of the United Nations (UN) and the three regional treaties of Europe, Africa and America. Chapter 6 examines international criminal justice, namely how it is established in the legal framework of the International Criminal Tribunal for Rwanda (ICTR), the International Criminal Tribunal for the former Yugoslavia (ICTY) and the International Criminal Court (ICC). Chapter 7 deals with the use of force, which covers the relevant rules in the UN Charter and international customary law, as well as the role of the UN Security Council.

The analysis in Chapters 3–7 is structured in the same way and seeks to provide answers to the following questions. First, the potential objectives of the international regimes outlined are considered. By examining the function of the regimes, it may be possible to understand why states accept regimes and constraints. Second, the degree of legalization of these international regimes is analyzed. This is measured in four dimensions: obligation, precision, delegation and state acceptance. Each international regime considered in the study is ranked pursuant to one of 16 combinations on the forms of international legalization described in section 1.2.1.5. Third, attention is given to gender bias in the surveyed regimes. Fourth, what processes and mechanisms for creating and enforcing law in the surveyed regimes is identified, including the role of non-state actors. Lastly, analysis of any identified differences between the regimes in relation to how power and law has been balanced is presented, with possible explanations for such differences. Particular attention is given in this as to whether a dominant state or hegemon had particular influence over emergence and design of the regimes surveyed.[12] Answering these questions contributes to understanding whether it is possible to have rules without a central authority to legislate, adjudicate and enforce international law.

The analysis in Chapters 3–7 is synthesized in Chapter 8, in which the overall conclusions of the study are presented.

12 Tallberg, Jonas and McCall Smith, James, 'Dispute settlement in world politics: States, supranational prosecutors, and compliance' *European Journal of International Relations* (2012) 1–27, p. 4.

1.1 Defining regimes

International relations scholars use terms such as "institutions", "regimes", "norms" and "organizations", rather than "treaties" and "international customary law".[13] Krasner has defined regimes as, "sets of implicit or explicit principles, norms, rules, and decision-making procedures around which actors' expectations converge in a given area of international relations".[14] Norms and principles define the essential character of a regime. This broad definition of regimes allows a shift of the focus of inquiry from the functioning of international organizations *per se* to the broader phenomenon of international cooperation.[15] Finlayson and Zacher hold that the principles of a regime are those prevailing beliefs that underlie states' policy orientations to a variety of issue areas. Principles may provide explanations for states' acceptance of behavioral prescriptions and proscriptions in an area of international relations, but they are not part of a regulatory framework *per se*. Norms specify general standards of behavior, and identify the obligations of states. Finlayson and Zacher divide them into substantive norms, which provide standards for drawing up specific behavioral prescriptions, and procedural norms, which provide guidelines regarding how states should design and use decision-making mechanisms. They argue that norms can be distinguished according to whether they are derived from the traditional structure of international politics (sovereignty norms), or from international interdependencies in particular issue areas that incline states to maximize welfare through collaboration (interdependence norms).[16]

Hafner-Burton, Victor and Lupu have noted that the functional perspective in studying international cooperation has been a productive way to generate hypotheses and focus empirical research on particular, practical aspects of international cooperation—including how the design of legal procedures and organizations affects outcomes.[17] Ginsburg and Shaffer argue that in many situations, problem-focused and power-based explanations may both have

13 Adamson, Fiona B. and Sriram, Chandra Lekha, 'Perspectives in International Law in International Relations' in Başak, Çali (ed), *International Law for International Relations* (Oxford: Oxford University Press, 2010), pp. 25–45, p. 25.

14 Krasner, Stephen D., 'Structural causes and regime consequences: regimes as intervening variables' in Krasner, Stephen D. (ed), *International Regimes* (Ithaca, NY and London: Cornell University Press, 1983), pp. 1–21, p. 2; see similar definition of international institutions in Goldstein, Judith L., Kahler, Miles and Keohane, Robert O., 'Introduction: Legalization and World Politics' in Goldstein, Judith L. et al. (eds), *Legalization and World Politics* (Cambridge, MA and London: MIT Press, 2001), pp. 1–15, p. 3.

15 Koh, 1997, p. 2625.

16 Finlayson, Jock A. and Zacher, Mark W., 'The GATT and the regulation of trade barriers: regime dynamics and functions' in Krasner, Stephen D. (ed), *International Regimes* (Ithaca, NY and London: Cornell University Press, 1983), pp. 273–314, p. 276.

17 Hafner-Burton, Emilie M., Victor, David G. and Lupu, Yonatan, 'Political Science Research on International Law: The State of the Field', 106 *American Journal of International Law* (2012) 47–97, p. 81.

relevance.[18] Moreover, most empirical research on international cooperation is organized on a functional basis by issue area—such as trade, human rights, arms control or the environment.[19] This approach to regimes is revisited later in the present book.[20]

1.2 How to compare legal regimes

1.2.1 Dimensions of legalization

Abbott, Keohane, Moravcsik, Slaughter and Snidal (henceforth Abbott and others) argue that three criteria are relevant when comparing international legal regimes: obligation, precision and delegation.[21] This typology on the dimensions of legalization is illustrated in Figure 1.1.

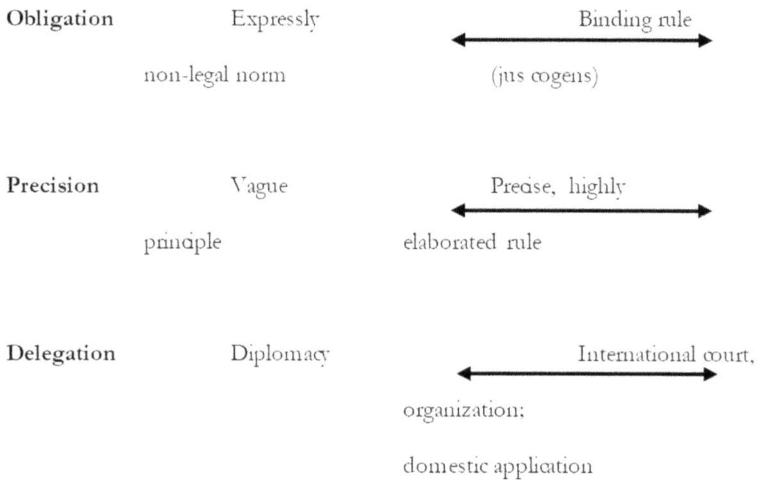

Figure 1.1 Dimensions of legalization

This book adopts the same approach with three changes: (a) obligation is primarily perceived as binary dimension and not as a continuum (section 1.2.1.1); (b) the additional criteria of acceptance of states is also used (section 1.2.1.4); and (c) the dichotomy "centralized system" versus "anarchy" is used instead of the ideal types "hard law" versus "anarchy" (section 1.2.1.5).

18 Ginsburg, Tom and Shaffer, Gregory, 'How Does International Law Work: What Empirical Research Shows' in Cane, Peter and Kritzer, Herbert (eds), *Oxford Handbook of Empirical Legal Studies* (Oxford: Oxford University Press, 2010), pp. 753–784, p. 756.

19 Hafner-Burton, Victor and Lupu, 2012, pp. 60–61.

20 Sections 2.1.2 on liberal institutionalism, 2.2.1 on the objectives of international law, 2.2.2 on legal fragmentation, 2.4 on the sociological study of international law

21 Abbott et al., 2001, pp. 17, 20 and 28; Goldstein et al., 2001, p. 3 who use the concept "international institutions".

1.2.1.1 Obligation

Obligation means that states or other actors are bound by a rule or commitment or by a set of rules or commitments. Fully legalized institutions bind states through law: their behavior is subject to scrutiny under the general rules, procedures and discourse of international law and, often, domestic law. Abbott and others provide the following indicators (operationalization) of obligation (see Table 1.1):[22]

Table 1.1 Indicators of obligation

High
Unconditional obligation
Political treaty
National reservations on specific obligations
Hortatory obligations
Norms adopted without law-making authority: recommendations and guidelines
Explicit negation of intent to be legally bound
Low

Abbott and others describe this as a "spectrum",[23] and Table 1.1 suggests that obligation is a continuum where there is "hard law" and "soft law". However, from a strict legal positivist perspective, either there is a legal obligation or there is not. Obligations under "soft law" are arguably a contradiction in terms.[24] Although norms characterized as "soft law" may be invoked by states and, as such, have some relevance, under this reasoning they tend to undermine the distinction between binding legal obligations and policy statements. An alternative would thus be to treat obligation as a binary dimension and not as a continuum. Article 38 of the International Court of Justice (ICJ) Statute is generally regarded as a complete statement of the sources of international law. The primary sources of international law are treaties, customary international law and general principles of law. A treaty is an international agreement concluded between two or more states. Customary international law consists of two elements: *usus* (consistent and general state practice) and *opinio juris* (recognition of states that a certain practice is obligatory). The third source, general principles of law, is ambiguous and contentious among legal scholars. A reasonable understanding is that general principles of law differ from other sources of law in the sense that they are not self-supporting as a source of law in themselves. They derive their normativity from other sources

22 Abbott et al., 2001, pp. 17 and 24–28.
23 Abbott et al., 2001, p. 26.
24 Weil, Prosper, 'Towards Relative Normativity in International Law', 77 *American Journal of International Law* (1983) 413–442, pp. 414, footnotes 7 and 416; and Stenhammar, Fredrik, *Riktade FN-sanktioner och rule of law i folkrätten* (Stockholm: Jure, 2008), pp. 42–47. Compare with Abbott, Kenneth W. and Snidal, Duncan, 'Hard and soft law' in Goldstein, Judith L. et al. (eds), *Legalization and World Politics* (Cambridge, MA and London: MIT Press, 2001), pp. 37–72.

of law, which may include treaty law, custom and national law but not natural law.[25] The extent to which "soft law" is intended to express vagueness in the rule's area of application[26] may, instead, be expressed in terms of "precision". There is debate among legal scholars whether treaty law or customary international law is likely to have the strongest impact on actual state practice.[27]

Hafner-Burton, Victor and Lupu notes challenge this strict legalistic approach, arguing that a central finding of political scientists:

> is that the choice of soft law does not necessarily reflect a failure to agree on hard law. Rather, states often favor soft law because it is less costly to negotiate, more adaptive in the face of uncertainty, and more readily adjusted to facilitate compromise between actors with differing interests and degrees of power. Indeed, these same factors explain why, looking across many areas of human interaction, contracts are often incomplete. Consequently, in such settings, soft law instruments not only are more convenient but can also be more effective than binding agreements.[28]

1.2.1.2 Precision

Precision means that the rules unambiguously define the conduct they require, authorize or proscribe. In other words, precision narrows the scope of reasonable interpretation. Disorder in international society does not necessarily reflect violation or non-existence of international law. Instead, it could reflect different views about an uncertain law.[29] Abbott and others operationalize precision in the following manner (see Table 1.2):[30]

25 Klamberg, Mark, *Evidence in International Criminal Trials: Confronting Legal Gaps and the Reconstruction of Disputed Events* (Leiden: Martinus Nijhoff Publishers, 2013), pp. 29–30.

26 Klabbers, Jan, 'Redundancy of Soft Law', 65 *Nordic Journal of International Law* (1996) 167–182, p. 168: "The term soft law … may concern … even the more flexible provisions of otherwise hard treaties", and pp. 179 and 181: "All this seems to drive us inevitably into the embrace of the binary code, which thinks only in terms of legal and illegal, binding and non-binding, black and white … Our binary law is well capable of handling all kinds of subtleties and sensitivities; within the binary mode, law can be more or less specific, more or less exact, more or less determinate, more or less wide in scope, more or less pressing, more or less serious, more or less far-reaching; the only thing it cannot be is more or less binding."

27 Kennedy, David, 'When Renewal Repeats: Thinking Against the Box', 32 *New York University Journal of International Law and Politics* (2000) 335–500, p. 352; Goodman, Ryan and Jinks, Derek, 'How to Influence States: Socialization and International Human Rights Law', 54 *Duke Law Journal* (2004) 621–703, pp. 675–676; Simmons, Beth A., *Mobilizing for Human Right: International Law in Domestic Politics* (Cambridge: Cambridge University Press, 2009), p. 363.

28 Hafner-Burton, Victor and Lupu, 2012, p. 73.

29 Henkin, 1979, p. 46.

30 Abbott et al., 2001, pp. 17 and 28–31. Compare with Pauwelyn, Joost and Elsig, Manfred, 'The Politics of Treaty Interpretation: Variations and Explanations Across International Tribunals' in Dunoff, Jeffrey L. and Pollack, Mark A. (eds), *Interdisciplinary Perspectives on International Law and International Relations: The State of the Art* (Cambridge: Cambridge University Press, 2013), pp. 445–473, p. 459, who discuss the "interpretation space" open to a court which is a function

Table 1.2 Indicators of precision

High
Determinate rules: only narrow issues of interpretation
Substantial but limited issues of interpretation
Broad areas of discretion
"Standards": only meaningful with reference to specific situations
Impossible to determine whether conduct complies
Low

The general assumption is that precision may offer a number of advantages. It constrains "self-serving auto-interpretation", discouraging free-riding and clearly defining what counts as cooperative behavior. It reduces potential interpretive disputes over whether a state has fulfilled its obligations, which in turn makes violations more costly. Provided that high precision raises the cost of defection, the credibility of commitment will increase. The act of ratifying a treaty with high levels of precision signals a willingness and capacity to comply. However, precision comes with a cost. It makes negotiations reaching agreement more difficult.[31] As such, while high precision may reduce post-agreement costs of managing and enforcing agreements, the adoption of such rules may entail significant contracting costs.[32] Thus, the standard assumption that precision yields more effective international legal institutions and rules has been challenged. It could be argued that imprecision, as with non-binding agreements, can lead to more cooperation because it allows for incomplete contracts, which may be unavoidable when interests diverge and uncertainty is high. The challenge thus becomes to obtain the advantages of flexibility while still sending credible signals.[33]

1.2.1.3 Delegation

Delegation means that third parties have been granted authority to implement, interpret, settle disputes and (possibly) to make rules. Abbott and others provide the following indicators of delegation (see Table 1.3).[34]

When disputing states decide whether to pursue arbitration or adjudication, they weigh the trade-off of pursuing an effective conflict management mechanism versus the costs of relinquishing decision control. Arbitration and adjudication are unlike other forms of dispute resolution because the states

of the precision or incompleteness of the legal text in question, see also Dunoff, Jeffrey L. and Pollack, Mark A., 'What Can International Relations Learn from International Law?' *Temple University Legal Studies Research Paper No 2012–14* (2013), p. 51.

31 Goodman and Jinks, 2004, pp. 677–678.

32 Abbott and Snidal, 2001, p. 50.

33 Hafner-Burton, Victor and Lupu, 2012, p. 74.

34 Abbott et al., 2001, pp. 17 and 31–34.

Table 1.3 Indicators of delegation

A. Dispute resolution
High
Courts: binding third-party decisions; general jurisdiction; direct private access; can interpret and supplement rules; domestic courts have jurisdiction
Courts: jurisdiction, access or normative authority limited or consensual
Binding arbitration
Non-binding arbitration
Conciliation, mediation
Institutionalized bargaining
Pure political bargaining
Low
B. Rulemaking and implementation
High
Binding regulations: centralized enforcement
Binding regulations with consent or opt-out
Binding internal policies; legitimation or decentralized enforcement
Coordination standards
Draft conventions: monitoring and publicity
Recommendations; confidential monitoring
Normative statements
Forum for negotiations
Low

pledge in advance to uphold the agreement they reach, labelling the procedure as binding. However, in contrast with domestic systems, there exists no third party with the automatic power to enforce an agreement. Thus, these measures are only binding so far as the states have pledged publicly to uphold a settlement/judgment.[35]

Gent and Shannon argue, based on empirical studies, that arbitration and adjudication are more effective mechanisms for ending territorial disputes than bilateral or non-binding third-party negotiations. Arbitration and adjudication garner higher reputation costs for breaking rules than other intervention techniques.[36] Evidence of reputation costs is found by Simmons, who shows that leaders who pledge to honor legalistic mechanisms of conflict management are more likely to uphold the decision than leaders who come into power after a decision is made. Chief executives who make commitments to arbitrate tend to keep them; those who did not (and possibly opposed them

35 Gent, Stephen E. and Shannon, Megan, 'Decision Control and the Pursuit of Binding Conflict Management: Choosing the Ties that Bind', 55 *Journal of Conflict Resolution* (2011) 710–734, pp. 711–712.

36 Gent, Stephen E. and Shannon, Megan, 'The Effectiveness of International Arbitration and Adjudication: Getting Into a Bind', 72 *The Journal of Politics* (2010) 366–380, pp. 367 and 369.

all along) do not have the same reputational stake.[37] A further reason why binding conflict management is efficient is that leaders can use the legality of binding conflict management to satisfy domestic opposition in several ways. Domestic audiences perceive concessions based on international law and judicial decisions as more legitimate than those offered in bilateral negotiations. It is more attractive to make concessions to a disinterested institution than to a political adversary.[38] Gent and Shannon acknowledge that although states value the effectiveness of binding procedures, they are reluctant to give up the decision control necessary to submit to arbitration or adjudication. Three factors may be identified that influence the willingness of states to give up decision control: (a) the importance of the issue to the disputants; (b) the availability of outside options; and (c) the history of negotiations. For the purpose of assessing these factors, Gent and Shannon investigated the prevalence of binding conflict management compared with other types of settlement attempts in disputed territorial, maritime and river claims in the Americas, Europe and the Middle East from 1816 to 2001. They controlled for joint democracy in the disputing states and whether the dispute was related to military conflict. They found that state leaders are less likely to sacrifice decision control if the source of the dispute is highly important, for example territory of strategic importance or with valuable resources. Further, powerful states that have outside options and can achieve a favorable outcome outside binding conflict management are less likely to risk an unfavorable outcome through arbitration or adjudication. Lastly, states are generally only willing to submit a territorial claim to arbitration if previous negotiations have led to some agreement about the disputed boundary.[39]

Tallberg and McCall Smith differentiate between two ideal types of dispute settlement: *interstate* and *supranational*. Adapting their definition, in interstate dispute settlement, the authority to sue states for non-compliance resides exclusively with states. By contrast, in supranational dispute settlement this authority is partly or entirely delegated to a commission, secretariat or other body with a prosecutorial function.[40] This is consistent with Tallberg's principal-supervisor-agent (P-S-A) model which he has used to explain supranational influence in European Union (EU) enforcement, where national governments of the EU member states (principals) have assigned to the EU Commission and European Court of Justice (supervisors) the task of enforcing compliance with EU law, as delegated to the individual members states

37 Simmons, Beth A, 'Capacity, Commitment, and Compliance: International Institutions and Territorial Disputes', 46 *Journal of Conflict Resolution* (2002) 829–856, p. 844; Simmons, 2009, p. 120.

38 Simmons, 2002, p. 834; Gent and Shannon, 2010, p. 369.

39 Gent and Shannon, 2011, pp. 711–712 and 716–728.

40 Tallberg and McCall Smith, 2012, pp. 4–5. See also Keohane, Robert O., Moravcsik, Andrew and Slaughter, Anne-Marie, 'Legalized dispute resolution: Interstate and Transnational' in Goldstein, Judith L. et al. (eds), *Legalization and World Politics* (Cambridge, MA and London: MIT Press, 2001), pp. 73–104.

(agents).[41] It is thus not only a question of having a court; it is also a question of who has the responsibility to monitor non-compliance and the power to initiate a complaint. Tallberg and McCall Smith claim that:

> empowerment of supranational prosecutors fundamentally alters the dynamics and outcomes of dispute settlement. Other things equal, systems relying on supranational prosecution of infringement cases will be more effective in addressing non-compliance, and more likely to mediate the impact of power asymmetries on dispute settlement outcomes, than systems relying exclusively on state-initiated complaints.[42]

Henkin identifies several reasons why states may be unwilling to submit to the jurisdiction of international states: they want to keep control of their own diplomacy over their interests; a preference for flexibility and possible compromise, rather than the all-or-nothing of a law suit; the delay and uncertainty of a law suit; a lack of confidence in foreign judges and a fear that the court might extend its authority and scope of law to strictly internal matters; a law suit may be considered an unfriendly act and a loss of case could represent a blow to national prestige.[43] Koremenos has examined a random sample of treaties to assess when and why states choose to delegate issues to international organizations. She employs a rational choice framework and finds that agreements that address complex cooperation problems, that is, problems characterized by uncertainty, prisoner's dilemma-like incentives to defect, and/or time inconsistency are more likely to include dispute resolution provisions.[44] Hafner-Burton, Victor and Lupu have noted that, in general, delegation is high when many states are involved, disputes are complex, and mechanisms have gained trust through decades of exercising delegated authority. A common problem with delegation of authority is how to keep under control the "agents" to whom authority is delegated. Successful delegation that enhances cooperation requires that important states have confidence that the agents remain loyal to the intended purpose of the cooperation. Lack of confidence in agents makes cooperation more difficult.[45]

To summarize, delegation deals with one of the main arguments of this book, namely who decides whether it is the general rules or the exceptions that are applicable in a given situation and how such decisions are enforced.

41 Tallberg, Jonas, *Making States Comply* (Lund: Studentlitteratur, 1999), p. 9.
42 Tallberg and McCall Smith, 2012, p. 5.
43 Henkin, 1979, pp. 186–188.
44 Koremenos, Barbara, 'If Only Half of International Agreements Have Dispute Resolution Provisions, Which Half Needs Explaining?', 36 *Journal of Legal Studies* (2007) 189–212; see also Koremenos, Barbara, 'Contracting Around International Uncertainty', 99 *American Political Science Review* (2005) 549–565: commented by Ginsburg and Shaffer, 2010, p. 758.
45 Hafner-Burton, Victor and Lupu, 2012, pp. 75–76.

1.2.1.4 *Acceptance of states*

Having outlined the typology of legalization created by Abbott and others, the question now turns to whether the three dimensions explained above are adequate to determine whether an issue area is legalized and institutionalized. More specifically, does this typology sufficiently factor in consideration of state acceptance?

Abbot and others use the concept *jus cogens* (unconditionally rules binding on all states at all times or peremptory norms) to designate the hardest form of *obligation*,[46] but few norms belong to this category of rules.[47] All other norms are dependent on state consent. This means that states have the discretion to decide whether they want to be subject to an international legal regime. How this discretion is actually used or not used, as in the number of states that have consented to be subjected to an international legal regime, is arguably an indicator to determine the level of legalization. The number of states that accept an international legal regime is indicative of the strength of that regime. A low number of states that are party to a treaty could be argued to be an indication that the level of legalization in that issue area is low.

Turning to the dimension of *delegation*, Abbot and others differentiate between courts with general jurisdiction and courts where the access or normative authority is limited or consensual. Moreover, they use a continuum from binding regulations, coordination standards to recommendations as indicators when it comes to rule-making and enforcement.[48] This continuum of indicators is recognition that delegation is dependent on state consent, but again the continuum does not clearly include any indicators on actual state consent. By the same reasoning as above, the number of states that accept delegation is, arguably, an important indicator of the strength of that regime.

Moreover, from a realist perspective, the acceptance of powerful states is crucial to the level of legalization in any regime because power is the primary source of order and rules in an international system.[49] For the same reasons that the number of states may be relevant to assess the strength of a regime, the same may be said about the level of acceptance from powerful states.

It would therefore be reasonable to either redefine "obligation" and/or "delegation" as dimensions of legalization in order to incorporate the level of state acceptance as an additional indicator, or to add a fourth dimension.

46 Abbott et al., 2001, pp. 20 and 26. See also Byers, Michael, *Custom, Power and the Power of Rules: International Relations and Customary International Law* (Cambridge: Cambridge University Press, 1999), pp. 13 and 183.

47 Shelton, Dinah, 'International Law and "Relative Normativity"' in Evans, Malcolm D. (ed), *International Law* (3rd edn, Oxford: Oxford University Press, 2010), pp. 141–171, pp. 147–151: the ICJ has discussed the concept in relation to use of force and genocide. Bring, Ove, Mahmoudi, Said and Wrange, Pål, *Sverige och folkrätten* (4th edn, Stockholm: Norstedts Juridik AB, 2011), pp. 16, 30 and 132 claim the concept is relevant for the prohibition on the use of force, genocide, slavery, and the use of chemical and biological weapons.

48 Abbott et al., 2001, p. 32.

49 Abbott and Snidal, 2001, p. 64.

For example, over time there has been a declining ratio of states that accept the compulsory jurisdiction of the ICJ. This fact makes Keohane, Moravcsik and Slaughter argue that, "[a]s measured by the level of legal obligation, legalization in the ICJ has moved backwards over the last half-century".[50] In this, they deduce that the number of states is relevant when determining the level of legalization. However, it is not obvious whether this is a question of "obligation", "delegation" or both. Thus, for the purpose of the present study, a fourth dimension of state acceptance is used.[51]

A common assumption in international law literature is that membership should be as broad as possible. The logic for universalism is often rooted in the idea that broader memberships are more representative and thus more legitimate. However, political scientists would argue that membership comes at a cost, and restricted membership can lead to more effective agreements for two reasons. The first advantage concerns enforcement. With cooperation based on a small group of states that are the most likely to cooperate, excluding free-riders, enforcement becomes easier. The second reason concerns contracting. Empirical research shows that membership involves a tradeoff: large memberships create potential gains from a wider application of common rules, but generate complexity and uncertainty.[52] Thus, regimes with few state parties may be stronger when it comes to other dimensions of legalization such as obligation, precision and obligation.

1.2.1.5 Variations in international legalization

Abott and others argue that, conceptually, states may combine any level of obligation, precision and delegation to produce an international legal regime suited to the specific needs of the states concerned. This creates eight possible combinations.[53] As this study adds a fourth dimension, there are 16 possible combinations. Table 1.4 illustrates the variety of international legalization. Obligation, precision, delegation and state acceptance are characterized as either high or low. Rows are arranged roughly in order of decreasing legalization, with legal obligation weighted most heavily, followed by delegation, precision and state acceptance, respectively. Abbott and others convincingly argue that a binary characterizations sacrifice the continuous nature of the dimensions of legalization, but the table usefully: (a) demonstrates the range of institutional possibilities; and (b) highlights the tradeoffs involved in weakening (or strengthening) particular elements. Abbott and others express the different forms of international legalization in a table, which has been adapted for the purposes of this study to take into account the fourth dimension of *state*

50 Keohane et al., 2001, p. 96.
51 Compare with Hafner-Burton, Victor and Lupu, 2012, pp. 72 and 77–79.
52 Hafner-Burton, Victor and Lupu, 2012, p. 77–78.
53 Abbott et al., 2001, p. 22.

Table 1.4 Forms of international legalization

	Type	*Obligation*	*Precision*	*Delegation*	*State acceptance*
Ideal type: centralized system					
	I	High	High	High	High
	II	High	Low	High	High
	III	High	High	High	Low
	IV	High	High	Low	High
	V	Low	High	High	High
	VI	High	Low	High	Low
	VII	High	High	Low	Low
	VIII	High	Low	Low	High
	IX	Low	High	High	Low
	X	Low	Low	High	High
	XI	Low	High	Low	High
	XII	High	Low	Low	Low
	XIII	Low	Low	High	Low
	XIV	Low	High	Low	Low
	XV	Low	Low	Low	High
	XVI	Low	Low	Low	Low
Ideal type: anarchy					

acceptance.[54] Abbott and others use "hard law" and "anarchy" as opposite ideal types. However, the present study finds it more fitting to use the dichotomy "centralized system" versus "anarchy", as even in an anarchic society rules (and law) may exist, but they are not created or enforced by a central authority, unlike in un-anarchic societies:

Row I in Table 1.4 corresponds to situations near the ideal type of full legalization—a centralized system. Abbot and others argue that the European Community (at that time signifying the European Coal and Steel Community, the European Economic Community and the European Atomic Energy Community, now the EU), the World Trade Organization (WTO) regime on the Agreement on Trade-Related Aspects of Intellectual Property Rights (TRIPS) and the ICC belong to this category. In the present study, it is argued in sections 6.2.4 and 8.2 that the ICC does not belong to this category. At the other end of the spectrum, systems in row XVI entail very low levels of legalization and are not legal institutions in any real sense, where concepts such as "balances of power" and "spheres of influence" are dominant. Here we approach the ideal type of anarchy prominent in international relations theory.[55] To characterize the regimes, the notations (O, P, D, A) are used to refer to the level of obligation, precision, delegation and state acceptance, respectively. Capital letters will be used for high levels (e.g. P), lower case letters for moderate levels (e.g. d) and dashes for low levels (-).[56]

54 Compare with Abbott et al., 2001, p. 21.
55 Adaptation of Abbott et al., 2001, p. 21–24.
56 Adaptation of Abbott and Snidal, 2001, p. 40.

The four dimensions on the form and strength of international legalization and their combinations are revisited in sections 3.2, 4.2, 5.2, 6.2 and 7.2.

1.3 Processes and mechanisms for creating and enforcing international law

To measure legalization in different dimensions is one way of discussing the relevance of international law. Another way to phrase it is to study processes and mechanisms for creating and enforcing international law, which partly overlaps with the issue of delegation. International law is, arguably, "essential to foreign policy and to diplomacy in that it provides mechanisms, forms, and procedures" by which states maintain their relations, carry on trade and other forms of intercourse.[57] The processes and mechanisms of the international system do not have to be identical to those in a domestic society in order to be an efficient and an effective system. Koh notes that, "[l]ike most laws, international rules are rarely enforced, but usually obeyed".[58] Even the realist Morgenthau admitted that, "during the four hundred years of its existence international law has in most instances been scrupulously observed ... to deny that international law exists as a system of binding legal rules flies in the face of all the evidence".[59]

It is, arguably, more relevant whether international law is reflected in the policies of states and in relations between states. International law is not dependent on a world parliament; instead, it is more significant whether law adapts to the needs of a changing society. Similarly, the absence of a mandatory judicial dispute settlement at the international level does not preclude the settlement of disputes in an orderly fashion. The impact of international law cannot merely be assessed whether it is enforceable. Equally important is whether law actually governs or influences state behavior and whether international behavior reflects key values of international law: peace, sovereignty and order. Usually, it is meaningful to speak of violation or compliance. The question whether international law is relevant for state behavior is more complicated. International law obviously influences behavior when it helps to deter violations. The influence of international law cannot be assessed by the number of violations alone. Also relevant is the record of observance of the law by states. Henkin argues that it is necessary to examine the operation of law on the working level of foreign ministries, notably how legal counsel within these ministries suppress or modify proposals that are deemed illegal before they reach the level of decision. He asserts that it is probably the case that, "almost all nations observe almost all principles of international law and

57 Henkin, 1979, p. 18.
58 Koh, 1997, p. 2603.
59 Morgenthau, Hans J., *Politics Among Nations* (1st edn published 1948; 2nd edn, New York, NY: Alfred A. Knopf, 1954), pp. 249–252.

almost all of their obligations almost all of the time".[60] Although Henkin is the most quoted on this point, Bull made a similar pronouncement two years earlier, when he stated that, "[i]f it were possible or meaningful to conduct a quantitative study of obedience to the rules of international law, it might be expected that most states obey most agreed rules of international law most of the time".[61] This should be understood as a rebuttal against the realist view of international order, where international law and organizations totally lack any intrinsic significance. Similarly, when Guzman discusses the role of international law, it is less about compliance with its rules, but more whether it changes the behavior of states.[62] A potential point of criticism is that Henkin does not merely think that it is difficult to obtain evidence and to evaluate the influence of international law. He states that, "[o]rder is not measurable, no purpose is served by attempts to grade it".[63] This book shares the assumption of Henkin that international law is relevant but differs in its attempt to show that order is measurable and that it is possible to grade legalization in terms of more or less.

It is, admittedly, difficult to conduct empirical studies on how state policy is influenced by international law. Policy is not always planned or deliberate; records on the process of decision-making are often not publicly available; and it is difficult even for the decision-makers to identify, analyze and weigh the elements of a decision. Further, the daily success of international law does not lend itself easy to a "case study".[64] A case study approach to examine specific rules of international law might enable a scholar to offer only limited generalizations about state adherence to international law; to examine the international legal system as a whole would clearly be too broad a study to undertake.[65]

A fundamental concept of the principle of rule of law is that the law of any society must apply to all its members. Byers describes the two main ways in which this can happen in a national legal system. First, law can be understood as imposed vertically from the state or sovereign above. Second, law can be understood as a multitude of horizontal, bilateral relationships between individuals or between the individual and the state. In the absence of an overarching sovereign, international society is frequently perceived as a multitude of horizontal, bilateral relationships between states. This has consequences for the processes and mechanisms for creating and enforcing international law.[66]

60 Henkin, 1979, pp. 26, 44, 46–47 and 246.

61 Bull, Hedley, *The Anarchical Society: A Study of Order in World Politics* (London: Macmillan, 1977), p. 137.

62 Young, Oran R. and Levy, Marc A., 'The Effectiveness of International Environmental Regimes' in Young, O.R. (ed), *The Effectiveness of International Environmental Regimes: Causal Connections and Behavioural Mechanisms* (Cambridge, MA: MIT Press, 1999), pp. 1–32, pp. 4–6; Guzman, Andrew, *How International Law Works: A Rational Choice Theory* (New York, NY: Oxford University Press, 2008), p. 8; comment by Thirlway, 2014, p. 203.

63 Henkin, 1979, pp. 49, 98 and 167.

64 Henkin, 1979, pp. 242–243.

65 Piper, 1968, p. 400.

66 Byers, 1999, p. 88.

Empirical studies suggest that different processes and mechanisms give rise to international law depending on the distinct domain of international law.[67] The predominant mechanisms used are reciprocity, coercion, persuasion and socialization.[68] Some authors use more expansive lists,[69] but for the reasons listed below, the present study utilizes a more consolidated list. As explained in section 1.4, the mechanisms at work may be uncovered by different means, including through case studies using process-tracing methods.[70]

1.3.1 Reciprocity

In the absence of a central authority with preponderant power, rules of international law to a large extent are upheld by measures of self-help, including the threat and use of force, by individual states. Obedience to law is the result of the interest a state perceives in reciprocal action by another state or states.[71] Reciprocity entails agreement between states to coordinate policy around international law standards to advance mutual interests, sometimes involving exchanges of reciprocal concessions on different issues. Reciprocity refers to "exchanges of roughly equivalent values in which the actions of each party are contingent on the prior actions of the others in such a way that good is returned for good, and bad for bad".[72] It may be practiced both in relation to cooperation and defection.[73] The risk that another state will exit the agreement rather than tolerate cheating can deter a would-be violator from cashing in on the short-term benefits of defection if that actor values future interactions.[74] Reciprocity is not only a social process, it also provides a basis for Roman, Germanic and Anglo-Saxon contract law, and treaty law.[75] Reciprocity may explain why laws or obligations that operate symmetrically between states—and as long as they continue to operate—are rarely violated.[76]

Reciprocity is a legal consequence of the formal equality of states in a system with no overarching sovereign. The concept of reciprocity involves the

67 Ginsburg and Shaffer, 2010, pp. 767–768.

68 Ginsburg and Shaffer, 2010, p. 767 use the concept "acculturation" instead of socialization. Compare with Berry, John W., 'Acculturation' in Grusec, Joan E. and Hastings, Paul D. (eds), *Handbook of Socialization: Theory and Research* (New York, NY: The Guildford Press, 2007), pp. 543–560, p. 543.

69 Braithwaite and Drahos list the following seven mechanisms used in the area of global business regulation: military coercion, economic coercion, systems of reward, modelling, reciprocal adjustment, non-reciprocal coordination, and capacity-building, Braithwaite, John and Drahos, Peter, *Global Business Regulation* (Cambridge: Cambridge University Press, 2000), pp. 532–549.

70 Ginsburg and Shaffer, 2010, p. 768.

71 Bull, 1977, pp. 131 and 139.

72 Keohane, Robert O., 'Reciprocity in International Relations', 40 *International Organization* (1986) 1–27, p. 8. See also Braithwaite and Drahos, 2000, pp. 21–22.

73 Axelrod, Robert, *The Evolution of Cooperation* (New York, NY: Basic Books, 1984), p. 118.

74 Simmons, 2009, pp. 116–117; Ginsburg and Shaffer, 2010, p. 767.

75 Braithwaite and Drahos, 2000, pp. 20–21.

76 Henkin, 1979, p. 54.

idea of bilateral relationships between at least formally equal parties. Can a legal system based on bilateral relations have generally applicable rules? Byers explains that if a bilateral relationship in respect of any particular rule is multiplied so that similar relationships in respect of the same rule exist between all states, the rule would seem to become general in application.[77]

To illustrate the principle of reciprocity, imagine the establishment of a regime on the admission of foreign nationals. Under the rules of the regime, all states will grant residence status to nationals of other regime states. If regime state A disobeys the rules, other states of the same regime could reciprocate and refuse to grant residence to nationals of state A. The reciprocal connection may induce all parties to comply with the rules of the regime.[78] Schwarzenberger and Brown list diplomatic immunity, extradition, commerce, communications and transport as examples where international law developed on the basis of reciprocity. Even in times of war, where dynamics of power dominate, some scope exists for the mechanism of reciprocity.[79] Reciprocity is an ambiguous term. Typically, it is perceived as a reaction in kind.[80] Braitwaithe and Drahos differentiate between cooperation based on reciprocal adjustment and non-reciprocal coordination. The former involves externalities that are reciprocal, for example when two states both pour pollution and both suffer from the consequences, while the latter concerns non-reciprocal externalities, for example industrial nations may get market access in exchange for providing security.[81] Reciprocity could entail that a state's violation or compliance is returned in kind, but not necessarily so. Violations of obligations in one area can be met by counter-measures in another area of interaction. For example, the United States (US) took action in several different fields as a reaction to the occupation of the US embassy in Tehran in 1979.[82] It is more reasonable to consolidate the two forms, as both reciprocal adjustment and non-reciprocal coordination entail mechanisms of reciprocity.[83] Moreover, Keohane argues that reciprocity can refer either to a policy pursued by a single actor or to a systemic pattern of action. He gives the concept of reciprocity two quite distinct meanings, specific versus diffuse reciprocity.

Specific reciprocity refers "to situations in which specified partners exchange items of equivalent value in a strictly delimited sequence. If any obligations exist, they are clearly specified in terms of rights and duties of particular

77 Byers, 1999, pp. 89–90.

78 Arend, Anthony C., *Legal Rules and International Society* (New York, NY and Oxford: Oxford University Press, 1999), pp. 121–122.

79 Schwarzenberger, Georg and Brown, E.D., *A Manual of International Law* (6th edn, Milton: Professional Books, 1976), p. 10.

80 Simmons, 2009, p. 117.

81 Braithwaite and Drahos, 2000, pp. 22–23 and 543–546.

82 *United States Diplomatic and Consular Staff in Tehran* (United States of America v Iran), ICJ, Judgment 24 May 1980, paras 30–32.

83 Ginsburg and Shaffer, 2010, pp. 767–768.

actors".[84] This is the typical meaning of reciprocity in economics and game theory.

Mathematicians were the first to develop game theory, primarily for use in economics. Later, other disciplines, such as political science, international relations, law, sociology and biology also employed game theory concepts. Game theory is a strand of rational choice theory. It is divided into cooperative and non-cooperative game theory, based on the enforceability of agreements and communication. Cooperative game theory assumes the existence of an institution capable of enforcing the agreements concluded between the players, whereas non-cooperative game theory assumes no such institution exists. In cooperative games, communication between the players is allowed, while in non-cooperative games, communication may or may not be allowed. Hirsch notes that prevailing international relations theory assumes that: (a) states are the central actors in the international system; (b) states are not subordinated to a central international authority to enforce cooperation; (c) states are egoists—they constantly try to maximize their interests; and (d) states are rational—they have consistent, ordered preferences, which derive from calculating the costs and benefits of alternative courses of action. Assumptions (b), (c) and (d) are consistent with those of non-cooperative game theory. Meanwhile, assumption (a) in no way contradicts any of the underlying premises of game theory.[85]

States may choose different strategies towards cooperation. A Nash-equilibrium is the combination of strategies, representing the best response of each player to the predicted strategies of the other players. Such equilibrium is called "strategically stable" or "self-enforcing" because no single actor is interested in deviating from the predicted strategy.[86] Morrow argues that institutions must be self-enforcing to be sustained. In terms of game theory, institutions must form an equilibrium of a game.[87] In other words, the goal of international law regimes should, arguably, be to promote cooperative norms, incentives and structures which at the same time are subject to a Nash-equilibrium. However, Axelrod and Keohane note that cooperation does not equal harmony. Harmony requires complete identity of interests, while cooperation takes place in situations that contain a mix of conflicting and complementary interests.[88]

84 Keohane, 1986, pp. 3 and 19.

85 Hirsch, Moshe, 'Game Theory, International Law, and Future Environmental Cooperation in the Middle East', 27 *Denver Journal of International Law & Policy* (1998) 75–119, pp. 78 and 80; see also Thompson, Alexander, 'Applying Rational Choice Theory to International Law: The Promise and Pitfalls', 31 *Journal of Legal Studies* (2002) 285–306.

86 Hirsch, 1998, pp. 76 and 80.

87 Morrow, James D., 'The Institutional Features of Prisoner of War Treaties', 55 *International Organization* (2001) 971–991, p. 973.

88 Axelrod, Robert and Keohane, Robert O., 'Achieving Cooperation Under Anarchy: Strategies and Institutions' in Oye, Kenneth A. (ed), *Cooperation Under Anarchy* (Princeton, NJ: Princeton University Press, 1986), pp. 226–254, p. 226.

Game theory models can either be zero-sum games, whatever one actor wins the other loses, or non-zero-sum games. Both type of models may include an element of competiveness. While gains and losses in zero-sum games have an absolute nature, actors would rather seek relative gains in non-zero games. For example, in military contexts the aim is to achieve superiority. Hirsch notes that pure zero-sum situations rarely arise in the international arena, if at all. Models of non-zero games include prisoner's dilemma, assurance games and coordination games. Prisoner's dilemma is a non-cooperative game where the Nash-equilibrium creates sub-optimal outcomes in one-shot games. Table 1.5 illustrates payoffs in prisoner's dilemma where, no matter what the other states does, defection yields a higher payoff than cooperation:[89]

Even if states have the possibility to communicate, they will gain by defection. However, international relations are not one-shot, they consist of infinite iterated games where cooperation creates long-term mutual benefit. Enforcement mechanisms may be valuable in this regard. Assurance games are less conflict-driven. There may be several Nash-equilibriums with equal gains for all gainers whereof one equilibrium creates the optimal outcome. Thus an optimal outcome may be achieved even in one-shot games, provided that the involved players all are rational, and that they communicate and cooperate. Coordination games are similar in the sense that they have several Nash-equilibriums, the difference is that one player dominates the other, which creates a distribution problem. Cooperation is possible but becomes more difficult under iterated conditions. Hirsch lists examples such as setting common standards for international communication, agreeing on the emergency radio frequency for civil aviation, and formulating an international system for the classification of goods for customs purposes.[90]

Robert Axelrod has focused on the game of prisoner's dilemma and developed a theory of cooperation which applies to states and relies heavily on specific reciprocity. It is not necessary to assume that state actions are rational. Action may be the result of complex bureaucratic politics involving complicated information protection and shifting coalitions. The important factor is how payoffs for the states are ordered.[91] States may play "tit-for-tat" on the basis of self-interest alone. For specific reciprocity to become successfully institutionalized, exchange must take place sequentially, rather than simultaneously. Based on game theory and social exchange theory, Keohane argues that reliance on simultaneous exchange alone provides an unsatisfactory basis for long-term relationships.[92] Three conditions principally determine whether

89 Adaptation of Axelrod, 1984, p. 8. See also Zagare, Frank C., 'Game Theory' in Williams, Paul D. (ed), *Security Studies – an introduction* (2nd edn, London and New York, NY: Routledge, 2013), pp. 45–62, p. 51.

90 Hirsch, 1998, pp. 82–94; Guzman, 2008, p. 41.

91 Axelrod, 1984, pp. 7–13, 17–18, 125 and 174; see interpretation by Keohane, 1986, p. 8.

92 Keohane, 1986, pp. 21 and 27. "Tit-for-tat" is defined by Axelrod as "the strategy of starting with cooperation, and thereafter doing what the other player did on the previous move", Axelrod, 1984, p. viii.

Table 1.5 Prisoner's dilemma

		State B	
		Cooperate	Defect
	Cooperate	A = 3, B = 3 Reward for mutual cooperation	A = 0, B = 5 A is the loser and tempted to defect
State A	Defect	A = 5, B = 0 B is the loser and tempted to defect	A = 1, B = 1 Punishment for mutual defection

the exercise of specific reciprocity leads to co-operation: the extent to which the players have interests in common; the "shadow of the future"; and the number of players in any given game.[93] A frequent objection to specific reciprocity concerns multilateral situations involving a large number of actors, in which collective, or public, goods are involved. Multilateral situations offer substantial incentives to behave as a "free-rider".[94] The question is why states still follow the rules.

In situations characterized by *diffuse reciprocity*, by contrast, "the definition of equivalence is less precise, one's partners may be viewed as a group rather than as particular actors, and the sequence of events is less narrowly bounded … diffuse reciprocity can be maintained only by *a widespread sense of obligation*".[95] In contrast to Axelrod, Keohane mentions obligations which are perceived as important. Diffuse reciprocity involves conforming to generally accepted standards of behavior. Keohane believes that diffuse reciprocity is rare. It only occurs within cooperative international regimes that link countries with extensive shared interests, such as European integration.[96] Compared to the conditions of cooperation for specific reciprocity, diffuse reciprocity is "only feasible when some norms of obligation exist: that is, when international regimes are relatively strong. These norms may express the actors' conceptions of their self-interest, but their conceptions of self-interest must be broad and their confidence in the good faith of others fairly great".[97] Byers perceives Keohane's introduction of diffuse reciprocity as advancement and adds an additional dimension, namely the connection between the sense of obligation, reciprocity and law. Byers perceives reciprocity not only as a general social concept, but also "as a principle of international law which plays an important role in qualifying applications of power in the development, maintenance and change of customary rules".[98]

93 Keohane, 1986, p. 24.
94 Keohane, 1986, p. 12.
95 Keohane, 1986, pp. 3 and 20 (emphasis added).
96 Keohane, 1986, p. 3.
97 Keohane, 1986, p. 25.
98 Byers, 1999, pp. 28–29.

Self-enforcing agreements rely on the mechanism of reciprocity. A self-enforcing agreement is one in which two or more parties adhere to the agreement as long as each gains more from continuing the agreement than from retracting it. It does not depend on third parties to enforce the terms of the agreement, it is enforced by shutting down or reducing the future flow of benefits. Self-enforcing agreements are stable over time if the implied costs of breaking the agreement counter-balance any short-term temptation to deviate unilaterally from the terms of the agreement. Reputational considerations may contribute to the stability of self-enforcing agreements. Reputational considerations are, arguably, less important when little interaction is required between the states. A realist would argue that self-enforcing agreements are the only stable agreements in an anarchic society.[99] Keohane has declared reciprocity as, "the most effective strategy for maintaining cooperation among egoists".[100] Bull argues that, "[i]t is only if power, and the will to use it, are distributed in the international society in such a way that states can uphold at least certain rights when they are infringed, that the respect for international law can be maintained".[101] To summarize, reciprocity is valuable for decentralized enforcement of cooperative agreements.[102]

In game theory, reciprocity is the key component.[103] Reciprocity can facilitate cooperative outcomes under iterated conditions. With the possible exception of global nuclear war, the assumption of international politics is future, continuous interaction between states. Under iterated conditions, the ability to distinguish between cooperation and defection by others and to respond can affect the power of reciprocity.[104] Iteration not only changes the outcome in the interaction between states in a given situation, it also changes the underlying cooperative structure.[105]

Axelrod's analysis assumes that states are capable of discriminating, i.e. they cooperate with some actors while not cooperating with others.[106] This is not always a reasonable assumption. For example, difficulties arise in cooperation in relation to international public goods because states cannot isolate their actions toward one state from another state, an example of this is restraining

99 Simmons, 2009, pp. 116–117.
100 Keohane, 1986, p. 2.
101 Bull, 1977, pp. 131–132.
102 Axelrod and Keohane, 1986, p. 246.
103 Axelrod, 1984, pp. 3–20.
104 Axelrod, 1984, pp. 7–12; Oye, Kenneth A., 'Explaining Cooperation under Anarchy: Hypotheses and Strategies' in Oye, Kenneth A. (ed), *Cooperation Under Anarchy* (Princeton, NJ: Princeton University Press, 1986), pp. 1–24, pp. 3–4 and 12; Snidal, Duncan, 'The Game Theory of International Politics' in Oye, Kenneth A. (ed), *Cooperation Under Anarchy* (Princeton, NJ: Princeton University Press, 1986), pp. 25–57, p. 48. See also Rapoport, Anatol and Chammah, Albert M., *Prisoner's dilemma: a study in conflict and cooperation* (Ann Arbor, MI: University of Michigan Press, 1965).
105 Snidal, 1986, p. 49.
106 Axelrod, 1984, pp. 140, 168–169 and 182; Snidal, 1986, p. 53.

the size of fishing catches in the high seas or air pollution. Institutions need to be designed which allow for discrimination.[107]

Axelrod states that when the use of a central authority is impossible or too expensive, the best method to rely upon is self-policing. He argues that cooperation can evolve in three stages: (a) cooperation can start even in a world of unconditional defection from cooperation. Cooperation may evolve from small clusters of actors who base their cooperation on reciprocity; (b) reciprocity thrives in a world with many different strategies of cooperation; and (c) once cooperation is established on the basis of reciprocity, it is less susceptible to being weakened by less cooperative strategies.[108]

Axelrod argues that principle of reciprocity has "the effect of promoting cooperation by establishing a direct connection between an actor's behaviour and anticipated future benefits".[109] Based on empirical findings in different fields, Axelrod argues that the most direct way to encourage cooperation is to make the interactions more durable, i.e. the actors should be in contact with each other for extended periods of time. Another way is to make the interactions more frequent. A good way to increase interaction between two actors is to keep other actors away or to break down the issues into small pieces.[110] If the assumption is that the principal actors are power-maximizing states, game theory subsumes the realist position. However, while game theory—similarly to realism—treats actors as rational actors, its empirical assumptions neither require that the key actors are states nor that they maximize power. Thus, with different assumptions game theory is equally consistent with other approaches to international relations.[111] It may bring together interdependence and realist positions in a common framework, and it can renovate the broader metaphors of "Hobesian anarchy" and "international organization".[112]

An important aspect of game theory is the ability to forgo short-run advantages for longer-run considerations, i.e. the individual actions of states can increase the collective outcome. The development of rules and institutions may be explained in terms of efforts to overcome the problems of collective action and achieving long-run benefits by altering the "rules of the game".[113] Cooperation according to game theory depends also on the context within which interaction takes place. Interaction takes place within the context of norms that are shared, sometimes explicitly, sometimes implicitly by the participants. This means that norms embedded in institutions may influence rational and self-interested actors.[114] The context or setting in the form of

107 Snidal, 1986, pp. 53–54.
108 Axelrod, 1984, pp. 20–21, 173 and 186.
109 Axelrod, 1984, pp. 13, 126–132 and 174, as formulated by Oye, 1986, p. 14.
110 Axelrod, 1984, pp. 129–132.
111 Snidal, 1986, pp. 35 and 38.
112 Snidal, 1986, pp. 56–57.
113 Snidal, 1986, pp. 39–40
114 Axelrod and Keohane, 1986, pp. 238–239 and 246.

institutions may be transformed in order to promote cooperation, for example by enlarging the shadow of future in terms of payoffs. The key is to make the long-term incentives for mutual cooperation greater than the short-term incentives for defection.[115] Axelrod and Keohane argue that regimes do not necessarily enforce rules in a hierarchical sense, but they do change patterns of transaction costs and provide information to participants, so that uncertainty is reduced.[116]

Oye argues that the explicit codification of norms can limit definitional ambiguity, clarifying standards of conduct, and defining cooperative and uncooperative behavior which permits more effective strategies of reciprocity.[117] The principle of reciprocity, arguably, operates better in scenarios with fewer states, rather than many actors, because of coordination problems and the fact that defection from cooperation by one state involves costs for all other states, which may, in turn, lead to subsequent, wholesale defection of even more states. One solution in systems with many states is the creation of rules and institutions that monitor compliance with collective enforcement mechanisms.[118]

Unconditional cooperation may appear as the morally correct strategy, but it provides an incentive for other actors to exploit any state that adopts such strategy. Axelrod admits that strategies based on reciprocity may not appear to be the height of morality compared to unconditional cooperation, but argues that it is the best strategy for building a system which prevents exploitative and predatory strategies.[119]

In summary, game theory may be relevant for posing interesting questions, but the theory cannot predict behavior in particular circumstances. It can, however provide general explanation of behavior in regime areas discussed in this study.[120] Klabbers is even more skeptical, arguing that game theory has the flawed assumption that states are unitary actors that engage in rational decision-making, maximizing individual interests.[121] Moreover, reciprocity is often understood as a relationship between two states—"tit-for-tat" as a means of influence. However, some norms are of an *erga omnes* nature. The violation of such norms is not only an offence against the individual state affected and/or the individual person directly offended, it is also a violation against all members of the world community. Examples of *erga omnes* norms include aggression, piracy, genocide, slavery, torture and racial discrimination.[122] In

115 Axelrod, 1984, pp. 124 and 134.
116 Axelrod and Keohane, 1986, p. 250.
117 Oye, 1986, pp. 16–17.
118 Oye, 1986, pp. 19–20.
119 Axelrod, 1984, pp. 136–137.
120 Snidal, 1986, p. 55.
121 Klabbers, 2004, p. 39.
122 *Barcelona Traction, Light and Power Company, Limited* (Belgium v Spain), ICJ, Judgment, 5 February 1970, paras 33–34. See also Malanczuk, Peter, *Akehurst's Modern Introduction to International Law* (7th rev edn, London and New York, NY: Routledge, 1997), pp. 58–60.

such cases, reciprocity may, arguably, only give a limited explanation. As such, coercion, persuasion and socialization appear more relevant in relation to *erga omnes* obligations.

1.3.2 Coercion

States may use coercive methods, such as punishment or reward, to get other states to agree to particular outcomes. Coercion can be exercised with positive incentives ("carrots" or inducements) and penalties ("sticks" or negative incentives). It can include military as well as economic means. By increasing costs, undesirable behavior is discouraged. This includes "agreements with teeth" or strong enforcement mechanisms such as the ICC via criminal sanctions, the UN Security Council via enforcement measures or linking compliance with financial or military aid.[123] Coercion does not necessarily involve any change in the target actor's underlying preferences but rather can involve a re-calculation of the cost-benefit for the target state. [124]

In the absence of effective international institutions, individual states should, arguably, be allowed to adopt measures which are normally unlawful, not only in defense of their self-interest pursuant to the principle of reciprocity but also to defend the public interest. As indicated in the section above, coercion may be a means to induce compliance with *erga omnes* obligations. Dawidowicz notes that the concept of *erga omnes* implies "that individual states can take third-party counter-measures to enforce the most serious breaches of international law".[125] This stance is reconcilable with Articles 48(1)(b) and 54 of the International Law Commission (ILC) draft articles on State Responsibility.[126] Dawidowicz lists as one of several examples the US grain embargo against the Soviet Union in response to its invasion of Afghanistan in December 1979.[127] A similar example would be the US-EU sanctions against Russia in response to its illegal annexation of Crimea and interventions in Eastern Ukraine in 2014. The absence of prior judicial determination as to whether a measure is a violation makes the use of third-party interventions more complex. Dawidowicz suggests that the starting point could be to rely on statements of the sanctioning state(s), protests from other states and existing institutional action, for example by the UN.[128]

123 Goodman and Jinks, 2004, p. 691.
124 Goodman and Jinks, 2004, pp. 633–634; Halliday, T. and Osinsky, P., 'Globalization and Law', 32 *Annual Review of Sociology* (2006) 447–470, p. 451; Ginsburg and Shaffer, 2010, p. 767; Hafner-Burton, Victor and Lupu, 2012, p. 52.
125 Dawidowicz, Martin, 'Public Law Enforcement Without Public Law Safeguards? An Analysis of State Practice on Third-Party Countermeasures and Their Relationship to the UN Security Council', 77 *British Yearbook of International Law* (2006) 333–418, pp. 342 and 344.
126 International Law Commission, Draft Articles on Responsibility of States for Internationally Wrongful Acts, November 2001, Supplement No. 10 (A/56/10).
127 Dawidowicz, 2006, pp. 349, footnote 77, pp. 363–366.
128 Dawidowicz, 2006, p. 350.

1.3.3 Persuasion

States may change their policies because they become persuaded of the "correct" or "appropriate" policy, by observing and learning from each other's policies. Persuaded actors internalize new norms and rules of appropriate behavior which redefine their interests and identities.[129] Persuasion may be defined as efforts by global institutions or powerful nations to convince other nations of the rightness of reforms that converge on global norms.[130] For expressive reasons and as a consequence of persuasion, states may ratify treaties to obtain legitimacy within the state but also vis-à-vis other states. Such expressive reasons may be of value, they demonstrate a commitment to the law.[131]

How is possible that states can be persuaded to consent to obligations that appear to be in conflict with their interests? Political science scholarship on the mechanisms of persuasion has focused on the role of rhetorical argument in international relations.[132] Goodman and Jinks highlight two factors that determine, in substantial part, the persuasiveness of counter-attitudinal messages: "framing", i.e. to frame an issue to resonate with already accepted norms, and "cuing", i.e. to target audiences to "think harder" about the merits of a counter-attitudinal message.[133] Empirical evidence suggests that actors often change their beliefs when, faced with new information, they systematically examine and defend their positions.[134] Braithwaite and Drahos describe two forms of persuasion as either as modelling through observational learning or as capacity building through technical assistance.[135] In essence, the distinction between these two forms comes down to whether a more or less direct mechanism of persuasion is used.[136]

When examining processes and mechanisms for creating and enforcing international law, persuasion is an alternative to more power-based explanations involving coercion or reciprocity. In their study of 13 areas of global business regulation, Braithwhite and Drahos conclude that the "most consistently important mechanism was modelling" (a form of persuasion). They find that the significance of modelling has been "neglected in the regulatory and international relations literature".[137]

129 Goodman and Jinks, 2004, p. 635; Ginsburg and Shaffer, 2010, p. 767.

130 Halliday and Osinsky, 2006, p. 451.

131 Cronin-Furman, Kate, 'Managing Expectations: International Criminal Trials and the Prospects for Deterrence of Mass Atrocity', 7 *International Journal of Transitional Justice* (2013) 434–454, p. 439.

132 Hafner-Burton, Victor and Lupu, 2012, pp. 56–57.

133 Goodman and Jinks, 2004, p. 637.

134 Zimbardo, Philip G and Leippe, Michael, *The psychology of attitude change and social influence* (New York, NY: McGraw-Hill, 1991), pp. 192–197.

135 Braithwaite and Drahos, 2000, pp. 539–542 and 546.

136 Ginsburg and Shaffer, 2010, p. 768.

137 Braithwaite and Drahos, 2000, p. 546, see also Table 22.1 on pp. 532–533, and Ginsburg and Shaffer, 2010, p. 769.

1.3.4 Socialization

Socialization can be defined as the "induction of new members ... into the ways of behavior that are preferred in a society".[138] In an international context, this only makes sense if the international system is defined as a society of states.[139] The process of behavioral learning among states is, arguably, different compared to such processes among individuals in terms of life-span. While an ordinary process for human infants to go through on a daily basis, the formation of a new state is an extraordinary event. Therefore, even though many scholars use the term "socialization", as does this book, the term "acculturation" may be considered in relation to states as it concerns existing members of a society. Acculturation shares many features with socialization. Berry describes acculturation as secondary socialization occurring after initial socialization into an original culture.[140] The mechanism is sometimes conflated (or even confused) with other mechanisms such as persuasion. Goodman and Jenks define acculturation as "the general process by which actors adopt the beliefs and behavioral patterns of the surrounding culture. This mechanism induces behavioral changes through pressures to assimilate – some imposed by other actors and some imposed by the self".[141] States may for expressive reasons (such as obtaining legitimacy) create and ratify treaties. As already stated, expressive reasons may be of value as they demonstrate a commitment to the law.[142]

It appears quite straightforward to distinguish socialization from coercion. However, socialization concerns a pursuit of social legitimacy that may involve social sanctions and rewards, such as shaming and back-patting. While both coercion and socialization may involve social costs, coercion differs in the sense that these social costs will translate into material costs. With the mechanism of socialization, the social costs in and of themselves influence thought and action. Socialization values the publication of best practices more highly than mechanisms operating under the logic of coercion.[143]

Axelrod argues that communities (in this context the society of states) using strategies based upon reciprocity can police themselves.[144] From this, it follows that states should teach each other to adopt reciprocity, i.e. a process of socialization.

Theories of socialization predict that socialization within a system will press toward increasing "isomorphism", that is, structural similarity across

138 Risse, Thomas and Sikkink, Kathryn, 'The Socialization of International Human Rights Norms into Domestic Practices: Introduction' in Risse, Thomas, Ropp, Stephen C. and Sikkink, Kathryn (eds), *The Power of Human Rights International Norms and Domestic Change* (Cambridge: Cambridge University Press, 1999), pp. 1–38, p. 11.

139 Ibid, p. 11. Bull, 1977, p. 13.

140 Berry, 2007, p. 543.

141 Goodman and Jinks, 2004, pp. 626–627 and 632.

142 Cronin-Furman, 2013, p. 439.

143 Goodman and Jinks, 2004, pp. 645 and 696.

144 Axelrod, 1984, pp. 138.

the system, cognitive and social pressures encouraging actors (such as states) to comply with social norms. Goodman and Jinks note that the convergence (across states) is accompanied by substantial and persistent "decoupling" (within states): official purposes and formal structure are disconnected from functional demands. Rather than correlating with local task demands, structural attributes and official goals of the state correlate in important ways with attributes and goals of other states in the world.[145]

However, state commitments at the international level are not necessarily implemented. If such international commitments do not fit the local needs of states, there is further decoupling between international convergence across states and the implementation within states.[146]

Structural isomorphism and decoupling contradicts realist theories that explain state behavior solely in terms of distribution of power. If distribution of power prevailed, it could be expected that poorer countries would be more inclined to yield to external pressure from powerful actors and adopt particular practices. Empirical studies on welfare and labor policy, civil rights guarantees, and public order maintenance summarized by Goodman and Jinks show that norm adoption does not correlate with the economic wealth or development of countries. Further, realist theory would suggest that powerful states would put pressure on weaker states to mimic their actions. However, evidence shows that mimicry frequently occurs regardless of whether there is external political pressure to conform. Lastly, theories involving coercion have difficulties explaining persistent decoupling; why would powerful states accept formal policy convergence across states without effective implementation within states?[147]

A related, still separate perspective is based on the premise that designs of international institutions are often not purely intentional. Instead, they are the result of prior historical choices and emerge, in part, through path dependence, earlier choices constraining later ones.[148]

Some of the processes and mechanisms described in the present section are revisited in section 2.4 on the sociological study of international law.

1.3.5 Non-state actors

According to a traditional understanding of international law, states are the main actors in international system. However, non-state actors such as transnational corporations (TNCs) and non-governmental organizations (NGOs) may influence and be actors in the international system. To various degrees, the international law may impose duties and obligations on such non-state

145 Goodman and Jinks, 2004, pp. 647–649.
146 Goodman and Jinks, 2004, p. 651.
147 Goodman and Jinks, 2004, pp. 652–653.
148 Hafner-Burton, Victor and Lupu, 2012, p. 82. On path dependence, see section 2.1.2 on liberal institutionalism.

actors.[149] Even though they are not parties to a dispute, non-state-actors may intervene or otherwise make submissions during international judicial proceedings. A very restrictive approach on the right to intervention might hinder or delay a development of the law, while a permissive approach might undermine states' control over the dispute or cause extra cost and work for the court.[150]

TNCs are usually regulated under national law. However, they may still exercise influence on the international level vis-à-vis states. Further, states may be internationally responsible for the acts of entities which, even if they are not state organs, are actually empowered by the law of the state to exercise elements of governmental authority.[151]

NGOs may influence regimes in different roles and manners: mobilizers of public opinion; providers of information about situations unknown for states; defenders of viewpoints that governments do not represent or under-represent; watchdogs or private enforcement agents; policy analysts and expert advisors to governments; and bridges between state and non-state actors connecting local and global politics. This interaction is, to various extents, regulated. For example, such explicit authority to engage with NGOs may be found in the UN Charter:[152] "[t]he Economic and Social Council may make suitable arrangements for consultation with non-governmental organizations which are concerned with matters within its competence".[153] These matters are revisited in sections 3.4, 4.4, 5.4, 6.4 and 7.4.

1.4 Applying social science methods to state behavior at the international level

1.4.1 Knowledge in legal research and international relations

Çali suggests that there are four different types of knowledge in the fields of international relations and international law: factual knowledge, empirical knowledge, conceptual knowledge and normative knowledge. In the context of this book, *factual knowledge* may, for example, involve information about which states have ratified a treaty or other facts as opposed to theories or

149 Clapham, Andrew, *Human Rights Obligations of Non-State Actors* (Oxford: Oxford University Press, 2006), p. 27.

150 Lindblom, Anna-Karin, *The Legal Status of Non-Governmental Organizations in International Law* (Uppsala: Uppsala University, 2001), p. 283.

151 Draft Articles on "Responibility of States for internationally wrongful acts", International Law Commission, 2001, Article 5; Claphman, p. 239.

152 Esty, Daniel C., 'Non-Governmental organizations at the World Trade Organization: Cooperation, Competition or Exclusion', 1 *Journal of International Economic Law* (1998) 123–147, p. 129; van den Bossche, Peter, 'NGO Involvement in the WTO: A Comparative Perspective', 11 *Journal of International Economic Law* (2008) 717–749, p. 722; Niemetz, Martin Daniel, 'Empowering Civil Society: How to Increase the Input of NGOs into Security Council Deliberation', 6 *Journal of Human Rights Practice* (2014) 69–88, pp. 70–71.

153 Charter of the United Nations, 26 June 1945, 1 UNTS XVI, Article 71.

personal interpretations. The two disciplines may apply different levels of detail to factual knowledge. *Empirical knowledge* may involve qualitative or quantitative research techniques. Empirical knowledge may involve theories and/or interpretations as opposed to factual knowledge. International law research is traditionally an outsider to the vocabulary of qualitative or quantitative research techniques. However, international law still involves collection and analysis of the actual practice of states in order to determine whether a norm of international customary law exists. The prospects of empirical research in relation to norms are revisited below. *Conceptual knowledge* involves the understanding of the concepts used for a systematic enquiry. Here there is a strong overlap between the two disciplines, where international relations borrows more from international law, for example concepts such as state, consent and self-determination. *Normative knowledge* concerns what *ought to be* or *should be* as opposed to factual or empirical knowledge. In international relations, this may involve domains such as ethics and political theory. Law is normally perceived as normative and takes a different approach compared to international relations. The starting point in international law is primarily what the law *is* (*de lege lata*) and not what the law *ought to* be (*de lege ferenda*). In other words, the focus of international law is normally the norms that *do* govern international affairs, not which rules *should* govern international affairs. This is a different way to look at international morality.[154]

How is possible to conduct empirical research in relation to norms? How can we examine whether and to what extent international law influences state behavior? What would be an appropriate research-design? To the extent that international lawyers collect empirical data, the mode of data collection and interpretation normally differs from social science research in general. While international lawyers focus on data that can be associated with recognized legal sources (treaties, international customary law and general principles of law), international relations scholars accept a broader range of sources.[155] However, if we want to examine whether and to what extent international law influences state behavior, we arguably need to apply similar logics and methods as social sciences in general, including qualitative as well as quantitative methods.

154 Başak, Çali, 'International Law for International Relations: foundations for Interdisciplinary Study' in Başak, Çali (ed), *International Law for International Relations* (Oxford: Oxford University Press, 2010), pp. 3–24, pp. 12–16. Compare with Eide, Asbjörn, 'International Law, Dominance, and the Use of Force', 11 *Journal of Peace Research* (1974) 1–20, p. 1, who distinguishes "between three different aspects of the scholar's approach to the world society: (1) the empirical description of the 'real' world, its political, economic, and social structure and the processes taking place within it; (2) the description of the legal order (positive international law) within this system; (3) the normative orientation held by the scholar, as well as by other persons, in regard to the world society".

155 Başak, International Law for International Relations: foundations for Interdisciplinary Study, 2010, p. 14.

1.4.2 Case-oriented versus variable-oriented research

Social science research involves a decision on the number of cases studied. Three general comparative methods are available when studying states: global comparisons, few-country comparisons and single-case studies.[156]

The main strengths of variable-based global analysis include statistical control to rule out rival explanations, extensive coverage of cases, the ability to make strong inferences, and the identification of "deviant" cases or "outliers".[157] Simmons explains that quantitative research has the potential to check whether understandings generated from case studies can be generalized. It can also suggest systematic ways in which our "theories" might be amended or conditioned.[158]

Small-sample country comparisons use a middle level of abstraction with fewer cases than the global comparative analysis. It is meant to uncover the empirical relationship between the presence of key explanatory factors and the presence of an observed outcome. This can be done by adopting two distinct types of research design: "most similar systems design" (MSSD) and "most different systems design" (MDSD). Drawing on J.S. Mill's "method of difference", MSSD compares different outcomes across similar countries which allows the isolation of those factors that may account for an outcome. In contrast, MDSD compares similar outcomes across different countries. Drawing on Mill's "logic of agreement", MDSD compares countries which share few common features and then focuses on those factors common across countries that may account for an outcome.[159]

Single case studies are good for examining causal mechanism and temporal factors, and can generate new hypotheses and test hypotheses.[160] Within the single case study process-tracing may be used as a tool to trace the causal mechanism (see section 1.4.4). However, as Hume cautioned, we can never establish beyond doubt causal relations.[161] That said, the single case study may afford greater weight to historical nuances and explanations, aspects that are brushed over with a quantitative approach.[162]

156 Landman, Todd, 'Social Science Methods and Human Rights' in Coomans, Fons, Grünfeld, Fred. and Kamminga, Menno T. (eds), *Methods of Human Rights Research* (Antwerp and Oxford: Intersentia, 2009), pp. 19–44, p. 31.

157 Ibid, p. 31.

158 Simmons, Beth A, 'From ratification to compliance: quantitative evidence on the spiral model' in Risse, Thomas, Ropp, Stephen C. and Sikkink, Kathryn (eds), *The Persistent Power of Human Rights: From Commitment to Compliance* (Cambridge: Cambridge University Press, 2013), pp. 43–59, p. 43.

159 Landman, 2009, pp. 33–34.

160 Landman, 2009, p. 36.

161 Hume, David, *An Enquiry Concerning Human Understanding (1748)* (Oxford: Oxford University Press, 2007), pp. 60 and 67–68; commented by Oneal, John R., Russett, Bruce and Berbaum, Michael L., 'Causes of Peace: Democracy, Interdependence, and International Organizations, 1886–1992', 47 *International Studies Quarterly* (2003) 371–393, p. 374.

162 Hathaway, Oona A., 'Do Human Rights Treaties Make a Difference?', 111 *Yale Law Journal* (2002) 1935–2042, p. 1939.

There is no omnipotent method and the choice of method is a function of the research question.[163] It is possible to combine quantitative methods with large N and single case studies.[164] By combining combine qualitative and quantitative research, we may study the same phenomena from different angles.[165]

1.4.3 Correlation and causality

The basic technique for measuring the influence of international law on state behavior would be to correlate statistically a dependent variable (behavior) with an independent variable (norm). However, given that self-interest can coincide with normative behavior, this approach can only demonstrate that norms do not influence behavior. Causes are by nature non-observable. It is only possible to gain partial and uncertain knowledge about them through careful empirical studies.[166] Goertz and Diehl argue that the observation of state behavior can only indirectly infer the importance of a norm. To demonstrate the importance of a norm, it is important to check for self-interest, a principle relevant for case studies as well as for correlational research.[167]

It has been noted that correlation between ratification of a treaty and subsequent state behavior does not necessarily mean that an international legal norm is the cause of state behavior. The difficulty to establish whether international law influences state behavior involves the possibility that states ratify a treaty as a consequence of a policy change. Thus, the policy change is the cause for ratification and not the result of a treaty norm. In such a case the ratification only has an expressive function. Does this mean that international law is irrelevant? Henkin provides a reasonable answer in that:

> [l]aw is generally not designed to keep individuals from doing what they are eager to do. Much of law, and the most successful part, is a codification of existing mores, of how people behave and feel they ought to behave. To that extent law reflects, rather than imposes, existing order … The effective law system … is not the one that punishes the most violators, but rather that which has few violations to punish because the law deters potential violators.[168]

163 Landman, 2009, p. 20.

164 Gent and Shannon, 2011, who first present quantitative data with a large N (pp. 722–728) and then reinforce their argument by studying "The Gulf of Venezuela Maritime Claim" (pp. 728–729).

165 Simmons, 2013, p. 44.

166 Holland, Paul, 'Statistics and Causal Inference', 81 *Journal of American Statistical Association* (1986) 945–960, p. 959; Teorell, Jan and Svensson, Torsten, *Att fråga och att svara* (Malmö: Liber, 2007), p. 65.

167 Goertz, Gary and Diehl, Paul F., 'Toward a Theory of International Norms: Some Conceptual and Measurement Issues', 36 *Journal of Conflict Resolution* (1992) 634–664, pp. 642–644.

168 Henkin, 1979, p. 93.

Similarly, Hafner-Burton, Victor and Lupu find that formal measures of compliance often do not reveal much about whether legal institutions actually have an effect because states can select and influence the content of agreements and which agreements they join. Instead, they find that some of the most effective legal institutions are those whose formal levels of compliance are very low.[169] They point to insights from political science literature and emphasize that compliance rates are subject to selection effects and must be analyzed accordingly. States may, in some cases, select to join treaties because they would honor them anyway or because they are sure they can comply. In other cases, states might join treaties that they do not intend to honor, knowing that no other actor will be able to enforce compliance.[170] Thus, it is rather selection effects that explain the noticeable compliance of a state and less the law itself. They argue that compliance alone often is an incomplete concept for analyzing the effects of international law on state behavior.[171]

Thus, quantitative methods that show correlation between treaty commitment and state behavior do not necessarily prove a causal relationship. However, they can eliminate many alternative explanations that initially appear to be more reasonable.[172]

1.4.4 Process-tracing

Process-tracing is defined by its ambition to trace causal mechanisms, to go beyond merely identifying correlations between independent variables (Xs) and outcomes (Ys). It involves an attempt to identify the intervening causal process—the causal chain and mechanism. Process-tracing is a systematic internal single case study. It is, arguably, similar to the fact-finding process of a court. Three variants can be identified: (a) theory-testing process-tracing deduces a theory from the existing literature and then tests whether the evidence shows that each part of a hypothesized causal mechanism is present in a given case; (b) theory-building process-tracing seeks to build general theoretical explanations from empirical evidence; and (c) explaining-outcome process-tracing attempts to craft a minimally sufficient explanation of a puzzling outcome in a specific historical case. Process-tracing cannot be presented in narrative form, although temporal sequences can be relevant in testing causal mechanisms. Instead, it should be presented as a step-by-step test of each part of a causal mechanism.[173]

A theory-testing case study may be divided in three steps. First, the causal mechanism between x and y is conceptualized based on existing theorization.

169 Hafner-Burton, Victor and Lupu, 2012, p. 50.
170 Hafner-Burton, Victor and Lupu, 2012, pp. 88–89.
171 Hafner-Burton, Victor and Lupu, 2012, pp. 88–89.
172 Simmons, 2009, p. 199.
173 Teroell och Svensson, 2007, p. 247; Beach, Derek and Brun Pedersen, Rasmus, *Process-Tracing Methods. Foundations and Guidelines* (Ann Arbor, MI: The University of Michigan Press, 2013), pp. 1–3 and 5.

Second, the causal mechanism is operationalized, i.e. theoretical expectations are translated into case-specific predictions of what observable manifestations each part of the mechanism should have if the mechanism is present in the case. Lastly, empirical evidence is collected which is used to test whether the hypothesized mechanism was present and whether the mechanism functioned as predicted or only in part. However, theory-testing process-tracing does not enable us to test the relative explanatory power of competing mechanisms in the situation where two or more mechanisms can be conceptualized.[174] Case-selection is commonly performed after a regular association between X and Y has been found with other methods (often large-*n* studies). If regression analysis has been used, cases that are on or close to a regression line that plots the actual dependent variable score against predicted scores are suitable candidates.[175] Theory-testing studies are often nested in a broader mixed-method research program where case-selection strategies are based on the results of larger-*n* analyses. In such cases, the theory used for process-tracing must be compatible with that tested in the large-*n* analysis.[176]

Theory-building process-tracing is utilized in two different research situations: (a) when we know a correlation between x and y, but lack knowledge regarding potential mechanisms linking the two (X-Y-centric theory building); and (b) when we know an outcome (Y), but are unsure about the causes (Y-centric theory building). The difference compared with theory-testing is that theory-building involves identifying the theory before the fact, as opposed to identifying the fact before theory. It seeks to build a mid-range theory describing a causal mechanism that can be generalized outside the individual case study to a bounded context (spatially or temporally bounded). Theory-building process-tracing is primarily an inductive method, but may include deductive elements in that the scholar seeks inspiration from the existing theoretical work in related fields.[177] Case-selection in X-Y-centric theory building is a typical case, i.e. where both X and Y are present. Case-selection in Y-centric theory building resembles deviant case selection strategy, namely when the outcome (Y) demonstrates a surprising value.[178]

Process-tracing may, through case-studies, be used to uncover processes and mechanisms that give rise to international law.[179] Another option involves counterfactual reasoning which may probe limitations of an explanation advanced, as well as to reinforce their potential validity.[180] It is a hypothetical exercise to predict how events would have unfolded had a few elements of the

174 Beach and Brun Pedersen, 2013, pp. 14–15.
175 Beach and Brun Pedersen, 2013, pp. 146–149.
176 Beach and Brun Pedersen, 2013, p. 157.
177 Beach and Brun Pedersen, 2013, pp. 16–17.
178 Beach and Brun Pedersen, 2013, pp. 154–156.
179 Ginsburg and Shaffer, 2010, p. 768.
180 Ahmedi, Idris, *The Remaking of American Strategy toward Iran and Iraq: Outline of a Theory of Foreign Policy Change* (Stockholm: Stockholm University, 2013), pp. 92–93.

event been changed, with a focus on varying conditions that seem important and/or manipulable.[181] In the context of the present study, a relevant question is whether a state that has a legal obligation would act the same way in absence of that legal obligation. Pursuant to the same logic, one might ask the following question in order to explore the significance of the UN: How might the 1930s and 1940s have evolved had the League of Nations been designed in the same way as the United Nations? However, due to its hypothetical nature and the complexity of societal events, this method is quite weak and should be seen only as a complement to other methods.[182]

How social science methods may be applied to evaluate the impact of norms is revisited in relation to international trade (section 3.4), environmental protection (section 4.4), human rights (section 5.4), international criminal justice (section 6.4) and the use of force (section 7.4), using reviews on the empirical research by other scholars.[183]

181 van Evera, Stephen, *Guide to Methods for Students of Political Science* (Ithaca, NY: Cornell University Press, 1997), p. 25.

182 George, Alexander L. and Bennett, Andrew, *Case Studies and Theory Development in the Social Sciences* (Cambridge, MA and London: MIT Press, 2005), pp. 230–231; Young and Levy, 1999, p. 18.

183 See overviews provided by Ginsburg and Shaffer, 2010, and Hafner-Burton, Victor and Lupu, 2012.

2 Approaches to international regimes, power and law

2.1 Perception of regimes and rules in international relations

Theoretical approaches and debates in international relations rarely refer explicitly to international law. When they do, international law is dealt with as a marginal issue. However, whilst the terminology, language and assumptions differ from that used by international lawyers, international relations theory engages with international law in an implicit but significant manner. International relations scholars focus less on the legal standards, more on shared understandings, agreements and institutions.[1] The next section describes different approaches to international law adopted in international relations theory, and how they relate to and complement each other.

2.1.1 Realism

As a discipline, international relations theory has historically repudiated the prescriptive worth of international law to matters dealing with "vital national interest" or "high politics". The classical realist view on international relations concentrates exclusively upon the dynamics of power politics and the "balance of power".[2] Pursuant to this view, the foundations of the international system are a given and cannot be changed as they are based on human nature. Neo-realism has a slightly different approach where the international system remains unchanged due to the structural dynamics of a state-based-system. Thus, international order is about the use of state power to advance state interests.[3]

As stated above, realism concentrates exclusively upon the dynamics of power politics and the "balance of power". When another power increases its capacities through either internal or external efforts, others have incentives to

1 Adamson and Sriram, 2010, pp. 26–27.

2 Boyle, Francis Anthony, *World Politics and International Law* (Durham, NC: Duke University Press, 1985), pp. 3 and 8; Mearsheimer, John J., 'The False Promise of International Institutions', 19 *International Security* (1994) 5–49, p. 9.

3 Koskenniemi, Martti, 'The Empire(s) of International Law: System Change and Legal Transformation', 8 *Austrian Review of International and European Law* (2003) 61–68, p. 64.

look to their own position.[4] Balance of threat theory, a close cousin of balance of power theory, predicts that states will usually align together against a state that combines great power, geographical proximity, offensive capability and policies that suggest malign intent. The balance of threat theory explicitly incorporates assessments of intentions into a decision to balance.[5]

According to realist theory, international law and organizations totally lack any intrinsic significance. International law, morality, ethics and ideology are mere components in the power equation, devoid of non-instrumental significance or prescriptive worth, subject to compulsory service as tools of power when deemed necessary for the vital interests of state.[6] International organizations reflect, rather than effect, world politics. The competing perspective of "idealism" is perceived as naïve in its view of power.[7]

Morgenthau evaluates international law according to three functions that any legal system must fulfil: legislation, adjudication and enforcement. The decentralized nature of international law weakens these three functions. Morgenthau states that, "[w]here there is neither community of interests nor balance of power, there is no international law".[8]

Regimes are, essentially, a reflection of the distribution of power in the world. They are based on the self-interested calculations of the great powers, and they have no independent effect on state behavior. Realists, therefore, believe that regimes are not an important cause of peace. They matter only on the margins.[9] The most powerful states in the system create and shape institutions so that they can maintain their share of world power, or even increase it. In this view, institutions are "arenas for acting out power relationships".[10] International law exists and is complied with only when it is in the interests of a hegemon or a few powerful states, which coerce less powerful states into accepting the regime and complying with it.[11] States create rules for self-interested reasons and will feel no reluctance about violating rules when they cease to be in the state's interest.[12]

4 Morgenthau, 1954, p. 5; Waltz, Kenneth N., *Theory of International Politics* (Reading: Addison-Wesley, 1979), p. 118; Boyle, 1985, pp. 3 and 8; Posen, Barry, 'European Union Security and Defense Policy: Response to Unipolarity?', 15 *Security Studies* (2006) 149–186, p. 153.

5 Walt, Stephen M., *The Origins of Alliances* (Ithaca, NY: Cornell University Press, 1987), pp. 17–33; Posen, 2006, pp. 154 and 162.

6 Boyle, 1985, p. 7; Arend, 1999, p. 116; Ginsburg and Shaffer, 2010, p. 754.

7 Boehmer, Charles, Gartzke, Erik and Nordstrom, Timothy, 'Do Intergovernmental Organizations Promote Peace?', 57 *World Politics* (2004) 1–38, p. 1; Adamson and Sriram, 2010, pp. 27–29.

8 Morgenthau, Hans J., 'Positivism, Functionalism, and International Law', 34 *American Journal of International Law* (1940) 260–284, pp. 274–275; Morgenthau, 1954, p. 252.

9 Mearsheimer, 1994, p. 7. Mearsheimer treats regimes and institutions as synonymous concepts (see footnote 13); see Navari, Cornelia, 'Liberalisms' in Williams, Paul D. (ed), *Security Studies – an introduction* (2nd edn, London and New York, NY: Routledge, 2013), pp. 32–47, pp. 44–45, who contrasts realism with liberalism.

10 Mearsheimer, 1994, p. 13.

11 Hathaway, 2002, p. 1945.

12 Adamson and Sriram, 2010, p. 29.

Neo-realism and structural realism stand for a more nuanced approach by acknowledging the claim of institutionalism that regimes are a feature of the international system, but reach different conclusions about the circumstance in which regimes emerge and are maintained. According to this perspective, rules and regimes come about when they serve the power interests of states. When these arrangements no longer serve those interests, they are abandoned.[13] To the extent that binding legal rules work, the structural and neo-realist would argue that such rules bind the weaker members of the system, and enforcement depends on the willingness of stronger powers to bear the costs of enforcement. Policies based on legalism as an approach to world politics are likely to collapse under pressure.[14] This strand of realism focuses on how states use their power capabilities in situations requiring coordination, and the way that costs and benefits derived from the regime are divided up.[15]

Realists make a convincing argument that the distribution of power and state interests are key for understanding international relations. However, pure realism is unrealistic. As this book shows, nations rely on international law, invoke it, observe it and are influenced by it. Even states that wish to escape from legal obligations are usually compelled to invoke legal principles in order to escape.[16] We cannot reject the effectiveness and existence of international law merely on significant, but still infrequent, violations committed by powerful and/or rogue states. Henkin suggests that international law is principally aimed at the mass of states; it is not effective against "the Hitlers".[17] Morgenthau describes the denial of the existence of international law as a misconception and "the result of the disproportionate attention that public opinion has paid in recent times to a small fraction of international law, while neglecting the main body of it".[18]

2.1.2 Liberal institutionalism

Liberal and institutionalist arguments are often intertwined as liberal institutionalism. When the two are disaggregated, certain elements can be noted. A central argument of liberal international relations theory is that domestic politics matters in order to understand a state's behavior at the international level. According this view, compliance depends significantly on whether or not the state can be characterized as "liberal" in identity, that is, a representative

13 Arend, 1999, p. 116; Hathaway, 2002, p. 1945.

14 Stein, Arthur A., 'Coordination and collaboration: regimes in an anarchic world' in Krasner, Stephen D. (ed), *International Regimes* (Ithaca, NY and London: Cornell University Press, 1983), pp. 115–140, pp. 116 and 127–129; Goldstein et al., 2001, p. 7; Little, Richard, 'International regimes' in Baylis, John, Smith, Steve and Owens, Patricia (eds), *The Globalization of World Politics* (5th edn, Oxford: Oxford University Press, 2011), pp. 294–307, pp. 296–297.

15 Stein, 1983, pp. 129–132; Little, 2011, pp. 296–297.

16 Henkin, 1979, pp. 4 and 20.

17 Henkin, 1979, pp. 4, 20 and 94.

18 Morgenthau, 1954, p. 251.

government, upholding civil and political rights guarantees, and the rule of law.[19] Institutionalism combines realist and liberal perspectives on international relations by focusing on the rational self-interest of states. They differ from realists in that they believe that international institutions can come to have an autonomous agency of their own. Because of the focus on rational self-interest, institutionalism easily incorporates to game theory,[20] described in section 1.3.1 on reciprocity.

A key question is why and when do states—even powerful states—accept international legal regimes when their autonomy would be less constrained without legalization? With a cost–benefit analysis, all states profit from international law in terms of order and stability. These advantages come at a price, however. International law limits freedom of action and autonomy. States may have different preferences, i.e. they have different cost–benefit analyses depending on domestic policies, as well as relative distribution of power. More powerful states tend to be less willing to give up their autonomy. However, even powerful states cannot commonly obtain what they want by force, but must offer something in return based on principles of reciprocity and compensation.[21]

Although liberal institutionalists in the past have avoided directly discussing international law, they have used the concept of international regimes and institutions, which has a close affinity to international law.[22] The use and definition of "regimes" adopted early on by most theorists required neither formal institutions nor enforcement powers. Much of the ensuing literature on regimes focused on informal cooperation and largely ignored traditional international organizations and international law. Later work in this field has adopted a broader view of institutions that encompasses law, as well as international legal institutions.[23] In essence, liberal institutionalism claims that regimes can have significant roles to play in the behavior of states.[24]

According to liberal institutionalism, it is more worthwhile to construct regimes instead of *ad hoc* agreements in order to avoid transaction costs and facilitate the operation of reciprocity.[25] Liberal institutionalists expect interstate cooperation to occur if states have significant common interests.[26] Stein argues that the same factors that explain regime formation (e.g. a common

19 Koh, 1997, p. 2633.
20 Adamson and Sriram, 2010, pp. 34–35.
21 Henkin, 1979, pp. 29–31.
22 Reus-Smit, Christian, 'International law' in Baylis, John, Smith, Steve and Owens, Patricia (eds), *The Globalization of World Politics* (5th edn, Oxford: Oxford University Press, 2011), pp. 278–292, p. 289. See also Dunoff and Pollack, 2013, p. 6.
23 Hathaway, 2002, p. 1949.
24 Arend, 1999, p. 121.
25 Keohane, Robert O., 'The demand for international regimes' in Krasner, Stephen D. (ed), *International Regimes* (Ithaca, NY and London: Cornell University Press, 1983), pp. 141–171, pp. 150–151; Keohane and Martin, 1995, p. 42; Goldstein et al., 2001, p. 13; Ginsburg and Shaffer, 2010, p. 754.
26 Keohane and Martin, 1995, p. 39.

interest) also explain regime maintenance, change and dissolution. Regimes are maintained as long as the patterns of interest that gave rise to them remain. Regimes may be maintained even after shifts in the interests that gave rise to them, as states do not continually calculate their interactions and transactions. Once in place, institutions serve to guide patterned behavior. Institutions may be required again in the future and the costs of destruction or reconstruction for short-term-changes may be too costly in the long term. They can also be maintained and sustained by tradition and legitimacy. Stein also states that institutions may change the perceived interests of a state,[27] a claim shared with constructivism.

Liberal institutionalists indicate two main routes for regime formation. The first route is with or without a dominant/hegemonic power. The theory of hegemonic stability holds that concentration of power in one dominant state facilitates the development of strong regimes, and that fragmentation of power is associated with regime collapse. However, regimes may still persist when a hegemon declines. When states move away from a competitive sub-optimal outcome, there is no incentive to defect from mutually collaborative strategies. The second route for establishing and maintaining a regime is the principle of reciprocity. Inspection and surveillance facilities become important for ensuing that states are operating within the parameters of a regime.[28] This does not mean that the distribution of power is irrelevant. Institutionalism theory "posits that international institutions are created in response to state interests, and that their character is structured by the prevailing distribution of capabilities".[29] Keohane and Martin argue that, "institutions make a significant difference in conjunction with power realities".[30] In response to the realist assertion that institutions are merely a tool for powerful states, it could be argued that international law may serve as a conduit for weak and powerful states alike to magnify their influence in terms of power. Recognizing the central role of power does not make international law irrelevant or imply that international law has no effect on its own.[31]

Institutionalism argues that institutions, once created, develop an identity and power of their own. Path dependency may constrain state behavior, even where states may wish to deviate from agreed rules. Their ability to reduce transaction costs, increase transparency and enable regularity and stability may constrain state behavior even after they cease to serve the original state interests. Institutionalists argue that states are usually more concerned with achieving *absolute gains* than *relative gains*, which means that powerful states may accept a relative loss, but overall absolute gain for all.[32]

27 Stein, 1983, pp. 137–139. See also Finlayson and Zacher, 1983, p. 305.
28 Keohane, 1983, p. 142; Little, 2011, p. 303.
29 Keohane and Martin, 1995, p. 47.
30 Keohane and Martin, 1995, p. 42.
31 Hafner-Burton, Victor and Lupu, 2012, p. 52.
32 Adamson and Sriram, 2010, p. 35; Hafner-Burton, Victor and Lupu, 2012, p. 82. On path dependence, see section 1.3.4. on socialisation.

What is the function of regimes? As indicated above, a possible condition for the formation and maintenance of a strong regime is that all states, especially the major powers, prefer a regulated environment to one in which all states behave individualistically.[33] The assumption is that international legal regimes can be explained in terms of their functional value, i.e. what benefits they provide to the actors involved.[34] The functional value corresponds to challenges of different types, including: (a) collective action problems (e.g. common environmental concerns); (b) coordination problems (e.g. harmonizing regulatory trade standards); (c) institutionalize and legitimize policy outcomes desired by particular states and other actors, advancing some positions over others; and (d) serve expressive functions (e.g. human rights law).[35] The function of the surveyed regimes is revisited in sections 3.1, 4.1, 5.1, 6.1 and 7.1.

2.1.3 Constructivism

Constructivists assume that the structure of the international system is a "social structure".[36] Ruggie holds that, "the system of states is embedded in a society of states, which includes sets of values, rules, and institutions that are commonly accepted by states and which make it possible for the system of states to function".[37] Wendt holds that:

> constructivists are structuralist ... Where neorealist and constructivist structuralisms really differ, however, is in their assumptions about what structure is made of. Neorealists think it is made only of a distribution of material capabilities, whereas constructivists think it is also made of social relationships. Social structures have three elements: shared knowledge, material resources, and practices.[38]

As social actors, states are influenced by international norms that prescribe what is considered to be appropriate and inappropriate behavior.[39]

In comparison with realism, the constructivist view on international relations conveys more optimism on the possibility to change the system. The interests of actors are not taken for granted; instead, contructivism

33 Jervis, Robert, 'Security Regimes' in Krasner, Stephen D. (ed), *International Regimes* (Ithaca, NY and London: Cornell University Press, 1983), pp. 173–194, p. 176.

34 Goldstein et al., 2001, pp. 6, 12 and 14.

35 Ginsburg and Shaffer, 2010, p. 756. See also Stein, 1983.

36 Arend, 1999, p. 127.

37 Ruggie, John Gerard, *Constructing the World Policy: Essays on International Institutionalism* (London and New York, NY: Routledge, 1998), p. 11; see also Arend, 1999, p. 127 and Dunoff and Pollack, 2013, p. 6.

38 Wendt, Alexander, 'Constructing International Politics', 20 *International Security* (1995) 71–81, pp. 72–73.

39 Adamson and Sriram, 2010, p. 37.

problematizes and relates them to the identities of the actors involved.[40] Wendt has made the observation that in the traditional game-theoretic analysis of cooperation, the structure of the game—of identities and interests—is exogenous to interaction and, as such, does not change. The norms that evolve from interaction are treated as rules and behavioral regularities which are external to the actors and which resist change because of the transaction costs of creating new ones. A constructivist analysis of cooperation would concentrate on how the expectations produced by behavior affect identities and interests. The process of creating institutions is one of internalizing new understandings of self and other, of acquiring new role identities, not just of creating external constraints on the behavior of exogenously constituted actors. Even if not intended as such, the process by which egoists learn to cooperate is at the same time a process of reconstructing their interests in terms of shared commitments to social norms.[41] In other words, there is a process of socialization of legal norms.[42]

Wendt makes a caveat, to say that the fact that structures are socially constructed is no guarantee that they can be changed. Sometimes social structures may constrain action so that transformative strategies are impossible. This is explained by the collective nature of social structures; structural change depends on changing a system of expectations that may be mutually reinforcing. Wendt argues that a key issue in determining policy-makers' responsibilities, therefore, is how much "slack" a social structure contains. Neo-realists would argue there is little slack in the system, and thus states that deviate from power politics will get punished or killed by the "logic" of anarchy. Instead, Wendt argues that such dangers have been greatly reduced by institutions such as sovereignty and democratic peace, and that there is therefore more possibility for change.[43]

2.1.4 The English School

The English School perspective on international law combines some of the views of both realists and constructivists, sharing many of the assumptions of the present book. The English School embraces the role of law, rules and norms in international society. It accepts realist premises regarding the nature of power in the international system at the same time as it identifies a place

40 Risse and Sikkink, 1999, pp. 8–9; Hafner-Burton, Victor and Lupu, 2012, p. 54.

41 Wendt, Alexander, 'Anarchy is what States Make of It: The Social Construction of Power Politics', 46 *International Organization* (1992) 391–425, pp. 416–417. See also Haas, Mark, 'The United States and the End of the Cold War: Reactions to Shifts in Soviet Power, Policies, or Domestic Politics?', 61 *International Organization* (2007) 145–179, p. 148; Amnéus, Diana, *Responsibility to Protect by Military Means – Emerging Norms on Humanitarian Intervention?* (Stockholm: Stockholm University, 2008), pp. 35 and 39.

42 Wendt, 1992, p. 415. See also Finlayson and Zacher, 1983, p. 311, Arend, 1999, p. 118, and Ginsburg and Shaffer, 2010, p. 754.

43 Wendt, 1995, p. 80.

for law and rule-governed behavior. A key concept of the English School of realism is that states exist in an "international society", where the exercise of power occurs within a normative context.[44] Within this international society, states "comply with international law for communitarian reasons: not solely because of cost-benefit calculations about particular transactions, but because particular rules are nested within a much broader fabric of ongoing communal relations".[45] Bull argues that although international society is an anarchical society with no world government, it is nonetheless based on shared institutions and values.[46] He elaborates on the connection between the international society and international law in the following:

> A *society of states* (or international society) exists when a group of states, conscious of certain common interests and common values, form a society in the sense that they conceive themselves to be bound by a common set of rules in their relation with one another, and share in the working of common institutions.[47]

All societies share three elementary goals: security against violence, the honoring of agreements and the stability of possession. Bull does not embrace natural law in arguing that these goals are rules binding for all men, rather it is an empirical description of all actual societies.[48] The term "international society" should be distinguished from "international system". Where states "are in regular contact with one another and where in addition there is interaction between them sufficient to make the behavior of each a necessary element in the in the calculations of the others", there is an international system.[49] An international society is something more in the sense that the states should conceive that they share certain common interests and common values. An international society presupposes an international system, but an international system may exist that is not an international society.[50] However, Bull argues that, "[t]he element of international society has always been present in the moderns international system because at no stage can it be said that the conception of the common interests of states, or common rules accepted and common institutions worked by them, has ceased to exert an influence".[51] Hurrell has advanced a view of international society similar to that advanced

44 Koh, 1997, p. 2634; Adamson and Sriram, 2010, p. 38; Armstrong, David, Farrell, Theo and Lambert, Hélène, *International Law and International Relations* (2nd edn, Cambridge: Cambridge University Press, 2012), p. 87.

45 Koh, 1997, p. 2617.

46 Bull, 1977, reference in Adamson and Sriram, 2010, pp. 46–51.

47 Bull, 1977, p. 13.

48 Bull, 1977, pp. 5–6; Buzan, Barry, 'From International System to International Society: Structural Realism and Regime Theory Meet the English School', 47 *International Organization* (1993) 327–352, pp. 327 and 331.

49 Bull, 1977, p. 12; Buzan, 1993, pp. 327, 331 and 340–343.

50 Bull, 1977, pp. 13–14.

51 Bull, 1977, p. 42.

by Bull. However, Hurrell has taken the additional step of recognizing the special character of international law, the legal specificity that distinguishes it from other aspects studied by international relations scholars:[52]

> Being a political system, states will seek to interpret obligations to their own advantage. But being a legal system that is built on the consent of other parties, they will be constrained by the necessity of justifying their actions in legal terms. It is for these reasons that it is important to make a clearer distinction than is common in regime theory between specifically legal rules and the working of the legal system within which they operate on the one hand, and the wide variety of other formal and informal norms and rules and the processes of negotiation, bargaining, or imposition that underpin them on the other.[53]

The English School concept of international society is not conceived as a separate perspective or theory such as realism, liberalism and constructivism. The concept of international society provides a context within which international relations occur, rather than a systematic theory. It also explicitly examines the origins of the current international order, in contrast to realism and liberalism.[54] In this context, Buzan notes that the English School is largely based on historical work. He argues that the English School should be complemented with a functionally based account,[55] which is consistent with the approach of this book.

2.1.5 Feminism

Feminist theory views international relations as a reflection of gendered power relations and, consequently, international law as a reflection of gendered international order.[56] Feminism does not represent a unified theory or method.[57] A central concern within feminist scholarship on international law is the structural bias in women's positions of inequality as being outside international law's remit. International relations feminists generally agree with the claim that gender hierarchies are socially constructed and maintained through power structures that work against the participation of women in, for example, foreign and national security policy-making.[58] Even though

52 Byers, 1999, p. 32.

53 Hurrell, Andrew, 'International Society and the Study of Regimes: A Reflective Approach' in Rittberger, Volker (ed), *Regime Theory and International Relations* (Oxford: Clarendon, 1993), pp. 49–72, p. 61.

54 Adamson and Sriram, 2010, p. 38; Armstrong, Farrell and Lambert, 2012, p. 117.

55 Buzan, 1993, pp. 327, 329 and 335–336.

56 Adamson and Sriram, 2010, pp. 41–43.

57 Gunnarsson, Åsa and Svensson, Eva-Maria, *Genusrättsvetenskap* (Lund: Studentlitteratur, 2009), p. 27.

58 Amnéus, 2008; pp. 59 and 71.

such broad contours may be identified, there is significant diversity in feminist engagement in international law, from post-structural and post-modern preferences to more materialist analyses.[59]

The feminist perspective is revisited in relation to trade (section 3.3), environmental protection (section 4.3), human rights (section 5.3), international criminal justice (section 6.3) and the use of force (section 7.3).

2.2 International law

2.2.1 Objectives of international law

It is assumed that international law, like other law, exists as a response to social needs.[60] These social needs may be expressed in different words, for example function, interests or objectives.[61] Such objectives may concern peace, security, cooperation, human rights, sovereignty and non-intervention.[62] International law cannot be reduced to either rules or objectives; it is both.[63] Individual sources of law, such as a treaty or a custom, express complementary

59 Buss, Doris and Manji, Ambreena, 'Introduction' in Buss, Doris and Manji, Ambreena (eds), *International Law: Modern Feminist Approaches* (Oxford: Hart Publishing, 2005), pp. 1–16, pp. 2 and 6.

60 Morgenthau, 1940, p. 274; Koskenniemi, Martti, *From Apology to Utopia: The Structure of International Legal Argument* (reissue, New York, NY: Cambridge University Press, 2005), p. 24.

61 Pound, Roscoe, *An Introduction to the Philosophy of Law* (rev edn, New Haven, CT and London: Yale University Press, 1954), p. 44; Lehrberg, Bert, *Praktisk juridisk metod* (Uppsala: I.B.A., 2006), p. 220.

62 Preamble of the UN Charter; compare with Schwarzenberger and Brown, 1976, pp. 35–36; Stenhammar, 2008, p. 87.

63 Lauterpacht holds that in order to achieve "completeness in the law the judge must consider not only the letter of the law, but also its spirit and purpose", Lauterpacht, Hersch, *The Function of Law in the International Community* (originally published Oxford: Clarendon Press, 1933; Clark, NJ:The Lawbook Exchange, 2000), pp. 64 and 86; Morgenthau, 1940, pp. 274 and 267–268; Damaška, Mirjan R., *The Faces of Justice and State Authority* (New Haven, CT and London: Yale University Press, 1986), p. 21: "[E]ven specific rules contain an element of indeterminacy and can be interpreted in light of underlying goals as to lead to desirable outcomes"; Tapani holds that it is "a well known fact that legal decision-making is at the same time normbound and goal-oriented (teleological)", Klami, Hannu Tapani, Alexy, Robert and Bergholtz, Gunnar, 'A Note on Heuristics, Justification and Argument' in Aarnio, Aulis (ed), *Justice, Morality and Society A Tribute to Aleksander Peczenik on the Occasion of his Birthday 16 November 1997* (Lund: Juristförlaget, 1997), pp. 211–220, p. 219; Koskenniemi, 2005, pp. 209 and 564: "Existing academic works seemed to me too focused on either the formal or the substantive without suggesting a plausible account of the relations between the two … My first ambition … necessitated that I resist the pull of either excessive 'formalism' or excessive policy-oriented 'realism'."; Palmer, Vernon Valentine, 'From Lerotholi to Lando: Some Examples of Comparative Law Methodology', 53 *American Journal of Comparative Law* (2005) 261–290, p. 265: "[T]he challenge of the postmodern critique could be called that of making context manageable and of developing an *organic method* which incorporates both law and social underpinnings into the same comparative act".

or competing objectives.[64] For example, sovereignty may be in conflict with human rights, a dilemma present in cases of armed interventions for humanitarian reasons.

The line of thinking that law aspires to fulfil certain objectives has been carried forward in relation to national law by von Jhering,[65] Geny,[66] Heck[67] and Pound.[68] They consider the emphasis on objectives as an assault on what was perceived as legal formalism. Pound also applied this approach to international law, which involved a criticism of nineteenth-century naturalism and positivism.[69] Elements from Pound's theory were incorporated in the policy approach of McDougal,[70] and later his student, Judge Higgins, former president of the ICJ.[71] The policy approach was based on the American theory of legal realism and a defense of international law against international relations scholars who viewed international law as naive.[72] In that sense, international law is no different from domestic law; both concern certain objectives. However, the policy approach is vulnerable to criticism because it tends to ignore questions about the validity or content of law. Even more serious criticism concerns the subjectivism of the policy approach in its discussion of goal values.[73] The fundamental goal of the international community was often set by reference to US national interests.[74] The policy approach seems to see law not as it is, but always as becoming, and to conflate what the law is with what the law ought to be. Henkin argues that this is not the way states commonly look at law in deciding their own policy or in reacting to the behavior of others. To say that law seeks to fulfil certain objectives which may correspond to a particular policy is not to say that the law depends on the policy of any particular state. Once law of agreement is made, the obligation to abide by it is independent of the wishes of any particular state.[75] A reasonable approach is to stay clear of formalism, as well as the extreme version of the policy

64 Pound, Roscoe, *Jurisprudence* (St Paul, MN: West Publishing, 1959), volume III, part 4, pp. 31 and 334; MacCormick, Neil, *Legal Reasoning and Legal Theory* (Oxford: Clarendon Press, 1978), p. 106; Smits, 2009, p. 50; Klamberg, 2013, pp. 5–12.

65 Jhering, Rudolph von, *Der Zweck im Recht* (5th edn (printed 1916), Leipzig: Breitkopf und Härtel, 1877), pp. 44–45 and 360–361.

66 Geny, François, *Méthode d'interprétation et sources en droit privé positif* (2nd edn, Paris: Librairie générale de droit & de jurisprudence, 1954)

67 Heck, Philipp, *Begriffsbildung und Interessenjurisprudenz* (Tübingen: J.C.B. Mohr, 1932), p. 133f.

68 Pound, 1959, volume I, part 1, p. 358 and volume III, part 4, p. 15.

69 Pound, Roscoe, 'Philosophical Theory and International Law', 1 *Bibliotheca Visseriana Dissertationum Ius Internationale Illustrantium* (1923) 71–90, p. 89.

70 McDougal, Myres, 'International Law, Power, and Policy: A Contemporary Conception', 82 *Collected Courses of the Hague Academy of International Law (Recueil des Cours Académie de Droit International de La Haye)* (1953) 137–259, pp. 80–188.

71 Higgins, Rosalyn, *Problems and Process: International Law and How We Use it* (Oxford: Oxford University Press, 1994), p. 1.

72 Koh, 1997, pp. 2616–2618.

73 Koskenniemi, 2005, pp. 205–206.

74 Koh, 1997, p. 2623.

75 Henkin, 1979, p. 40.

approach. An attempt is made to portray the law as something more than its formal rules, but still strong in normative force. Rules cannot foresee every courtroom situation. They should be a framework, not a straitjacket. As stated above, law cannot be reduced to either rules or objectives; it is both.[76]

International law should be deconstructed in legal regimes keeping in mind that they together as a system still form a unity. A regime is not necessarily defined on the basis of its formal designation, but rather on what real and potential situations it aims to solve.[77] A regime may reflect several and overlapping objectives. A key assumption is that there is a *structural tendency* for a certain objective within a regime.[78] For example, when dealing with international trade, liberalization of trade is the main objective of the current regime, which is balanced against other objectives, such as environmental protection. The objectives of the surveyed regimes are revisited in sections 3.1, 4.1, 5.1, 6.1 and 7.1.

2.2.2 Legal fragmentation

The international system may be seen as a centralized system, fragmented entity or anarchy. As indicated earlier, this study claims that the international system is fragmented into sub-regimes that recognize different objectives (referred to below as principles by the ILC). By adopting the position between a centralized system and anarchy, it follows that there are some legal rules and institutions, although their relevance varies depending on the sub-regime.

The study-group of the ILC on fragmentation has in its report responded

76 Klamberg, 2013, p. 8.

77 An alternative to the term "specific procedural activity" could have been "function". However, the term "function" is sometimes used interchangeably with "purpose" which would make it difficult to distinguish from the term "objective" used in the present study. Zweigert, Konrad and Kötz, Hein, *Introduction to Comparative Law* (2nd edn, Oxford: Clarendon Press, 1987), pp. 5 and 30–36; Husa, Jaakko, 'Farewell to Functionalism or Methodological Tolerance?', 67 *Rabels Zeitschrift für ausländisches und internationales Privatrecht* (2003) 419–447, pp. 429–430. For accounts of functionalism in international law, see Falk, Richard A., 'New Approaches to the Study of International Law', 61 *American Journal of International Law* (1967) 477–495, pp. 491–493; see also May, Richard and Wierda, Marieke, *International Criminal Evidence* (New York, NY: Transnational Publishers, 2002), p. xv, and Koskenniemi, 2005, p. 523 footnote 15. A second alternative to the term "specific procedural activity" could have been "legal institution", a translation of *rättsinstitut* (Swedish) and *rechtsinstitut* (German). "Institut" in a Swedish legal context means "a group of legal rules that concern a specific need", translation from Bergström, Sture et al., *Juridikens termer* (9th edn, Stockholm: Liber, 2002), p. 89. However, the term "legal institution" appears to convey a meaning different from what is sought.

78 Kettler, David, *Domestic regimes, the rule of law, and democratic social change* (Berlin: Galda and Wilch, 2001), p. 85: "A regime may be said to intend a preferred type of outcome, but this design will be established in a structural tendency, subject to even quite important exceptions, and not in a purely instrumental machinery". Compare with Koskenniemi, Martti, 'Hegemonic Regime' in Young, Margaret A. (ed), *Regime Interaction in International Law Facing Fragmentation* (Cambridge: Cambridge University Press, 2012), pp. 305–324, p. 317, who discusses it in terms of "structural bias".

on the perceived emergence of new and special types of law, "self-contained regimes" and geographically or functionally limited treaty systems. The study-group argues that each rule-complex or "regime" comes with its own principles, its own form of expertise and its own "ethos", not necessarily identical to the ethos of neighboring specialization. They reflect the differing pursuits and preferences that actors in a pluralistic and global society have.[79] The approach of the ILC study group is similar to the approach of regime theory in international relations described above. Fragmentation is not a destructive phenomena *per se*, it could also be a sign of maturity reflecting the complexity and pluralism of international law.[80] A key explanation for this fragmentation is that there has never been a single global legislature or mandatory world court with general jurisdiction to mold a unified body of international law. Nor have states expressed the will to create such a system.[81]

Some legal scholars and practitioners perceive fragmentation as a threat which, *inter alia*, might undermine the authority of the ICJ. Others argue that the diversification provides space for exploration and experimentation, which is in an important prerequisite for the development of the law. The diversification of fora for dispute settlement is, arguably, conducive to an environment in which more international issue are authoritatively resolved by a multitude of international courts and organs.[82]

2.2.3 Regime interaction

2.2.3.1 Beyond technical coordination

Whatever the pros and cons may be, the phenomenon of fragmentation appears to be a reality of the international system. Regimes such as trade,

79 *Fragmentation of International Law: Difficulties Arising from the Diversification and Expansion of International Law*, Report of the Study Group of the International Law Commission, finalized by Martti Koskenniemi, UN Doc A/CN.4/L.682, 2006, paras 15–16; see also Cappelletti, Mauro, *The Judicial Process in Comparative Perspective* (Oxford: Clarendon Press, 1989), p. xiii: "[T]he world of humans … is composed of … the coexistence of contradictory values and principles, institutions and processes"; Vasiliev, Sergey, 'General Rules and Principles of International Criminal Procedure: Definition, Legal Nature, and Identification' in Sluiter, Göran and Vasiliev, Sergey (eds), *International Criminal Procedure Towards a Coherent Body of Law* (London: Cameron May, 2009), pp. 19–91, pp. 22–23.

80 Fogdestam Agius, Maria, *Interaction and delimitation of international legal orders* (Uppsala: Uppsala universitet 2013), p. 4.

81 Young, Margaret A., 'Introduction: the Productive Friction between Regimes' in Young, Margaret A. (ed), *Regime Interaction in International Law Facing Fragmentation* (Cambridge: Cambridge University Press, 2012), pp. 1–19, p. 2.

82 Charney, Jonathan I., 'Is International Law Threatened by Multiple International Tribunals?', 271 *Recueil des Cours* (1998), pp. 347 and 351; Stahn, Carsten and van den Herik, Larissa, '"Fragmentation", Diversification and "3D" Legal Pluralism: International Criminal Law as Jack-in-the Box?' in van den Herik, Larissa and Stahn, Carsten (eds), *The Diversification and Fragmentation of International Criminal Law* (Leiden and Boston, MA: Martinus Nijhoff Publishers, 2012), pp. 21–89, pp. 30–32.

human rights and environmental protection may in certain situations be in harmony, but may be in conflict with each other in different situations. They are neither fully integrated nor completely separated. Isolation of a regime may reflect a wish of states to protect their dominance. The differing mandates, principles, structures and non-identical state membership of regimes may lead to lack of coordination. Global problems, however, are not limited in scope to single regimes and this potentially creates conflicting norms between regimes. Young argues that the functional differentiation of regimes (envisaged in section 1.1 on defining regimes and section 2.2.2 on legal fragmentation) may lead to path dependency, higher transaction costs, "tunnel vision" and even "solipsistic and imperial" tendencies within regimes.[83] Snidal argues that international regimes are not independent of the existing global legal and political structure, they are "nested" so that the fabric of one provides the foundation of the other.[84] If international law is fragmented in regimes, how do the regimes interact? Young notes that regime theory "has tended to analyze single regimes, rather than regime interaction", although there is now a growing body of scholarship on regime interaction.[85] Regime interaction is relevant at different stages of international law-making, adjudication and enforcement, in the setting of agendas for new negotiations, during the ongoing norm elaboration within regimes and even for the domestic policy coordination between state ministries and departments.[86] More specifically, conflict clauses or declarations of mutual supportiveness may be introduced in international treaties as instructions to the parties. Examples of conflict clauses include the rule of *lex specialis derogat legi generali* (the primacy of the specific over the general, a more specific treaty will usually override the application of the general treaty), and the principle of *lex posterior derogat legi priori* (primacy of a more recent treaty over an earlier one). Moreover, international courts may, whether or not at the request of the parties, in their decisions approach overlapping regimes that are relevant for the dispute at hand.[87] However, regime interaction is, arguably, more than a question of technical coordination. One assumption is that there is a "harmony of interests" in the international system, a logical conclusion of which is that conflicts between states or between regimes emanate from problems of knowledge, not of political value. With a different assumption, clashes of interests or values between regimes are not about knowledge, but about radically incompatible preferences. Technical coordination will only enjoy weak authority where the chosen solution will be subject to chal-

83 Young, Introduction, 2012, pp. 10–11; Young, Margaret A., 'Regime Interaction in Creating, Implementing and Enforcing International Law' in Young, Margaret A. (ed), *Regime Interaction in International Law Facing Fragmentation* (Cambridge: Cambridge University Press, 2012), pp. 85–110, p. 85.
84 Snidal, 1986, p. 45.
85 Young, Introduction, 2012, p. 7.
86 Young, Introduction, 2012, p. 1.
87 Agius, 2013, pp. 5–6 and 715; Young, Introduction, 2012, p. 3.

lenges of being arbitrary. With the second assumption, "regime interaction" cannot be reduced to mere technical coordination.[88] This means that at a certain point either the "law-makers" (states) or the "adjudicators" (courts) must make a choice between interests. This should, arguably, be done in a transparent manner.

Johnsson and Urpelainen have developed a theory of regime integration and separation which highlights the nature of spillovers between issues. Positive spillovers exist when cooperation in one issue area aids the pursuit of objectives in another issue area. Negative spillovers exist when cooperation in one issue area impedes this pursuit in another issue area. They challenge the conventional wisdom which suggests that both positive and negative spillovers foster greater integration. Johnsson and Urpelainen argue that negative spillovers encourage integration, whereas positive spillovers do not. States integrate not to exploit positive spillovers between issues, but to mitigate negative spillovers. To test their theory, they examined the degree of integration or separation among environmental regimes, a study revisited later.[89]

2.2.3.2 Regime interaction and hegemony

The balancing point of interaction between international regimes is not necessarily permanent. Koskenniemi notes that much of the practice of international relations and international law is constituted by their efforts to develop rules, techniques and strategies to fortify the middle zone against collapse, and to make life there as good as possible. The concept of "hegemony" involves an acceptance that there is no permanent "ultimate" or "rational" ground in which conflicts between regimes are to be resolved. "Hegemony" should be understood as a universalization strategy or effort to appear as a representative of the universal. Koskenniemi argues that such strategies are commonplace in the international system (as well as in political life more generally).[90] Regimes are developed through the informal expansion of their vocabularies in academia and in bureaucracies, creating dominant frameworks and templates for the identification of problems and broad principles for their resolution.[91] Regimes on international trade, environmental protection and the use of force are all engaged in universalization strategies, trying to make their body of law, special knowledge and interest appear as representative of the general knowledge and common interest.[92]

88 Koskenniemi, 2012, pp. 307–308.

89 See section 4.4 on processes and mechanisms for creating and enforcing international environmental law; Johnson, Tana and Urpelainen, Johannes, 'A Strategic Theory of Regime Integration and Separation', 66 *International Organization* (2012) 645–677, pp. 645–646.

90 Koskenniemi, 2012, pp. 309–310.

91 Koskenniemi, 2012, pp. 317–319.

92 Koskenniemi, 2012, p. 315.

An alternative to full integration or complete separation is the creation of regime hybrids, such as "sustainable development", "human security" or "corporate social responsibility". The hegemonic nature of the struggle between regimes in this may be hidden in a vocabulary of technical cooperation in order to avoid an open politicization that would threaten the control of the process by the experts.[93]

2.2.3.3 Regime interaction in the creation, implementation and enforcement of international law

Young has highlighted empirical evidence of regime interaction in the creation, implementation and enforcement of international law relating to fisheries. Her study concerns the institutional collaboration and normative overlap between organizations such as the WTO, the United Nations Food and Agriculture Organization (FAO), and the Secretariat for the Convention on the International Trade in Endangered Species of Wild Fauna and Flora (CITES). She notes that: (a) the relevant laws were largely developed at different times; (b) the laws are implemented by different institutions, which have different powers of enforcement and relative strengths; (c) there is no uniform ratification of these laws by all states; and (d) these laws aim to fulfill particular sets of preferences within the international legal system, which may not be in harmony. She explains how regime interaction may erupt at different stages of law-making, settlement of disputes and enforcement. The legal bases and legitimacy of regime interaction are categorized into three broad concepts: parallel membership, mutual agreement of states and institutional arrangements (either formal or informal, within and between the organizations themselves). Regime interaction through parallel membership and mutual agreement is based on state consent and thus respects the principle of state sovereignty. To the extent that institutional arrangements explicitly allow for regime interaction,[94] such arrangements are also in conformity with state sovereignty. Interaction may also be based on a more informal basis, namely on implied powers, discussed in the next section.[95]

2.2.3.4 Implied powers

According to the doctrine of implied powers, international organizations (institutions) may, in addition to powers explicitly attributed to them, use so-called "implied" powers. The concept of implied powers is based on the rationale that the powers of an international organization constitute the means

93 Koskenniemi, 2012, pp. 319–320.

94 For example Rome Statute of the International Criminal Court, 17 July 1998, 2187 UNTS 90, Article 2, which allows the ICC to enter into relationship with the UN. See also Articles 13(b) and 16.

95 Young, Regime Interaction, 2012, pp. 85, 88–92 and 95–99.

through which an organization fulfills its purposes vis-à-vis its members.[96] The doctrine of implied powers derives its origin from teleological interpretation and the wording of Article 31(1) of the Vienna Convention on the Law of Treaties (VCLT), "in light of its object and purpose". According to this doctrine, an organization is not limited to such acts or rights as are specified in its constituent instrument.[97] Chaumont holds that implied powers "while not textually provided for by the creators of the organization, have been recognized or accepted by the member states within a certain period of life of the organization as auxiliary or subordinate means to accomplish the permanent ends for which the organization was founded".[98] The doctrine of implied powers is well accepted in international law.[99] The ICJ recognized it in express terms when it stated in the *Reparation for Injuries* case that:

> [u]nder international law, the Organization must be deemed to have those powers which, though not expressly provided in the Charter, are conferred upon it by necessary implication as being essential to the performance of its duties ... the rights and duties of an entity such as the Organization must depend upon its purposes and functions as specified or implied in its constituent documents and developed in practice.[100]

Functions and powers, if not provided for, may be implied only if they are necessary to fulfil the purposes of the organization.[101] Judge Hackworth expressed in his dissenting opinion in the *Reparation for Injuries* case that, "[p]owers not expressed cannot freely be implied. Implied powers flow from

96 Rama-Montaldo, Manuel, 'International Legal Personality and Implied Powers of International Organizations', 44 *British Yearbook of International Law* (1970) 111–156, p. 153. See comment in Klamberg, 2013, pp. 74–76.

97 Sevastik, Per, 'Reflections on the Interpretation of the UN Charter and its Binding Force' in Svanberg-Torpman, Katinka and Amnéus, Diana (ed), *Peace and Security* (Lund: Studentlitteratur, 2004), pp. 23–51, p. 39.

98 Chaumont, Charles M., 'La Signification du Principe de Spécialité des Organisations Internationales' in Rolin, Henri (ed), *Mélanges offerts à Henri Rolin Problèmes de droit de gens* (Paris: A. Pedone, 1964), pp. 55–66, p. 59; see also Sevastik, 2004, p. 39.

99 Sarooshi, Danesh, 'The Powers of the United Nations International Criminal Tribunals', 2 *Max Planck Yearbook of United Nations Law* (1998) 141–167, p. 144, footnote 7; Bohlander, Michael, 'The influence of academic research on the jurisprudence of the International Criminal Tribunal for the Former Yugoslavia – A first overview', 3 *The Global Community Yearbook of International Law and Jurisprudence* (2003) 195–209, p. 226; Klabbers, Jan, *An Introduction to International Institutional Law* (2nd edn, Cambridge: Cambridge University Press, 2009), pp. 59–64.

100 *Reparation for Injuries Suffered in the Service of the United Nations*, ICJ, Advisory Opinion, 11 April 1949, pp. 180 and 182.

101 Rama-Montaldo, pp. 153–154; Martines, Francesca, 'Legal Status and Powers of the Court' in Cassese, Antonio, Gaeta, Paola and Jones, John R.W.D (eds), *The Rome Statute of the International Criminal Court* (Oxford: Oxford University Press, 2002), pp. 203–218, p. 216; Sluiter, Göran, *International Criminal Adjudication and the Collection of Evidence: Obligations of States* (Antwerpen, Oxford and New York, NY: Intersentia, 2002), p. 28; Crawford, James, *Brownlie's Principles of Public International Law* (8th edn, Oxford: Oxford University Press, 2012), p. 188.

a grant of expressed powers, and are limited to those that are 'necessary' to the exercise of powers expressly granted".[102] Judge Hackworth thus disagreed with the majority and held that the majority used an unduly wide version of the implied powers doctrine. However, it is the wider majority version that is often thought to prevail.[103]

Young argues that the principle of implied powers is highly relevant to the phenomenon of fragmentation in international law. When regimes are dependent on other regimes, such as the WTO's proposed reliance on standard-setting and benchmarking functions in the fishery subsidy disciplines, intergovernmental organizations (IGOs) will have the discretion to learn and apply norms and facts from external sources because such collaboration is necessary for their functions. She notes that using implied powers in the context of regime interaction is controversial, as it suggests that not only states, but also organizations may contribute to the change and evolution in international law. States need to be involved as stakeholders, involved in mechanisms exercising scrutiny and involved review, in order to maintain the legitimacy of international institutions.[104]

2.2.4 Subjects of international law

Traditionally, it was held that only states were subjects of international law. Whatever role other agents, such as individuals, groups, international organizations or IGOs might play, they could figure in international law only as objects of it and not as subjects. The evolution of international law, particularly after the end of World War II, has made individuals, groups, international organizations and IGOs into subjects of international law in the sense that they are not merely affected by the rules of international law, but may also have duties and rights conferred upon them.[105]

2.3 Relationship between power and law

If international law exists as a response to social needs, as suggested in section 2.2.1, the relationship between power and law becomes relevant. The distribution of power may explain why certain rules are adopted, how they are interpreted and implemented. Hans Morgenthau and Carl Schmitt are both interesting for this study because they were both lawyers by training who examined the relationship between power and law.

Morgenthau set out in his early writings for a functional theory of international law intended to develop systematically concepts and methods capable

102 *Reparation for Injuries Suffered in the Service of the United Nations*, ICJ, Advisory Opinion, dissenting opinion by Judge Hackworth, 11 April 1949, p. 198.

103 Klabbers, 2009, pp. 60–61.

104 Young, Regime Interaction, 2012, pp. 100 and 103–107.

105 Bull, 1977, p. 129.

of conveying the legal characteristics, as well as the functional dependence on political factors, of political international law.[106] Scheurerman has noted that Morgenthau never fully developed this theory and his early writings are devoid of an adequate discussion of the interplay between justice and a workable system of legality, the existing state system and international law.[107] Morgenthau appears to share some assumptions of this study, namely: (a) law is based on interests; and (b) he differentiates between different areas, regimes of law. In the first regard, he argues that:

> [i]nternational law owes its existence to identical or complementary interests of states, backed by power as a last resort, or, where such identical interests do not exist, to a mere balance of power which prevents a state from breaking these rules of international law. Where there is neither community of interests nor balance of power, there is no international law.[108]

When it comes to regimes, Morgenthau distinguishes in his early as well as later writings between technical matters, non-political international law on the one hand and international law dealing with political matters on the other hand.[109] Oye notes that international relations between states can approximate both a Hobbesian state of nature and a Lockean civil society.[110] Other scholars make a similar distinction, arguing that economic and resource areas are more likely candidates for effective regimes. Security regimes are considered especially difficult to achieve compared to other areas.[111] Henkin states that there are areas of international relations for which there are no relevant norms, but it is very exceptional with cases where it is impossible to determine whether a state is in compliance or violation.[112] Even some institutionalists have made the assertion that international politics can be divided into two realms—security and political economy—and that liberal institutionalism mainly applies to the latter. However, Keohane and Martin argue that it is not the predominant view of institutionalist literature. They argue together with Axelrod that a single framework of analysis can throw light on both political-economic

106 Morgenthau, 1940, p. 274, p. 280.

107 Scheuerman, William E., 'A theoretical missed opportunity? Hans J. Morgenthau as Critical Realist' in Bell, Duncan (ed), *Political Thought and International Relations: Variations on a Realist Theme* (Oxford: Oxford University Press, 2008), pp. 50 and 53.

108 Morgenthau, 1940, p. 274, p. 275; repeated in Morgenthau, 1954, p. 252.

109 Morgenthau, 1940, p. 274, p. 279; Morgenthau, 1954, pp. 256–257; Koskenniemi, Martti, *The Gentle Civilizer of Nations: The Rise and Fall of International Law 1870–1960* (Cambridge: Cambridge University Press, 2001), p. 464.

110 Oye, 1986, p. 1.

111 Jervis, Robert, 'Cooperation Under the Security Dilemma', 30 *World Politics* (1978) 167–214, pp. 194 and 199–209; Jervis, 1983, pp. 173–176; Axelrod and Keohane, 1986, p. 226; Lipson commented by Mearsheimer, 1994, p. 16; Arend, 1999, p. 122; Goldstein et al., 2001, p. 2.

112 Henkin, 1979, p. 41.

relationships and military-security relationships. Institutionalist theory should be highly applicable to security issues because its argument revolves around the role of institutions in providing information.[113] This study shares the view that a single framework of analysis can be used. However, such analysis highlights that the degree of legalization varies between different realms (in the present study: regimes).

Turning to Schmitt, the present author is cognizant of the problematic nature of Schmitt and his writings because of his association with the Nazis in the Third Reich, anti-Semitism, radical anti-universalism and critique of liberalism. However, international relations as a discipline has incorporated some Schmittian insights that may still be relevant to the study of international relations and international law. Leftist critics of liberalism have appropriated him in a recent revival, but many of his thoughts on the use of force might as well be described as realist. Chandler writes that, "Schmitt was the forerunner of political realism, as exemplified in the work of Hans Morgenthau, E. H. Carr and Hedley Bull. Like all three of these later writers, he appreciated that while power relations could not be legislated or wished away, they could be managed".[114] For Schmitt,"[t]he justification of war does not reside in its being fought for ideals or norms of justice, but in its being fought against a real enemy".[115] Another submission of Schmitt is his definition of the sovereign, namely "he who decides on the exception", that is to say, on "whether there is an extreme emergency as well as what should be done to counter it".[116] This is relevant for the discussion on the relationship between delegation and distribution of power.

In the same manner as law and power are juxtaposed, law and policy are often contrasted, suggesting that law is obligatory and policy is voluntary. A more reasonable approach would be that, "law and policy are not in meaningful contrast ... All law is an instrument of policy, broadly conceived".[117] A

113 Keohane and Martin, 1995, p. 43; Axelrod and Keohane, 1986, pp. 227 and 231.

114 Chandler, David, 'The Revival of Carl Schmitt in International Relations: The Last Refuge of Critical Theorists?', 37 *Journal of International Studies* (2008) 27–48, p. 45; Koskenniemi, 2001, p. 424; Wrange, Pål, *Impartial or Uninvolved? The Anatomy of 20th Century Doctrine on the Law of Neutrality* (Visby: Elanders, 2007), p. 499.

115 Schmitt, Carl, *The Concept of the Political* (trans. from Der Begriff der Politischen (1932), Chicago, IL and London: The University of Chicago Press, 1996), p. 49. Schmitt writes on pp. 27–28: "The political enemy need not be morally evil or aesthetically ugly; he need to appear as an economic competitor, and it may even be advantageous to engage with him in business transactions. But he is, nevertheless, the other, the stranger; and it is sufficient for his nature that he is, in a specially intense way, existentially something different and alien, so that in the extreme case conflicts with him are possible ... The enemy is not merely any competitor or just any partner of a conflict in general. He is also not the private adversary whom one hates. An enemy exists only when, at least potentially, one fighting collectivity of people confronts a similar collectivit".

116 Schmitt, Carl, *Political Theology. Four Chapters on the Concept of Sovereignty* (trans. from Politische Theologie: Vier Kapitel zur Lehre von der Souveränität (1922/1934), Cambridge, MA and London: MIT Press, 1922), pp. 5–7; Koskenniemi, 2001, p. 428.

117 Henkin, 1979, p. 90.

response to realism is that it misconceives the purpose of law. Henkin argues that:

> [l]aw is generally not designed to keep individuals from doing what they are eager to do. Much of law, and the most successful part, is a codification of existing mores, of how people behave and the feel they ought to behave. To that extent law reflects, rather than imposes, existing order … The effective law system … is not the one than punishes the most violators, but rather that which has few violations to punish because the law deters potential violators.[118]

2.4 Sociological study of international law

This book concerns the relationship between the scholarly disciplines of international relations and international law. Legal studies and sociology are two separate scholarly disciplines which are opposed in method and aims. Legal studies concerns the art of government through rules, its concern is prescriptive and technical. Sociology is concerned with the scientific study of social phenomena, its concern is explanatory and descriptive. Yet both disciplines are concerned with the whole range of social relationships and typically seek to view these phenomena as part of, or potentially part of, an integrated social structure. Law is the practical craft of systematic control of social relations and institutions. Sociology is the scientific enterprise that seeks systematic knowledge about them. Both sociology and law are concerned with norms, rules that prescribe the appropriate behavior for people in a given situation. The study of conflict and conflict resolution are central in both disciplines. The sociological study of law is sometimes perceived as either a part of sociology or legal studies, in some countries legal sociology is a separate scholarly discipline.[119] Normally, the disciplines of law and sociology focus on relationships within a state on a domestic level. The difference with international relations and international law is that the main study subject is states and their relationships at an international level. Koh has noted that although the phenomenon of obedience to law "has been studied in the domestic law context by psychologists, philosophers, anthropologists, and domestic lawyers, it has received far less direct attention in the international realm".[120] As indicated above, international law is prescriptive while the main concern of international relations is the causes and consequences of international cooperation and, increasingly, international legalization.[121] The assumption is that international law is not a self-contained abstraction: rather, it is a fabric for

118 Henkin, 1979, p. 93.

119 Cotterrell, Roger, *The Sociology of Law: An Introduction* (2nd edn, London, Dublin, Edinburgh: Butterworths, 1992), pp. 4–5; Landman, 2009, p. 25.

120 Koh, 1997, p. 2603.

121 Dunoff and Pollack, 2013, p. 1. See also Hafner-Burton, Victor and Lupu, 2012, p. 48.

international society established by and continuously evolving through the interaction of states. This means that any inquiry into the role of law must take into account the state of "the system"—the character of international society and of the law at a given time. Both international law and international relations look different depending on the period studied, whether it is the Peace of Westphalia; the birth of international institutions around the end of World War I; the establishment of the UN, proliferation of nation-states, the decades of the cold war;[122] the fall of the Berlin wall with fewer international and more non-international armed conflicts; and the era post the 9/11 terrorist attacks.

Cotterell notes that his book *The Sociology of Law* covers the law within states and not the "internationalization of law".[123] He does not even mention the relationships between states and international law. Considering that Cotterell's book is a standard in the field, there at first appears to be a gap in academia. It is argued here that there is no gap, the concerns of and relationship between the disciplines international relations and international law are the same as the relationship between law and sociology described above. Morgenthau called for a functional theory of international law that arrives at a real scientific understanding of the material element of legal rules. In his early writings, he argued that "realist" jurisprudence is, in truth, "functional" jurisprudence,[124] which may be seen the precursor to his subsequent contribution to realism in international relations. He emphasized the "particular relationship between the rules of international law and their sociological context".[125] However, Morgenthau decided in his call for a "functional jurisprudence" to avoid using the term "sociological jurisprudence". The latter concept was under the influence of Professor Pound's writings, and as such associated with the idea of "social engineering", which Morgenthau perceived as a "very premature proposition".[126] Regardless of labelling, an expansion in the use of methodological tools is called for. Traditional legal scholarship tends to assume, rather than examine, the efficacy of international law and cooperation. A methodological expansion would mean that legal scholars would take the reach and efficacy of international law as empirical questions, to be neither assumed (as in traditional doctrinal scholarship) nor explained away as unimportant (as in the realist tradition of international relations).[127] When setting out with a similar program, Henkin found that "almost all states observe almost all their obligations almost all of the time".[128] Downs, Rocke and Barsoom question such observations; state compliance with international agreements may generally

122 Henkin, 1979, pp. 5 and 7.
123 Cotterrell, 1992, p. 287.
124 Morgenthau, 1940, p. 274.
125 Morgenthau, 1940, p. 272.
126 Morgenthau, 1940, p. 274, footnotes 42 and 43.
127 Ginsburg and Shaffer, 2010, p. 755.
128 Henkin, 1979, pp. 47 and 246.

be quite good because states may choose to consent to obligations with which it is easy to comply.[129]

Turning back to mainstream legal sociology, it suggests that there is a process of legal socialization, i.e. mechanisms or processes by which commitment to law is developed in the individual. Cotterell argues that there is a sequence of three levels and six stages in orientation of the individual to law. The first level includes the stage of conformity merely to avoid punishment and the further "hedonistic stage" of conformity to obtain reward. If there is neither punishment nor a reward, the individual will, arguably, not obey the rules. This squares well with realist assumptions about power of states and international law. Realism appears to accept this first level, namely that states react to stimuli such as punishment and rewards, but reject other means of committing states to international law. The second level involves conformity to rules because they are rules. Its initial stage is conformity to please others followed by the stage of conformity to do "one's duty" or to express respect for authority. The third level is that of supporting moral principles as such, apart from any demands of authority. The "social contract" stage involves upholding constitutionalism and the process that guards social stability and orderly process of change. Its ultimate stage is one of obeying only when law reflects ethics.[130] Liberal institutionalists and constructivists would probably be more willing to accept that states could be committed to international law through the second and third levels described above. They are also more willing to accept that regimes and institutions may guide patterned behavior, be maintained and sustained by tradition and legitimacy. Stein also states that institutions may change the perceived interests of a state.[131]

To rephrase this: to assert the validity of a rule of international law concerns reasoning on the normative plane and not on an empirical or factual one. But to the extent the rule actually influences state behavior, it is also part of the social reality.[132]

This brings us to the conclusion that international relations as a discipline analyzes the relevance of international law in similar ways and for similar purposes as legal sociologists confront national law. Adapting the insights of legal sociology in relation to states and their relations with each other does not necessarily mean that a particular rule or regime actually determines a state's behavior and actions in a given situation. That remains an empirical question. Therefore, it is argued that international relations—to the extent the discipline considers the impact and relevance of legal rules—is the sociology of international law. International relations fills the gap left open by legal sociologists, such as Cotterell. This would, for example, mean that

129 Downs, George W., Rocke, David M. and Barsoom, Peter N., 'Is the Good News about. Compliance Good News about Cooperation?', 50 *International Organization* (1996) 379–406, p. 383; commented by Ginsburg and Shaffer, 2010, p. 770.

130 Cotterell, 1992, pp. 141–142. Compare with Koh, 1997, p. 2600, footnote 3.

131 Stein, 1983, pp. 137–139. See also Finlayson and Zacher, 1983, p. 305.

132 Bull, 1977, p. 128.

the subfield of security studies—to the extent it considers the impact and relevance of legal rules—is the sociological study of the law on the peaceful settlement of disputes[133] and the law on the use of force.[134] While realism is skeptical towards the prescriptive worth of international rules, liberal institutionalism and constructivism tend to give international rules and regimes a greater role.

133 UN Charter, Chapter VI.
134 UN Charter, Chapter VII.

3 International trade

3.1 Function of the regime

This chapter focuses on the GATT. The original treaty was signed in 1947, coming into force in 1948 and as a result of negotiations concluded 1994, became a part of the WTO in 1995 (henceforth GATT 1994). The WTO is a permanent organization and legal entity with two main functions. First, it is a forum for trade negotiations. Second, it has an advanced dispute settlement system and provides access to sanctions.[1] The central norm of the GATT/WTO regime is liberalization of trade of goods, which in turn increases trade flows.[2] There are other relevant interests discussed as exceptions in section 3.2.2, which operate as ends in themselves or as constraints to trade liberalization. Even though international trade is sometimes portrayed as a positive-sum game, the legal regime also reflects and expresses the conflict in competition among nation-states and market actors for economic advantage.[3]

3.2 Dimensions of legalization

3.2.1 Degree to which World Trade Organization rules are obligatory

Although international trade law is a highly developed field of law, few norms relating to international trade can be discerned as international customary law and/or general principles of international law. The assumption is that states are free to define the terms upon which they allow access to their market for foreign goods.[4] This means that only states that have ratified the relevant treaties are subject to the rules of the regime.

1 Åhman, Joachim, *Trade Liberalisation, Health Protection, and the Burden of Proof in WTO Law* (Göteborg: Handelshögskolan vid Göteborgs universitet, 2011), p. 104; Tallberg and McCall Smith, 2012, pp. 2–3.

2 Finlayson and Zacher, 1983, p. 282.

3 Halliday and Osinsky, 2006, p. 460.

4 Zamora, Stephen, 'Is There Customary International Economical Law?', 32 *German Yearbook of International Law* (1989) 9–42, pp. 28 and 34; Langlet, David, *Prior informed consent and hazardous trade: regulating trade in hazardous goods at the intersection of sovereignty, free trade and environmental protection* (Alphen aan den Rijn: Kluwer Law International, 2009), p. 217.

3.2.2 Precision of the rules

The GATT 1994 contains three main normative principles which have the purpose of promoting free trade. The first principle is the principle of Most Favored Nation (MFN) treatment as formulated in Article I of the GATT. This principle provides that any advantage, favor, privilege or immunity granted by any WTO member to any product originating in or destined for any other country shall be accorded immediately and unconditionally to the like product originating in or destined for the territories of all other members. The second principle is the principle of national treatment under Article III, which provides that WTO members shall not apply internal taxes, other internal charges, and laws, regulations and similar requirements so as to afford protection to domestic production. The third principle is the principle on the general elimination of quantitative restrictions as formulated in Article XI, which provides that WTO members shall not institute or maintain any prohibitions or restrictions other than duties, taxes or other charges on the importation from or exportation of products to any other member.

There are exceptions that exempt a state from these obligations under certain conditions. These exceptions are divided in two broad groups: general exceptions and security exceptions.

The general exceptions concern, *inter alia*, the protection of public morals; the protection of human, animal or plant life or health; customs enforcement; the enforcement of monopolies; the protection of patents, trademarks and copyrights; the prevention of deceptive practices; the protection of national treasures of artistic, historic or archaeological value; the conservation of exhaustible natural resources; to ensure essential quantities of such materials to a domestic processing industry during periods when the domestic price of such materials is held below the world price as part of a governmental stabilization plan; and the acquisition or distribution of products in general or local short supply.[5]

The security exceptions provide that a number of measures may be exempted from the general obligations of the GATT. A WTO member may refuse to disclose any information which it considers contrary to its essential security interests. The security exceptions also cover actions relating to fissionable materials; traffic in arms, ammunition and implements of war; and taken in time of war or other emergency in international relations. Lastly, the obligations shall not be construed to prevent any member from taking any action in pursuance of its obligations under the UN Charter for the maintenance of international peace and security.[6]

5 General Agreement on Tariffs and Trade, adopted 15 April 1994, 55 UNTS 194, 1867 UNTS 187 (GATT), Article XX.
6 GATT, Article XXI.

There are also special rules on restrictions to safeguard the balance of payments,[7] customs unions and free-trade areas[8] and developing countries.[9] This means, *inter alia*, that developed countries give developing countries non-reciprocal preferential treatment for products originating from them and that developing countries exchange concessions among them.[10]

3.2.3 Delegation of some functions to a third party

The WTO agreement appears to place all members on an equal footing with the principle of one-member one-vote.[11] However, it masks the actual practice of WTO decision-making which favors powerful majorities or parity of interests. The major interests' norm reflects the belief of many member states, according to which those with the most obvious stake in a given issue or negotiations should exercise dominant influence in related decision-making. It also signifies a perception that the most powerful states have, almost by definition, the largest stakes in regime negotiations and activities, and therefore are entitled to exert a degree of influence proportional to their role.[12] As such, albeit seeming equal on first glance, decision-making in the WTO regime is power-oriented.

The WTO dispute settlement procedure consists of multiple stages at which conflicts may be resolved. The different stages include consultation, panel proceedings, appellate review proceedings, and implementation and enforcement. In the first stage, the complainant seeks to settle disputes through consultation with the defendant.[13] In the event that consultations are held, neither the Dispute Settlement Body (DSB), nor any other WTO bodies will be involved.[14] There has been a long-running struggle between trade "legalists", those seeking third-party adjudication of trade disputes under clear legal rules, and trade "pragmatists", those supporting nonbinding forms of dispute resolution that allows more scope for power and diplomacy.[15]

The current WTO system for settling trade disputes stems from 1995, when the WTO replaced the GATT. The major purpose of dispute settlement in the GATT was "to maintain, or to restore, the balance of advantages in trade terms", as opposed to determining whether a rule has been violated

7 GATT, Article XII.
8 GATT, Article XXIV.
9 GATT, Part IV.
10 Loibl, Herhard, 'International Economic Law' in Evans, Malcolm D. (ed), *International Law, 722–751* (3rd edn, Oxford: Oxford University Press, 2010), p. 735.
11 WTO Agreement, Article IX(I).
12 Finlayson and Zacher, 1983, pp. 278 and 302; Footer, Mary, *An Institutional and Normative Analysis of the World Trade Organization* (Leiden and Boston, MA: Martinus Nijhoff, 2005), pp. 107–108 and 157.
13 Understanding on Rules and Procedures Governing the Settlement of Disputes, Article 4(1)–(6).
14 Åhman, 2011, p. 108.
15 Abbott et al., 2001, p. 5; van den Bossche, 2008, p. 312.

and mete out a punishment.[16] The GATT dispute settlement system was diplomatic and power-oriented, because it gave defendant states the right to veto the adoption of panel reports and the authorization of sanctions. The Dispute Settlement Understanding (DSU) of the WTO was a distinct step in the direction of legalism for several reasons:[17] (a) it guarantees the right to a binding panel ruling;[18] (b) it includes a standing Appellate Body to review panel decisions;[19] (c) deadlines for compliance with adopted rulings are specified;[20] and (d) if compliance does not occur on time, bilateral sanctions are automatically authorized up to the level of economic injuries sustained by the complainant.[21] The notion of a "binding panel ruling" should be qualified for two reasons. First, panel reports have to be confirmed by the DSB, a body made up of all WTO members, "unless a party to the dispute formally notifies the DSB of its decision to appeal or the DSB decides by consensus not to adopt the report".[22] Second, if a panel report is appealed and the Appellate Body makes a legal finding, the panel report is adopted by the DSB, "unless the DSB decides by consensus not to adopt the Appellate Body".[23] The requirement that reports have to be adopted by the DSB is different compared to other international courts where decisions and judgment are directly binding for the parties involved.[24] However, the requirement that a report has to be adopted by the DSB is more of a formality and thus of less relevance.

The power-oriented nature of the WTO-regime also has consequences for dispute-resolution. Even though all states formally are equal, form is not everything. There is an interaction between law and politics.[25] Ginsburg and Shaffer find that US and European public and private actors have been the most influential in the economic and regulatory fields. They explain this influence by tracing it to the power that the US and the EU wield because of the size of their markets and the desire of other countries to gain access to them.[26] Byers argues that, "[p]ower derived from wealth gives some states the capacity to impose trade sanctions and to withstand them,

16 Curzon, G. and Curzon, V., 'The Management of Trade Relations in the GATT' in Shonfield, A. (ed), *International Economic Relations of the Western World 1959–1971* (London: Oxford University Press, 1976), pp. 143–244, p. 206; Finlayson and Zacher, 1983, p. 289.

17 Keohane et al., 2001, p. 82; Bown, Chad P., 'Participation in WTO Dispute Settlement: Complainants, Interested Parties, and Free Riders', 19 *World Bank Economic Review* (2005) 287–310, p. 292; van den Bossche, 2008, pp. 170 and 312; Tallberg and McCall Smith, 2012, p. 8.

18 DSU, Article 6.

19 DSU, Article 17.

20 DSU, Article 21.

21 DSU, Article 22.

22 DSU, Article 16(4).

23 DSU, Article 17(14).

24 See for example Statute of the International Court of Justice, San Francisco 26 June 1945, 1 UNTS XVI, Article 57, and UN Charter, Article 94(1) on the ICJ.

25 Keohane et al., 2001, pp. 101 and 103.

26 Ginsburg and Shaffer, 2010, pp. 767–770.

to withhold MFN status or not to care whether the status is granted".[27] Similarly, Bown has found that the self-enforcing nature of the WTO system requires "that complainant countries have the retaliatory capacity to threaten to impose economic sanctions on respondents that fail to comply with WTO rulings".[28] Empirical data indicates that poor and powerless members do not participate in the dispute settlement mechanism which may be explained by the institutional bias in the rules and procedures. There is substantial evidence that retaliation threats affect the likelihood and size of trade liberalization of the respondent and some evidence that panel rulings of guilty also induce economic compliance.[29] It is not only a question of market power, however. Busch, Reinhardt and Shaffer have examined legal capacity of WTO members (i.e. professional staff, bureaucratic organization at home, bureaucratic organization in Geneva, experience handling general WTO matters, and involvement in WTO litigation). Their conclusion is that asymmetric challenges still exist for developing countries: whilst increased legalization may alleviate some of the challenges raised in the distribution of economic power between developed and developing countries, it raises new ones over the distribution of legal capacity.[30] Similarly, Maton and Maton use regression analyses to test for correlation between the success of complainants in dispute settlement and a variety of factors, which they hypothesize represent the capacity of states to influence Panels and the Appellate Body. These factors include dimensions of political and economic power, the impact of the relative practical capacities of states in dispute settlement proceedings, and the formation of coalitions of states in support of a particular complainant or respondent. They find few significant correlations exist between the independent variables and the dispute outcomes. Their conclusion is that the judicial institutions of the dispute settlement mechanism are independent from member state influence. The one reliable correlation found in their analyses demonstrates that a complainant state does have substantial advantage in Panel proceedings if it has previously participated in more disputes than the respondent.[31] In other words, the complainant advantage in winning cases is not explained by such external factors as economic power and involvement of third parties.[32]

In summary, the WTO dispute settlement system is an example of "inter-state dispute settlement" using the terminology of Tallberg and McCall

27 Byers, 1999, p. 5.

28 Bown, 2005, pp. 287–288 and 300.

29 Bown, 2005, pp. 288, 291–292 and 308.

30 Busch, Marc, Reinhardt, Eric and Shaffer, Gregory, 'Does Legal Capacity Matter? A Survey of WTO Members', 8 *World Trade Review* (2009) 559–577, pp. 576–577. See also Ginsburg and Shaffer, 2010, p. 758, and Halliday and Osinsky, 2006, p. 462.

31 Maton, John and Maton, Carolyn, 'Independence under Fire: Extra-Legal Pressures and Coalition Building in WTO Dispute Settlement', 10 *Journal of International Economic Law* (2007) 317–334.

32 Ginsburg and Shaffer, 2010, p. 766.

Smith, given that states have to initiate the complaints.[33] One way of compensating for disparities in power and capacity to retaliate would be to introduce a WTO-sponsored supervisor with the task of enforcing compliance with WTO law and panel rulings—in other words, making the system more supranational.

3.2.4 State acceptance

The WTO has 159 members, including major powers such as the US, Russia, China, Brazil, Japan, India and the EU (including all of its member states).[34]

3.3 Feminist perspective on international trade law

Beveridge has noted the near-absence of any gender perspective on trade and the WTO, and that the WTO is perceived as gender-neutral. The relationship between gender and the economy has been addressed most thoroughly in the development studies field. Gender-based analyses of poverty have been an important part of gendered economic perspectives. Development and international relations theorists have offered various explanations for the exclusion of the gender perspective from dominant trade policy debates. The dominant explanation is the assumed neutrality of orthodox liberal trade theories and economic policies. The current form of globalization has acted to privilege particular sectors over others. The construction of the relationship between trade and social issues is founded on a dichotomy between the "economic" and the "social" which is itself deeply gendered. Feminist critique challenges this dichotomous approach to economic and social management, arguing that policies which do not take gender into account may fail and allocate resources ineffectively.[35] It therefore challenges the image of international trade law as a neutral set of rules, regulations and processes. The current trade regime presents non-discrimination and market liberalization as objectives of the WTO, while social objectives are justified as exceptions or exclusions. Beveridge notes that quantitative restrictions to trade which are contrary to Article XI of the GATT might be justified under Article XX as "necessary to protect human life or health" or "public policy". This is the presumed justification for national laws prohibiting trafficking in women and children, regulating inter-country adoption trade, regulating the import and distribution of pornographic materials and contraceptive drugs. If such measures are challenged before a WTO panel, the restrictions would be acceptable if they satisfy the "necessity" test found in Article XX.

33 Tallberg and McCall Smith, 2012, p. 5, who also describe the ICJ as interstate dispute settlement. See section 1.2.1.3 on delegation.

34 Members and Observers of the WTO, website checked 10 May 2013.

35 Beveridge, Fiona, 'Feminist Perspectives in International Economic Law' in Buss, Doris and Manji, Ambreena (eds), *International Law: Modern Feminist Approaches* (Oxford: Hart Publishing, 2005), pp. 174–201, pp. 176–180.

This means that states must argue the case for exception and protection of social interests which may prejudice the pursuit of national policy preferences. The construction of the WTO provisions replicates and strengthens the distinction made between international/domestic in international law, and in doing so it disguises the gendered nature of international economic law.[36] Orthodox legal analysis suggests that since WTO jurisprudence from the DSB increasingly is recognizing environment as a valid policy objective justifying accommodation, the same would apply to gender. From a feminist perspective, several concerns may be raised with this. First, a process where claims are balanced is inherently uncertain. Such approaches that do not explicitly endorse equality laws and policies may have a chilling effect on government action. Second, this system leaves significant power to judges who often are trade specialists and may be ill-equipped to make judgments about social policy. Third, the discretion of the DSB is limited by the WTO agreements. While there is reference to "sustainable development" in the preamble of the WTO agreement which may be relevant for trade and environment cases, no such reference is made to gender equality or the advancement of women.[37] If the aim is to engender the WTO, one needs to identify the relevant issues and measures. In relation to trade policies, the Beijing Platform for Action requires states to "[s]eek to ensure that national policies related to international and regional trade agreements do not have an adverse impact on women's new and traditional economic activities",[38] to "[e]nsure that all corporations, including transnational corporations, comply with national laws and codes, social security regulations, applicable international agreements, instruments and conventions, including those related to the environment, and other relevant laws",[39] and to "[c]reate non-discriminatory support services, including investment funds for women's businesses, and target women, particularly low-income women, in trade promotion programmes".[40] The platform points to how trade may incorporate a gender perspective.

3.4 Processes and mechanisms for creating and enforcing trade law

Trade rules provide a good example of stable self-enforcing agreements relying on the mechanism of reciprocity.[41] The principles of MFN and

36 Ibid, pp. 182–184.

37 *US-Import Prohibition of Certain Shrimp and Shrimp Products* (India, Malaysia, Pakistan, Thailand), Report of the Panel, 15 May 1998, WT/DS58/R, 98-1710; Report of the Appellate Body (AB-1998–4), 12 October 1998, WT/DS58/AB/R, 98-3899; Beveridge, 2005, pp. 185–186.

38 United Nations, Fourth World Conference on Women, Declaration and Platform for Action 1995, UN Doc A/CONF 177/20, 15 September 1995, Article 165(k).

39 Ibid, Article 165(l).

40 Ibid, Article 173(d); commented by Beveridge, 2005, pp. 191–192.

41 Keohane, 1986, pp. 1 and 3–4.

national treatment may be perceived as aspects of reciprocity.[42] Simmons argues that the market access rules of the WTO are largely respected, even in the absence of WTO enforcement power, because the parties have an ongoing interest in free trade. Reciprocity in the trade context means that a state's violation or compliance will be returned in kind. Denial of market access and the risk of being portrayed as an unreliable trade partner to the parties concerned, as well as other states, diminish the temptation of defection for short-term gains.[43]

The operation of trade regimes may be seen as specific as well as diffuse reciprocity—a distinction made by Keohane.[44] Keohane perceives unconditional MFN treatment as diffuse reciprocity, "Third parties no longer demand reciprocity for concessions given to others: these are extended automatically. The demand for equivalent contingent concessions is abandoned provided that each partner remains sufficiently loyal to the norms of the regime to be 'in good standing'".[45] The existence of diffuse reciprocity is, arguably, especially relevant for multilateral trade agreements involving customs unions and free-trade areas where even comparatively small states can expect powerful states with which they trade to comply with the rules.

As stated earlier, game theory has a close affinity to the principle of reciprocity.[46] Game theory may be used as a tool to analyze trade negotiation or settlement of disputes. Trade barriers between two states may be analyzed with the assumption that mutual free trade carries advantages for both states. However, if either country unilaterally eliminates its barriers, it would find itself facing terms of trade that would hurt its economy. In fact, under the assumptions of the prisoner's dilemma game, whatever one state does, the other state is better off retaining trade barriers, leading to a worse outcome than would have been possible had both states cooperated with each other.[47] The GATT/WTO principles of reciprocity and non-discrimination may alleviate the prisoner's dilemma which occurs when each country sets its trade policy unilaterally according to a terms-of-trade logic.[48]

As Snidal argues, separation of trade issues in the WTO framework, recognition of states as relevant decision-makers, and acceptance of restraint from force in deciding trade disputes all reflect theoretical assumptions as to which aspects of a trade regime can be taken as "given" for analysis of international trade.[49]

42 Braithwaite and Drahos, 2000, p. 21.
43 Simmons, 2009, p. 117.
44 See section 1.3.1 on reciprocity.
45 Keohane, 1986, p. 23.
46 See section 1.3.1 on reciprocity.
47 Axelrod, 1984, pp. 7–9.
48 Goldstein, Judith L., Rivers, Douglas and Tomz, Michael, 'Institutions in International Relations: Understanding the Effects of the GATT and the WTO on World Trade', 61 *International Organization* (2007) 37–68, p. 40.
49 Snidal, 1986, pp. 45–46.

Conybeare examines through the use of game theory the relevance of three dimensions that may promote or inhibit cooperation in relation to international trade: structure, iteration and numbers. First, the structure of payoffs of cooperation is influenced by, among other things, transaction costs.[50] Institutions may, arguably, reduce transaction costs.[51] In relation to iteration, Conybeare notes that the GATT rules on the arbitration of trade disputes (as in the US-European Economic Community 'chicken war' of the 1960s) help to insulate a particular dispute from affecting future relationships in other trade areas, mainly by constraining the scope and magnitude of permissible retaliation. Paradoxically, this may reduce the incentive to cooperate in the dispute at hand.[52] Lastly, increasing the number of states involved increases the likelihood of defection and free-riding, i.e. where actors take advantage of cooperation of others, while they themselves defect. MFN clauses may create severe public-good problems in systems with many states, as illustrated in the 1920s when the major trading state, the US, itself attempted to free-ride by refusing to negotiate tariff reductions while claiming benefits (through the MFN clause) of other states. One solution is to construct institutionalized rules, and regimes to constrain free-riding, involving coordinated retaliation against large powers. Institutional incentives, such as in the GATT system, may raise the payoff of cooperation and the costs of defection by way of the reciprocity principles (rewarding concessions by other countries with concessions of equal value) and retaliation (sanctions—including revocation of MFN status against free-riders).[53] To state that the principle of reciprocity operates does not necessarily mean that concessions have to be made in kind. Ginsburg and Shaffer note that in international trade negotiations, states obtain trade concessions of importance to them by offering reciprocal trade concessions in other sectors.[54]

Hafner-Burton, Victor and Lupu have found that the area where political science has advanced the most in measuring the effects of international institutions and addressing the problem of counterfactuals is trade. The central conclusion from that research is that the GATT/WTO system has been associated with higher flows of trade and greater economic efficiency only for some members, but the debate is far from settled.[55] Ginsburg and Shaffer have similarly noted that the question of whether international trade law matters have attracted considerable empirical attention, and their explanation is that this area of international law is particularly legalized. In addition, economists have long been interested in international trade matters and have

50 Conybeare, John, 'Trade Wars: A Comparative Study of Angla-Hanse, Franco-Italian, and Hawley-Smoot Conflicts' in Oye, Kenneth A. (ed), *Cooperation Under Anarchy* (Princeton, NJ: Princeton University Press, 1986), pp. 147–172, pp. 147–148.

51 Keohane, 1983, p. 150–151; Axelrod and Keohane, 1986, p. 238; Keohane and Martin, 1995, p. 42; Goldstein et al., 2001, p. 13; Ginsburg and Shaffer, 2010, p. 754.

52 Conybeare, 1986, pp. 150–151.

53 Conybeare, 1986, pp. 151–152 and 164–171; Axelrod and Keohane, 1986, pp. 234–235.

54 Ginsburg and Shaffer, 2010, pp. 768.

55 Hafner-Burton, Victor and Lupu, 2012, p. 90

applied their methodological tools to studying them. Their survey of empirical work is divided in two groups: (a) the impact of international trade law on trade commitments and trade flows; and (b) the effect of the WTO dispute-settlement system on member state compliance and member state practice.[56] The following sections partly follow these categories.

3.4.1 Impact of international trade law on trade flows

As stated earlier, the aim of the GATT/WTO regime is to increase trade flows. Rose surprisingly finds little evidence that countries joining or belonging to the GATT/WTO have different trade patterns from outsiders. He does not find that all multilateral institutions have been ineffectual. By way of example, the Generalized System of Preferences (GSP), extended from the countries in the northern hemisphere to developing countries, approximately doubles trade. The institutions were neither performing according to theory nor living up to their mandates. Rose relied on the standard "gravity" model of bilateral trade, which explains (the natural logarithm of) trade with (the logs of) the distance between the countries and their joint income. He augmented the basic gravity equation with a number of extra conditioning variables that affect trade, in order to account for as many extraneous factors as possible. These include: culture (e.g. whether a pair of countries share a common language), geography (e.g. whether none, one, or both are land-locked countries), and history (e.g. whether one colonized the other). Once other factors have been taken into account, he compared trade patterns for countries in the GATT/WTO with those outside the system. Rose offers two potential explanations why the GATT/WTO does not seem to have had much of an impact on trade. First, the GATT/WTO has not typically forced most countries to lower trade barriers, especially developing countries that have received "special and differential treatment". Second, members of the WTO seem to extend MFN status unilaterally to countries outside the system, even though they are under no WTO formal obligation to do so. In conclusion, Rose describes the negative result as an "interesting mystery".[57]

Rose's article caused a stir in both academic and policy circles and generated multiple follow-up attempts to validate or overturn the surprising result. Tomz, Goldstein and Rivers argue in two separate articles that many countries are mistakenly classified by Rose as outside the GATT, even though they were *de facto* members with similar rights and obligations. They show that not counting such countries as GATT members systematically underestimates the effect of the GATT on trade flows.[58] The GATT/WTO regime has had

56 Ginsburg and Shaffer, 2010, p. 776–778.

57 Rose, Andrew K., 'Do You Really Know that the WTO Increases Trade', 94 *American Economic Review* (2004) 98–114, pp. 98–99, 102–104 and 110–112.

58 Tomz, Michael, Goldstein, Judith L. and Rivers, Douglas, 'Do We Really Know That the WTO Increases Trade? Comment', 97 *American Economic Review* (2007) 2005–2018.

a positive impact on trade flows once one includes its effects on colonies, newly independent states, and provisional applicants. Goldstein, Rivers and Toms find that the GATT/WTO boosted trade among signatories, and it exerted a similarly large effect on colonies and newly independent states that had not acceded but, nonetheless, possessed the rights and obligations of members. Some institutions give standing, i.e. rights and obligations, not only to formal members, but also to territories and groups that never signed the agreement. Article XXVI:5(a) of the GATT specifies that when sponsored by their metropole, colonies could receive and give the benefits of membership. With much of the world under colonial rule in the late 1940s when the GATT was first agreed, this clause greatly expanded the scope of the agreement beyond the original signatories. Although not all countries extended benefits to their colonial possessions, most did, making these colonial participants the largest group of partakers of the early GATT/WTO. Non-member participants have thus received the core rights of the GATT/WTO, that is, access to other markets on MFN terms, and they reciprocated that right to other members of the organization. Goldstein, Rivers and Toms therefore argue that non-member participants should be included in any analysis of the effects of the GATT/WTO. They also use the gravity model and note that empirical researchers tend to drop colonies and territories from their data sets, which may obscure important and relevant patterns. Their conclusion is that trade among those with standing (including *de facto members*) in the GATT/WTO was considerably higher than what one would predict, based purely on proximity, national income, and other non-political variables.[59] Rose replied that he had concerns about the meaning, plausibility and robustness of the results of Tomz, Goldstein and Rivers, but conceded that they were right that whilst most colonies are not formal members they are covered by the GATT, and that he should have coded them accordingly.[60]

Allee and Scalera warn against oversimplification that obscures the diversity of countries' experiences within the regime. They classify the current members of the GATT/WTO into three groups according to how each state joined. The starting point is the *early* members, the approximately three dozen countries which joined the GATT at its outset and in the years immediately following. A second group is comprised of the *automatic* joiners, i.e. countries which joined effortlessly after receiving their independence from an existing GATT member. The final group, and the one most worthy of deeper examination, is the large collection of *rigorous acceders* which joined after a comprehensive process of scrutiny and commitment-making spanning several

59 Goldstein, Rivers and Tomz, 2007, pp. 38, 39, 41, 42, 47, 63 and 64. See also Allee, Todd L. and Scalera, Jamie E., 'The Divergent Effects of Joining International Organizations: Trade Gains and the Rigors of WTO Accession', 66 *International Organization* (2012) 243–276, p. 246; Dutta, Pushan, Mihova, Ilian and Van Zandtb, Timothy 'The effect of WTO on the extensive and the intensive margins of trade', 91 *Journal of International Economics* (2013) 204–219.

60 Rose, Andrew K., 'Do We Really Know That the WTO Increases Trade? Reply', 97 *American Economic Review* (2007) 2019–2025.

years. They find that those states that join via the rigorous accession process receive significant trade gains post-membership, and this is particularly true for those that had the most rigorous accessions and that engaged in the greatest commitments to further liberalization. Similarly, the early joiners, which made significant tariff reductions in their own right, also experience greater trade volumes, particularly in the years relatively soon after joining. In contrast, there is no evidence that automatic joiners, which joined without pledging any liberalization, experience increased trade. Their central argument and conclusion is that the trade gains from WTO membership are contingent on the way in which each state joined the organization.[61]

Kim argues that to evaluate accurately the role of the GATT/WTO on trade promotion, only trade in commodities and sectors that are actually under the influence of that organization should be taken into account. Therefore, Kim excludes agriculture, textile and oil trade from consideration, as they are not dealt with under the GATT/WTO rules. As a result, the benefit of the GATT's/WTO's promotional efforts is pronounced, increasing trade by approximately 30 per cent for member countries.[62]

3.4.2 Effect of the World Trade Organization dispute-settlement system on compliance and member practice

International trade law pays significant attention to incentives to defect. Several empirical studies suggest that the GATT/WTO regimes' dispute-settlement system is efficient in terms of compliance.[63] GATT/WTO members have largely complied with the dispute-settlement system's rulings. Hudec's comprehensive analysis of GATT dispute resolution shows that the system successfully resolved 88 per cent of legally valid claims.[64] Busch and Reinhardt find similarly high success rates under the more judicialized WTO system. They examine 600 GATT/WTO disputes from 1948 to 1999 and note that the effectiveness of the regime disproportionately manifests itself in the form of settlement, either at the stage of consultations or during panel proceedings prior to a ruling. In the data surveyed, they find that three-fifths of all disputes end prior to a panel ruling, and most of these without a request for a panel even being made. A key question in their study is whether the defendant liberalized the disputed trade policy practices, conceding to some or all of the complainant's demands, as opposed to whether a ruling (if there was one) favored one side or the other. They find counter to conventional wisdom that democracies, even controlling for their (typically) greater market power, are less likely to comply. Once the GATT/WTO has thrown

61 Allee and Scalera, 2012, pp. 247, 249, 263 and 271.

62 Kim, Myeong Hwan, 'Does the WTO promote trade? Further evidence', 19 *The Journal of International Trade & Economic Development* (2010) 421–437, pp. 423–424 and 430.

63 Ginsburg and Shaffer, 2010, p. 776–778.

64 Hudec, Robert E., *Enforcing International Trade Law: The Evolution of the Modern GATT Legal System* (Salem, NH: Butterworth Legal Publisher, 1993), p. 353.

down the gauntlet, it will be harder for a government that is highly sensitive to public opinion to cave in. Less Developed Countries (LDCs) are more likely to comply with adverse rulings than their comparably-sized, but more developed, counterparts.[65] Taking these findings into account, Ginsburg and Shaffer conclude that although the evidence suggests that the system is not biased from a formal perspective, there is evidence of some bias in the law-in-action as regards settlements, illustrating the continued relevance of different forms of power disparities among members.[66] Others make similar findings that the EU and the US break the rules or drag their feet when rules conflict with public sentiment or commercial interests. Their economic power gives them the ability to break international law without consequences. European trade barriers on genetically modified organisms, beef hormones and bananas are illustrative examples.[67] As indicated above, a country's ability to retaliate, its legal capacity as well as its international political economy relationships matter in relation to dispute settlement.[68] Reciprocity is often perceived as particularly potent in relation to international trade law. Busch and Reinhardt nuance this by arguing that domestic institutions and domestic actors also have a role in these regimes. They note that even without a credible threat by a complainant to seek authorization to retaliate, a definitive legal opinion from the institution may empower groups in the defendant state who oppose the disputed measure.[69]

3.4.3 International trade and non-governmental organization involvement

The WTO/GATT framework lacks detailed rules on the role of NGOs. Article V(2) of the Marrakech Agreement establishing the WTO provides in a very broad manner that, "The General Council may make appropriate arrangements for consultation and cooperation with non-governmental organizations concerned with matters related to those of the WTO". Further to Article V(2), the General Council adopted in 1998 guidelines which "recognizes the role NGOs can play to increase the awareness of the public in respect of WTO activities".[70] NGOs have been invited and attended WTO's Ministerial Conferences.[71] Other examples of NGO involvement include the

65 Busch, Marc and Reinhardt, Eric, 'Bargaining in the Shadow of the Law: Early Settlement in GATT/WTO Disputes', 24 *Fordham International Law Journal* (2000) 158–172, pp. 159–160, 162 and 168.

66 Ginsburg and Shaffer, 2010, pp. 776–778.

67 Posner, Eric A., *The Perils of Global gelaism* (Chicago, IL: The University of Chicago Press, 2009), p. 116.

68 Bown, 2005, pp. 287–288, 291–292, 300 and 308. See section 3.2.3 on the delegation of some functions to a third party.

69 Busch and Reinhardt, 2000, p. 165.

70 Guidelines for arrangements on relations with Non-Governmental Organizations, Decision adopted by the General Council on 18 July 1996, WT/L/162

71 Van den Bossche, 2008, pp. 726–727.

WTO Secretariat sponsoring and organizing various symposia for NGOs to express their ideas and concerns towards global problems of trade and development. However, in contrast to most other international organizations, the WTO does not allow NGOs to participate in its decision-making processes. They lack the formal power to influence decisions and policies of WTO. However, Daujotas notes that NGOs may exert influence through other means, such as assisting states, applying public pressure and lobbying. He illustrates this by reference to the WTO TRIPS agreement and the pharmaceutical industry. There was concern that the agreement would limit developing countries in accessing affordable medicines for life-threatening diseases such as HIV/AIDS, malaria, and tuberculosis. NGOs played a substantial role in promoting an amendment, with grounds for exceptions to the TRIPS agreement intended to secure the right and access to affordable medicine for citizens of developing countries.[72] Moreover, the WTO DSU grants the DSB the right to "seek information and technical advice from any source which it deems appropriate",[73] which may include NGOs.[74] This can be done in the form of *amicus curiae* briefs. Lindblom notes that such intervention appear more controversial in the WTO context compared to other fields of international law, which she explains by the considerable commercial interests at stake. It appears as WTO members believe that NGO involvement can affect the outcome of a dispute.[75]

The most important reason for the empowerment of NGOs in the international trade regime is the phenomenon of globalization. Van den Bossche notes that the WTO is the primary international organization concerned with trans-border trade and thus at the forefront of the multilateral efforts to manage and regulate economic globalization. He advances four arguments in favor of (greater) NGO involvement in WTO activities: (a) NGO participation will enhance the WTO decision-making process because NGOs will provide information, arguments and perspectives that governments do not bring forward; (b) NGO participation will increase the legitimacy of the WTO; (c) transnational interests and concerns may not be adequately represented by any national government and thus by allowing NGO involvement in WTO discussions, the WTO would hear about important issues which are international in nature; and (d) hearing NGOs at the WTO can thus compensate for the fact that NGOs are not always heard at the national level in every country.[76]

Esty discusses risks with NGO involvement at the WTO, more specifically special interest manipulation. There is a risk with lobbying that certain interests will exert disproportionate influence, slow the decision-making

72 Daujotas, Rimantas, 'Defining the Extent of NGO's Participation in the WTO', 3 *Organizational Forms ejournal* (2011), pp. 5–8.

73 DSU, Article 13(1).

74 Daujotas, 2011, pp. 11–12; van den Bossche, 2008, pp. 735–742.

75 Lindblom, 2001, p. 305.

76 van den Bossche, 2008, pp. 718–720.

processes, distort policy outcomes and cause inefficient results. In many cases, governments need to trade off competing domestic interests to strike agreements that liberalize trade. States must give up the particularized interests of certain industries or groups—especially inefficient industries hiding behind tariff barriers or other protectionist walls—to obtain benefits for the general public. It may be easier to go behind closed doors in order to cut such deals. Moreover, many NGOs are unsympathetic to the central tenet of the regime: trade liberalization efforts. For example, protectionist, environmental groups and labor unions are often fundamentally opposed to free trade. However, Esty argues that the fear of special interests of NGOs is overblown. Special interests are already present at the WTO in the form of business entities. Potential remedies include disclosure requirements and rules that spell out when and where lobbying is appropriate.[77] Another concern about the role of NGOs in the WTO relates to their representativeness and accountability. It may be difficult to ascertain how many and which people a particular group represents.[78]

To conclude, although progress may be observed in WTO engagement with NGOs, involvement of NGOs in policy-making, implementation, enforcement and dispute settlement is still modest.[79]

3.5 Tension between power and law

The potential weakness in that the rules of the WTO-regime on goods are only binding on state parties is compensated by the fact that the vast majority of major trading nations, major powers and other states—in total 159 states—are parties to the GATT and other central WTO agreements.[80] Finlaysson and Zacher consider that GATT (and thus also WTO) has depoliticized trade relations.[81] If their conclusion is correct, an additional plausible conclusion would be that trade has been de-securitized.

The potential weakness in the regime, rather, relates to the numerous possibilities of exceptions and power-of-balance factors when it comes to delegation, including dispute resolution, rule-making and enforcement. Finlaysson and Zacher note that norms and rules are largely the product of preferences of the strong, but once established an international regime may well limit the policy freedom of those who originally created it.[82]

77 Esty, 1998, pp. 138–139 and 147.
78 Esty, 1998, p. 141.
79 van den Bossche, 2008, p. 747.
80 Langlet, 2009, p. 217.
81 Finlayson and Zacher, 1983, p. 314.
82 Finlayson and Zacher, 1983, p. 313.

4 Environmental protection

4.1 Function of the regime

International environmental law deals with collective environmental concerns, including: (a) upstream–downstream problems in which one state exports harm to others;[1] (b) common areas located beyond the jurisdiction of states, such as the high seas, Antarctica or outer space; (c) common heritage which concerns certain resources that lie beyond the jurisdiction of all states, such as the non-living resources of the seabed; and (d) common concern of humankind, which relates to global environmental problems such as climate change or the conservation of biological diversity.[2] The challenge with common areas and common heritage is that they are not subject to the jurisdiction of any one state, so all states can potentially access and exploit these resources. It is difficult to exclude other actors from using a resource that is open in this way, but when any actor uses the resource, the amount left for others is diminished. Unless the access is regulated, its resources may be overexploited and destroyed, a phenomenon described as a "tragedy of the commons". While the concepts of common areas and common heritage are both limited by their geography and resources, the notion of common concern is more open ended. It is a global matter targeted at specific environmental processes.[3] In relation to climate change, the objective is to achieve "stabilization of greenhouse gas concentrations in the atmosphere at a level that would prevent dangerous anthropogenic interference with the climate system".[4]

1 Hafner-Burton, Victor and Lupu, 2012, p. 65.

2 Brunnée, Jutta, 'Common Areas, Common Heritage, and Common Concern' in Bodansky, Daniel, Brunnée, Jutta and Hey, Ellen (eds), *The Oxford Handbook of International Environmental Law* (Oxford: Oxford University Press, 2007), pp. 550–573, pp. 552–553.

3 Ibid, pp. 557 and 561–564.

4 UN Framework Convention on Climate Change (UNFCCC) adopted 9 May 1992, 1771 UNTS 107, Article 2.

4.2 Dimensions of legalization

There is no uniform and clearly delineated regime on international environmental protection. Instead, there are several international institutions with considerable variation in legal status, competences and tasks that address this area. Hey has grouped international institutions that participate in global environmental governance into the following categories: (a) treaty-based institutions; (b) UN specialized agencies; (c) UN General Assembly (UNGA) bodies; and (d) institutions based on cooperative arrangements between other international institutions.[5] However, these four categories do not cover the entire, composite regime relating to international environmental protection, and this chapter is therefore structured differently.

This chapter focuses on the international collective environmental concerns highlighted above. The first concern is upstream–downstream problems, which involve the duty of a state not to allow or tolerate any activity carried out within its jurisdiction that may cause damage to the environment of other states or of areas beyond its national jurisdiction.[6] This is also known as the "no harm" principle.[7] The second concern of common areas is illustrated by analysis of the regime on the high seas. Third, the concept of common heritage is studied in the context of the regime of the "area", the seabed and ocean floor beyond the limits of national jurisdiction. Lastly, the Kyoto Protocol is an example of a regime which addresses a common concern of humankind and aims at limiting greenhouse gas emissions. This choice of environmental concerns and related rules is done to illustrate the variety of the regime, its rules and mechanisms.

4.2.1 Degree to which international environmental law is obligatory

Having set out above the environmental concerns to be surveyed, consideration now turns to the extent are these concerns regulated by obligatory rules. The principle that states have "the responsibility to ensure that activities within their jurisdiction or control do not cause damage to the environment of other States or of areas beyond the limits of national jurisdiction" is formulated in Principle 21 of the Stockholm Declaration on the Human Environment and repeated in Principle 2 of the Rio Declaration on Environment and Development.[8] This principle has also been acknowledged by the ICJ. In

5 Hay, Ellen, 'International Institutions' in Bodansky, Daniel, Brunnée, Jutta and Hey, Ellen (eds), *The Oxford Handbook of International Environmental Law* (Oxford: Oxford University Press, 2007), pp. 749–769, pp. 750–752.

6 Beyerlin, Ulrich, 'Different Types of Norms in International Environmental Law: Policies, Principles and Rules' in Bodansky, Daniel, Brunnée, Jutta and Hey, Ellen (eds), *The Oxford Handbook of International Environmental Law* (Oxford: Oxford University Press, 2007), pp. 425–448, p. 439

7 Brunnée, 2007, pp. 552 and 555.

8 Declaration of the United Nations Conference on the Human Environment, adopted 16 June 1972 in Stockholm; Rio Declaration on Environment and Development, adopted 14 June 1992 in Rio de Janeiro.

the *Pulp Mill* case, the ICJ stated that states have the obligation "to use all the means at its disposal in order to avoid activities which take place in its territory, or in any area under its jurisdiction, causing significant damage to the environment of another State".[9] It reaffirmed its previous holding that this obligation is "part of the corpus of international law relating to the environment".[10] In other words, the "no harm" rule is an obligation on all states based on customary international law.[11]

Turning to the protection of the marine environment on the high seas, Part XII of the United Nations Convention on the Law of the Sea (UNCLOS) codifies and expands upon the existing obligation of states to protect and preserve the marine environment (Article 192). States shall take measures to prevent, reduce and control pollution of the marine environment (Article 194). States shall also cooperate in formulating and elaborating international rules, standards and recommended practices and procedures for the protection and preservation of the marine environment (Article 197).

As indicated, common areas, such as the high seas, are subject to open access for all states. In practice, this access tends to correspond to states' technological and financial resources. The concept of common heritage of humankind is a response to this and aims to ensure equitable sharing of benefits.[12] Part XI of UNCLOS states that the "Area", namely the seabed and ocean floor beyond national jurisdictions, and its resources, are the common heritage of mankind (Article 136). It follows that no state shall claim or exercise sovereignty or sovereign rights over any part of the Area or its resources (Article 137). An international institution (the Authority) shall adopt appropriate rules, regulations and procedures for the prevention, reduction and control of pollution and other hazards to the marine environment (Article 145). Activities in the Area shall be carried out for the benefit of mankind as a whole, and the Authority shall ensure that there shall be the equitable sharing of financial and other economic benefits derived from activities in the Area (Article 140).

UNCLOS is binding as a treaty on its 166 states parties.[13] A significant portion of the obligations in UNCLOS also have status as customary international law.[14]

9 *Pulp Mills on the River Uruguay* (Argentina v Uruguay), ICJ, Judgment, 20 April 2010, para 101.

10 *Legality of the Threat or Use of Nuclear Weapons*, ICJ, Advisory Opinion, 8 July 1996, para 29; Brunnée, 2007, p. 555

11 Langlet, 2009, p. 51; Redgwell, Catherine, 'International Environmental Law' in Evans, Malcolm D. (ed), *International Law* (3rd edn, Oxford: Oxford University Press, 2010), pp. 657–688, p. 663.

12 Brunnée, 2007, p. 562.

13 UN Division for Ocean Affairs and the Law of the Sea, Chronological lists of ratifications of, accessions and successions to the Convention and the related Agreements as at 29 October 2013, available at www.un.org/depts/los/reference_files/chronological_lists_of_ratifications.htm (accessed 18 September 2014).

14 Churchill, Robin and Lowe, Vaughan, *The Law of the Sea* (Manchester: Manchester University Press, 1999), pp. 16–22: "The UN regime for the seas is already almost universally accepted"; Aust, Anthony, *Handbook of International Law* (Cambridge: Cambridge University Press, 2005),

The UN Framework Convention on Climate Change (UNFCCC) establishes a number of key principles regarding the global response to climate change, including the idea that the response should take into account the principles of equity, sustainable development, precaution and cost-effectiveness.[15] This was followed by more specific obligations in the Kyoto Protocol to the UNFCCC, i.e. a commitment by industrialized nations to reduce their greenhouse gas emissions by specified amounts during the period from 2008 to 2012, with the overall aim of reducing their emission by at least 5 per cent below 1990 levels.[16] The Kyoto Protocol is explicitly based on the principle of "common but differentiated responsibility",[17] which means that different commitments apply to developed, compared to developing, states parties.

4.2.2 Precision of the rules

The "no harm" principle appears together with the partly opposing principle of national sovereignty. Principle 21 of the Stockholm Declaration not only provides that states have a responsibility not to cause harm to the territory of other states, but also that, "States have ... the sovereign right to exploit their own resources pursuant to their own environmental policies". There is thus an inherent tension between sovereignty and the "no harm" principle which creates room for interpretation and ambiguity. A literal interpretation of Principle 21 implies that *no* damage may be caused, which would be irreconcilable with numerous technologies and practices of the industrialized society. Thus, the exact level of prevention is less clear.[18]

The UNCLOS regime on protection and preservation of the marine environment is supplemented with several other, more specific treaties. These treaties add precision to states' obligations to varying degrees. For example, the Convention on the Prevention of Marine Pollution by Dumping of Wastes and Other Matter (London Convention)[19] initially listed in Annex I substances that could not be dumped at sea, while Annex II listed substances that could be dumped with a permit. The presumption was that non-listed substances could be dumped. The regime has been progressively tightened where the presumption has been reversed, with the consequence that only

pp. 298–299: "most of the Convention's provisions represent customary international law"; Bring, Mahmoudi and Wrange, 2011, p. 273; Crawford, 2012, p. 296.

15 Rowlands, Ian H., 'Atmosphere and Outer Space' in Bodansky, Daniel, Brunnée, Jutta and Hey, Ellen (eds), *The Oxford Handbook of International Environmental Law* (Oxford: Oxford University Press, 2007), pp. 315–336, p. 328.

16 Kyoto Protocol to the UN Framework Convention on Climate Change adopted 11 December 1997, 2303 UNTS 148, Article 3.

17 Ibid, Article 10 and as indicated by Annex B to the protocol with quantified emission limitation or reduction commitment per state.

18 Langlet, 2009, pp. 50–52.

19 Convention on the Prevention of Marine Pollution by Dumping of Wastes and Other Matter, adopted 29 December 1972, 1046 UNTS 120.

listed substances can be dumped.[20] In other words, fewer exceptions have created greater precision in the London Convention.

The Kyoto Protocol includes flexibility mechanisms which, arguably, increase the discretion of states in executing their obligations. For example, Article 6 provides that one developed state party may transfer to, or acquire from, any developed state party emission reduction units. This means that a country may increase its allowable emissions by a paying another country. In addition, Article 17 permits an emissions trading system. Many states and environmental groups raised concerns over these flexibility mechanisms during the negotiations of the Protocol.[21] In addition, some developed states, such as Canada and Japan, received during subsequent negotiations reduced obligations, with their original emissions limits being amended in order to secure participation. [22]

4.2.3 Delegation of some functions to a third party

Taking into account some variation between different environmental regimes, most have mechanisms to ensure compliance in the form of at least one compliance committee to the underlying multilateral environmental agreement and reporting back to the plenary body set up by that agreement (often dubbed the Conference of the Parties (COP) or Meeting of the Parties (MOP)).[23] Compulsory dispute settlement is rare in environmental agreements. Options for judicial dispute settlement, for example by the ICJ, are generally limited by the requirement that all parties must accept the Court's jurisdiction.[24]

UNCLOS is unusual in this respect. Disputes relating to the high seas may be brought to the International Tribunal for the Law of the Sea (ITLOS), the ICJ or an arbitral tribunal.[25] The Seabed Disputes Chamber of ITLOS has jurisdiction under Part XI of UNCLOS and the Annexes relating thereto in disputes with respect to activities in the Area.[26]

Article 18 of the Kyoto Protocol provides that compliance "procedures and mechanisms to determine and to address cases of non-compliance ... entailing

20 Ibid, Article 4(1)(1); Freestone, David and Salman, Salman M.A., 'Ocean and Freshwater Resources' in Bodansky, Daniel, Brunnée, Jutta and Hey, Ellen (eds), *The Oxford Handbook of International Environmental Law* (Oxford: Oxford University Press, 2007), pp. 337–361, p. 347.

21 Rowlands, 2007, p. 331.

22 Barrett, Scott, 'Economic Theory of Environmental Law' in Bodansky, Daniel, Brunnée, Jutta and Hey, Ellen (eds), *The Oxford Handbook of International Environmental Law, 231–261* (Oxford: Oxford University Press, 2007), pp. 231–261, pp. 233–234.

23 Klabbers, Jan, 'Compliance Procedures' in Bodansky, Daniel, Brunnée, Jutta and Hey, Ellen (eds), *The Oxford Handbook of International Environmental Law* (Oxford: Oxford University Press, 2007), pp. 995–1009, p. 998.

24 Brunnée, 2007, pp. 570–571.

25 United Nations Convention on the Law of the Sea, adopted 10 December 1982, 1833 UNTS 3, Articles 287 and 288.

26 Ibid, Articles 187 and 188.

binding consequences shall be adopted by means of an amendment to" the Kyoto Protocol. No such amendment exists, which weakens the regime.[27]

4.2.4 State acceptance

UNCLOS has 166 state parties, which include major powers such as the Russian Federation, China, France and the United Kingdom (UK), whereas the US is a non-state party.[28] The same major powers, but slightly fewer state parties—145 in total—have ratified the Agreement relating to the implementation of Part XI of UNCLOS which concerns the Area. The Kyoto Protocol has 192 state parties, again the US being a non-state party.[29]

4.3 Feminist perspective on international environmental law

Rochette argues from a feminist perspective that international environmental law is not equipped to address environmental problems, but rather the current structures and assumptions of the regime enable the continuing decline of the planet. She raises two reasons for this position. First, the gendered state system as represented in international law distinguishes between hard law and soft law. The soft law that addresses some of the root causes of environmental problems (such as the Rio Declaration[30]) are offset by the harder legal recognition of a state's sovereign right to exploit its resources set out in binding treaties. Second, the legal framework is based on the liberal equality paradigm that does not address the structural barriers to women's participation in environmental decision-making.[31]

4.4 Processes and mechanisms for creating and enforcing international environmental law

Mitchell notes that legal scholars often asses effects of international environmental agreements in terms of the extent to which states comply with their commitments. International relations scholars tend to examine international environmental agreements effects through a broader set of questions. Mitchell argues that a strict focus on compliance creates two analytical problems. First, it conflates coincidental compliance and treaty-induced compliance. Second,

27 Barrett, 2007, p. 234.

28 Chronological lists of ratifications of, accessions and successions to the United Nations Convention on the Law of the Sea as at 3 October 2014.

29 Status of Ratification of the Kyoto Protocol, last visit 8 October 2014.

30 Rio Declaration, 1992; Agenda 21: programme for Action for Sustainable Development, signed 14 June 1992, UN Doc A/CONF 151/26/Rev 1.

31 Rochette, Annie, 'Transcending the Conquest of Nature and Women: A Feminist Perspective on International Environmental Law' in Buss, Doris and Manji, Ambreena (eds), *International Law: Modern Feminist Approaches* (Oxford: Hart Publishing, 2005), pp. 203–235, pp. 204–205, 220–224.

the assumption that non-compliance equals a lack of an international environmental agreement's influence is misleading. States may make real efforts to promote an agreement's goal, but fall short of total compliance, and as such the agreement may still have impacted on state behavior compared to a regime with weaker or no rules.[32]

Studying effectiveness of rules often involves counterfactual reasoning—what would have happened if the law was absent? Researchers on international environmental cooperation have difficulties in identifying and measuring the counterfactual because behavior and environmental quality are affected by several factors, including economic growth, technological development and institutions.[33]

4.4.1 Environmental protection and game theory

Game theory may explain the difficult obstacles to cooperation in the field of environmental protection. In the prisoner's dilemma, where the choice is between "pollute" or "abate", without the ability to coordinate, each player's strategy will be to pollute.[34]

In an interdependent world, one state's behavior often imposes unintended costs and other externalities on other states. It is crucial to distinguish between asymmetric externalities on the one hand and symmetric externalities on the other hand. Asymmetric externalities may be illustrated by states sharing a river. Each state pollutes, but also uses the water for drinking. Some states are upstream, creating asymmetries in at least two respects. First, they are asymmetric in creating problems (externalities) for the others, the upstream states create problems for those downstream, but are unaffected by the pollution from the downstream states. Second, they have different preferences for solving the problem because the downstream states prefer mitigation, while the upstream states do not. This makes it more difficult, but not impossible, to create regimes because upstream states prefer no institution in the absence of compensation. Instead of relying on reciprocity, downstream states with economic, political or other capabilities may rely on broader linkages, if necessary with other regimes, involving coercive sanctions or

32 Bernauer, Thomas, 'The Effect of International Environmental Institutions: How We Might Learn More', 49 *International Organization* (1995) 351–377, pp. 361 and 377; Mitchell, Ronald B., 'Compliance Theory' in Bodansky, Daniel, Brunnée, Jutta and Hey, Ellen (eds), *The Oxford Handbook of International Environmental Law* (Oxford: Oxford University Press, 2007), pp. 893–921, pp. 894–895. See also Rehbinder, Eckard, 'Obstacles to national implementation of the Convention on Biological Diversity' in *Fågelperspektiv på rättsordningen: Vänbok till Staffan Westerlund* (Uppsala: Iustus Förlag, 2002), pp. 375–385, p. 377 on compliance and implementation in a broad sense; Guzman, 2008, p. 8; Thirlway, 2014, p. 203; section 1.3 on processes and mechanisms for creating and enforcing international law.

33 Hafner-Burton, Victor and Lupu, 2012, p. 90.

34 Danish, Kyle W., 'International Relations Theory' in Bodansky, Daniel, Brunnée, Jutta and Hey, Ellen (eds), *The Oxford Handbook of International Environmental Law* (Oxford: Oxford University Press, 2007), pp. 205–230, p. 211; Guzman, 2008, p. 42.

positive rewards. The only available means for weak downstream states is an exchange of side payments for cooperation in order to confront a stronger upstream state and resolve the problem. Pollution of the Rhine River by chlorides is an example of classic asymmetric externality. The tragedy of commons noted above applies to situations with symmetric externalities. In these cases, states may differ in their preferences for regime design, but all prefer some institution to none. When facing symmetric externalities, states prefer mutual cooperation to the status quo, which predisposes states toward narrow institutions that rely on issue-specific reciprocity. Mitchell and Kailbach perceive that to the extent the International Convention for the Regulation of Whaling and the International Whaling Commission have influenced states, they did so through issue-specific reciprocity. States may "opt out" and invoke the standard withdrawal clause to escape from the agreement, but at other times engage in reciprocal but decentralized "tit-for-tat" behavior, either to avoid being taken advantage of or to enforce the agreement.[35] The problem with greenhouse gas emissions is arguably also a symmetric tragedy of commons where most states are both perpetrators and victims of global warming.

Barrett notes that the issue of economic externalities are common both to environmental issues in a domestic or international setting. However, he argues that concerns in relation to environmental protection in a vertical domestic system, such as optimal targets (cost–benefit analysis), instrument choice (market versus command and control, taxes versus trade emission permits, etc) and cost-effectiveness, may be less relevant in the horizontal system of international environmental law. The most important question, instead, is enforcement. The Kyoto Protocol is similar to a domestic system based on "cap and trade" of greenhouse emissions. However, as an international treaty, it is voluntary and its enforcements have to be self-enforcing. Participation is a huge problem, for example the US is not participating.[36]

With assumptions based on the tragedy of commons, the prospects for cooperation are pessimistic unless strong, formal enforcement mechanisms are in place. However, states have afforded more attention to enforcement issues in recent decades. In addition, there is emerging research that has identified conditions under which collective action to manage common resources is likely to arise even in the absence of formal mechanisms for contracting, monitoring and enforcement. There are several examples of effective collective action in local settings because the players are more likely to know each other, making it easier to monitor and sanction defectors.[37] Gibson, Williams and Ostrom mention the argument that:

35 Mitchell, Ronald B. and Keilbach, Patricia M., 'Situation Structure and Institutional Design: Reciprocity, Coercion, and Exchange', 55 *International Organization* (2001) 891–917, pp. 891–892, 895, 901, 906 and 916.

36 Barrett, 2007, p. 233.

37 Hafner-Burton, Victor and Lupu, 2012, p. 64, footnote 88.

> high levels of social capital, as commonly understood, should decrease both the uncertainty and costs (transaction costs) to individuals and so increase the odds of reaching and maintaining a collective solution, and low levels of social capital might impede, or at least be neutral to, individuals engaged in such efforts. Groups with high levels of social capital should find it easier to sustain the regular monitoring of rule conformance needed for long-term sustainability.[38]

Is it reasonable to expect that the same logic applies to states though? As mentioned in section 1.3.1 on reciprocity, the ability to distinguish between cooperation and defection by others and to respond can affect the power of reciprocity. In other words, even if formal mechanisms are absent, effective enforcement may be possible if: (a) the number of states involved is low; (b) it is possible to distinguish between cooperation and defection; and (c) states have means for sanctioning defectors.

As indicated above, game theory may explain how states address these problems through institutionalized cooperation. This may be relevant to problems involving the tragedy of commons where the involved states can choose whether to cooperate or defect. If it is a problem, based on the logic of prisoner's dilemma, all states will have a long-term gain in mutual cooperation. Is the same logic also applicable for cases of asymmetrical situations with the example of upstream–downstream problems in which one state exports harm to others? Hafner-Burton, Victor and Lupu note that in such cases, only the downstream state has an interest in cooperation (such as stricter policies to reduce water pollution); the upstream state is generally indifferent or even gains, such as by exporting noxious effluents. As already indicated, the standard solution to these problems is for the downstream state to establish a system of incentives, such as payments, that change the behavior of upstream polluters.[39] The question is what leverage the downstream state has. It is difficult for the downstream state to retaliate or defect within a self-contained regime, i.e. it cannot play a strict "tit-for-tat" strategy with responses in kind. The distribution of costs and benefits in asymmetric externalities makes actors reluctant to join an institution and encourages them to violate institutional rules. This suggests that distribution problems are not always separable from—and, indeed, sometimes drive—enforcement problems.[40] Instead, the downstream state may rely on what Braitwaithe and Drahos describe as non-reciprocal coordination with counter-measures in another regime and area of interaction.[41] For example, the downstream state may withhold trade cooperation in order to counter environmental pollution.

38 Gibson, Clark C., Williams, John T. and Ostrom, Elinor, 'Local Enforcement and Better Forests', 33 *World Development* (2005) 273–284, p. 274.
39 Hafner-Burton, Victor and Lupu, 2012, p. 64–65.
40 Mitchell, Keilbach, 2001, p. 892.
41 Braithwaite and Drahos, 2000, pp. 22–23 and 543–546; see section 1.3.1 on reciprocity.

Section 2.2.3 on regime interaction introduces the theory of Johnsson and Urpelainen on regime integration and separation. The central argument of the theory is that negative spillovers encourage integration, while positive spillovers do not. They noted that environmental regimes lie between the extremes of integration and separation. In order to test their theory, Johnsson and Urpelainen examined the regimes surrounding ozone depletion, climate change, deforestation and desertification. They held multiple factors constant in the observations. All regimes pertained to the same issue of environmental degradation and lack of strong enforcement mechanisms, and the observations analyzed range between same time period of time—the late 1980s and early 1990s. The regimes for these four issues differ widely in their relationships with one another. Some are integrated hierarchically, some merely overlap, and some are starkly separate. Substantial negative spillovers exist between ozone depletion and climate change. For example, to heal the ozone layer, countries banned certain ozone-depleting substances, but they substituted these banned substances with others that are potent greenhouse gases. Substantial positive spillovers exist between deforestation and climate change. Because forests are natural carbon sinks, forest preservation mitigates climate change. After empirically studying regime-pairs in terms of factors such as structural coordination and funding, they find that only the climate change-ozone pair displays meaningful integration. There is a lack of integration between the climate change and forests regimes. These results confirm their original theory.[42]

In summary, some parts of the regime for environmental protection are self-enforcing when states can police each other based on reciprocity. However, when dealing with upstream-downstream problems and global challenges such as climate change, other strategies are necessary. Linking with other regimes becomes an important part of creating and enforcing international environmental law, especially when there are negative spillovers between efforts to combat one area and another, such as the example of ozone depletion and climate change.

4.4.2 Non-state actors

NGOs have become an important actor in international environmental law-making.[43] NGOs attend almost every intergovernmental conference and meeting held within the framework of environmental agreements or intergovernmental organizations. Principle 10 of the Rio Declaration has been particularly influential for this development.[44] It provides the following:

42 Johnson and Urpelainen, 2012, pp. 645–647, 649–650, 663 and 665–673.

43 Spriro, Peter J., 'Non-Governmental Organization and Civil Society' in Bodansky, Daniel, Brunnée, Jutta and Hey, Ellen (eds), *The Oxford Handbook of International Environmental Law* (Oxford: Oxford University Press, 2007), pp. 770–790, p. 771.

44 Ebbesson, Jonas, 'Public Participation' in Bodansky, Daniel, Brunnée, Jutta and Hey, Ellen (eds), *The Oxford Handbook of International Environmental Law* (Oxford: Oxford University Press, 2007), pp. 681–703, pp. 683–684.

> Environmental issues are best handled with the participation of all concerned citizens, at the relevant level. At the national level, each individual shall have appropriate access to information concerning the environment that is held by public authorities, including information on hazardous materials and activities in their communities, and the opportunity to participate in decision-making processes. States shall facilitate and encourage public awareness and participation by making information widely available. Effective access to judicial and administrative proceedings, including redress and remedy, shall be provided.

Several UN bodies, such as the UN Environment Programme and the Commission on Sustainable Development, have adopted accreditation programs that apply to NGOs.[45]

The right to access to justice in environmental matters is made most explicit in the Aarhus Convention and the North American Agreement on Environmental Cooperation (NAAEC).[46] State parties have an obligation under the Aarhus Convention to ensure that: (a) any person who considers that his or her request for environmental information has been ignored, wrongfully refused, inadequately answered, or otherwise not dealt with in accordance with the provisions of that Article, has access to a review procedure before a court of law or another independent and impartial body established by law; (b) concerned members of the public have the right to challenge the substantive and procedural legality of any decision, act or omission concerning specific activities; and (c) members of the public have access to administrative or judicial procedures to challenge acts and omissions by private persons and public authorities which contravene provisions of its national law relating to the environment.[47] The approach to access to justice in the NAAEC is even broader in scope than that of the Aarhus Convention.[48] State parties shall ensure that interested persons may request competent authorities to investigate alleged violations of its environmental laws and regulations, and persons with a legally recognized interest under its law in a particular matter have appropriate access to administrative, quasi-judicial or judicial proceedings. The NAAEC also requires that parties provide private access to remedies, including the ability to sue private actors for damages, to request the competent authorities to take appropriate enforcement action, and to seek injunctions.[49] It also contains due process guarantees.[50]

45 Ibid, pp. 689–690.

46 Ibid, pp. 700–701.

47 Convention on Access to Information, Public Participation in Decision-making and Access to Justice in Environmental Matters (Aarhus Convention), adopted 25 June 1998, 2161 UNTS 447, Articles 4, 6 and 9.

48 Ebbesson, 2007, p. 701.

49 North American Agreement on Environmental Cooperation, adopted 8, 9, 12 and 14 September 1993, 32 ILM 1480, Article 6.

50 Ibid, Article 6.

Other key non-state actors include corporations which are central actors in international environmental law. Industry engages far more than states directly in degrading the environment, as well as in prevention and remedying their harms. From this follows that: (a) corporations will seek to influence law-making, implementation and enforcement of environmental law; and (b) environmental law will only be effective to the extent it controls the behavior of corporations. However, international law is still state-centered.[51]

Drahis and Braihwaite describe how corporations may approach international environmental protection in two different ways. The first approach concerns the economic dynamics of the race to the bottom. States with the weakest environmental protection may attract corporations seeking lower costs in order to maximum tax revenue and employment. In contrast, the second approach contains no contradiction between economics and environmental protection. Consumers will respond to and reward environmentally friendly companies creating a competitive advantage for such companies.[52] However, Ratner notes that corporate attitudes cannot be grouped simply in anti-regulation and pro-regulation. All corporations seek certainty in legal regimes and a new regulation may be more attractive than uncertainty.[53] Moreover, other factors than domestic environmental standards may be more relevant for corporations, such as labor costs, infrastructure, the domestic legal system in a wider sense and proximity to markets.

The involvement of non-state actors is patchy, but their participation has influenced international environmental law in a broad sense, this regime is not limited to defining emission standards, technical requirements and measures to reduce pollution. It is also concerned with access to justice, governance and democratic structures in international and national contexts.[54]

4.5 Tension between power and law

The regime for environmental protections fits well with the explanation of liberal institutionalism. Even if states are self-interested, they will sometimes sacrifice their autonomy in order to establish regimes where gains from cooperation exceed the gains of unilateral action. Regimes provide a tool to address market failures by taking into account economic externalities.[55]

Danish notes that threads of constructivism can be found in much of the literature on international environmental regimes. For example, the Young and Levy edited book deals not only with the utilitarian impact of environmental regimes, but also their social and constitutive impacts (regimes

51 Ratner, Steven R., 'Business' in Bodansky, Daniel, Brunnée, Jutta and Hey, Ellen (eds), *The Oxford Handbook of International Environmental Law* (Oxford: Oxford University Press, 2007), pp. 807–828, p. 808.

52 Braithwaite and Drahos, 2000, pp. 267–270 and 279.

53 Ratner, 2007, pp. 810–811.

54 Ebbesson, 2007, p. 702.

55 Danish, 2007, p. 209.

as "bestowers of authority", "learning facilitators" and "role definers").[56] In addition, states may, for expressive reasons, create and ratify treaties on environmental protection to obtain legitimacy. In other words, ratification may be a means for states to express their position in the international community.[57]

In relation to the framework on legal regimes set up by Abbot and others set out in section 1.2, Danish puts the Kyoto protocol in the "high" spectrum of legalization because of its well-specified obligations, staffed secretariat and relatively strong enforcement mechanism.[58] The UNCLOS dispute settlement is, arguably, also in the high spectrum, as there is no default permitted and mandatory mechanisms for disputes relating to upstream-downstream problems.

56 Young and Levy, 1999, pp. 23–26, commented in Danish, 2007, p. 217.

57 Compare with section 5.4.1 on the expressive function of human rights law.

58 Danish, 2007, p. 219. Danish appears to do this assessment based on formal criteria. In practice, the regimes appear to be weaker.

5 Human rights

5.1 Function of the regime

There are different views on the precise nature and role of human rights. The concept may be viewed as negative rights, offering protection against state interference and abuse of government power, or as also including positive rights involving protection against other private entities and claims of benefits from the state. The concept of human rights is closely related to ethics and morality. In this, rights that reflect the values of a community will generally have the most chance of successful implementation. Regardless, international human rights law concerns the relationship between the individual and the state, which constrains the state in what it can do and how it should use its resources. The main purpose of international human rights law is to protect individuals. Human rights law differs from other fields of international law in several regards. First, state consent to human rights is, arguably, difficult to explain in terms of solving common problems of cooperation or coordination between states. Unlike other fields of international law, human rights law primarily serves idealistic ends, not particular national interests. Second, states may promote and protect human rights within their territory without necessarily coordinating their efforts with other states. Third, although human rights law becomes entangled in international politics, it contradicts the traditional premise of international law that how a state treats its own citizens is a matter of domestic jurisdiction.[1] When a state violates a human rights norm, no other state directly suffers harm. Rather, the primary concern of human rights law is what happens inside a state.

Different human rights address different needs. This part of the study will focus on the core UN human rights treaties, the main regional human rights treaties and the institutions associated with these treaties. Consistent with the argument made in section 2.2.1 on the objectives of international law, human rights law is a product of competing interests. Much of international human rights law codifies state's interests, rather than human interests,[2] as illustrated

1 Henkin, 1979, p. 228; Goodman and Jinks, 2004, pp. 628–629.

2 Forsythe, David P., 'Human Rights Studies: On the Danges of Legalistic Asssumption' in

by the fact that several specific human rights may be subject to restrictions in order to satisfy state interests.

5.2 Dimensions of legalization

5.2.1 Degree to which rules are obligatory

In addition to the nine international human treaties of the UN,[3] there are several regional human rights treaties.[4] The degree of ratification varies which, to some extent, is compensated by the fact that core human rights, such as the prohibitions against racial discrimination and torture, are also rights under international customary law.[5] However, states with different types of ideologies and political structures place different values on different rights. Thus, not all rights are universally obligatory even when considering international customary law. The discretion of states to prioritize certain rights in their structure is amplified by the lack of precision, as explained in the next section.

5.2.2 Precision of rules

Human rights law protects several different rights, not all of which are absolute. The possibilities to make exceptions or limit the exercise of these rights will impact on the precision of the rules.

Some rights are of a relative nature and can be restricted if certain requirements are met, namely that the interference must have a legal basis, pursue

Coomans, Fons, Grünfeld, Fred. and Kamminga, Menno T. (eds), *Methods of Human Rights Research* (Antwerp; Oxford: Intersentia, 2009), pp. 59–76, p. 63.

3 Convention on the Elimination of All Forms of Racial Discrimination, 660 UNTS 195, adopted 21 December 1965; International Covenant on Civil and Political Rights adopted 16 December 1966, 999 UNTS 171; International Covenant on Economic, Social and Cultural Rights adopted 16 December 1966, 993 UNTS 3; Convention on the Elimination of All Forms of Discrimination against Women, adopted 18 December 1979, 1249 UNTS 13; Convention against Torture and Other Cruel, Inhuman or Degrading Treatment or Punishment adopted 10 December 1984, 1465 UNTS 85; Convention on the Rights of the Child, adopted 20 November 1989, 1577 UNTS 3; International Convention on the Protection of the Rights of All Migrant Workers and Members of Their Families, adopted 18 December 1990, 2220 UNTS 3; International Convention for the Protection of All Persons from Enforced Disappearance, 20 December 2006, 2715 UNTS; Convention on the Rights of Persons with Disabilities, 13 December 2006, 2515 UNTS 3.

4 European Convention for the Protection of Human Rights and Fundamental Freedoms adopted 4 November 1950 as amended by Protocol No 11, 213 UNTS 221; American Convention on Human Rights adopted 22 November 1969, 1144 UNTS 123; African Charter on Human and Peoples' Rights, adopted 27 June 1981, 1520 UNTS 217.

5 Chinkin, Christine, 'Sources' in Moeckli, Daniel, Shah, Sangeeta and Sivakumaran, Sandesh (eds), *International Human Rights Law* (Oxford: Oxford University Press, 2010), pp. 103–123, pp. 110–113: "Treaties and custom coexist and despite the wide adherence by states to human rights treaties, customary international law retains some considerable importance as a source of human rights law."

a legitimate aim, be necessary in a democratic society and proportionate.[6] In times of public emergency which threatens the life of the nation and the existence of which is officially proclaimed, states may take measures derogating from some of their treaty obligations.[7] Both specific restrictions taken in the normal course of events and general restrictions during public emergency widens the discretion of states. A handful of rights are absolute and cannot be restricted in any circumstances, such as the prohibition against torture. In relation to these rights, the precision of the state's obligation is high. The rights of aliens may also be restricted in relation to political activities and, under certain circumstances, they may be expelled.[8] Furthermore, states may make reservations to human rights treaties.[9] States may enter into human rights commitments through ratification as a reputational move or as a part of a political bargain. When doing so, they may enter reservations, which means that parts of the human rights treaty becomes meaningless for them.[10] Obvious examples are reservations to the Convention on the Elimination of All Forms of Discrimination against Women (CEDAW), where religious and traditional values are given precedence over gender equality and some have argued such reservations go against the core of CEDAW. From a feminist perspective, although CEDAW is a landmark treaty, it does not explicitly address some of the most serious violations such as violence against women.[11] However, it should be noted that reservations are not allowed which are incompatible with the object and purpose of human rights treaties.[12]

The European Court of Human Rights (ECtHR) has in its case law introduced the doctrine of margin of appreciation. This doctrine may be perceived as an expression of moral relativism, based on the notion that each society is entitled to a certain amount of latitude in resolving the inherent conflicts between individual rights and national interests or among different moral convictions.[13] This is yet another manner where the discretion of the state is widened to the potential loss of the individual's rights. This may be illustrated by national restrictions on the right to wear a veil in public, which have been

6 For example ICCPR, Articles 17–19, 21–22; ECHR, Articles 8–11.

7 ICCPR, Article 4; ECHR, Article 15.

8 ECHR, Article 16; Protocol No 4, Articles 3–4; Protocol No 7, Article 1.

9 ICCPR, Article 4; ECHR, Article 57. In case the issue of reservations are not regulated, the general rules in the Vienna Convention on the Law of Treaties, adopted 23 May 1969, 1155 UNTS 331, Articles 2(1)(d) and 19–23.

10 Başak, Çali, 'International Human Rights Law' in Başak, Çali (ed), *International Law for International Relations* (Oxford: Oxford University Press, 2010), pp. 281–305, p. 289.

11 Chinkin, Christine, Wright, Shelley and Charlesworth, Hilary, 'Feminist Approaches to International Law: Reflections from Another Century' in Buss, Doris and Manji, Ambreena (eds), *International Law: Modern Feminist Approaches* (Oxford: Hart Publishing, 2005), pp. 17–46, p. 22.

12 Vienna Convention on the Law of Treaties, Article 19(c).

13 Benvenisti, Eyal, 'Margin of Appreciation, Consensus, and Universal Standards', 31 *International Law and Politics* (1999) 843–854, pp. 843–844.

accepted by the ECtHR with reference to the states' margin of appreciation.[14] As Benvinisti argues, the universal aspirations of human rights are, to a large extent, compromised by the doctrine of margin of appreciation. International human rights organs other than the ECtHR have, for the most part, avoided a systematic use of the margin of appreciation doctrine.[15] The moral relativism of the ECtHR becomes paradoxical in consideration of the debate between universalism and cultural relativism, where advocates of the later portray the human rights project as colonial, Euro-centric universalism. Mutua challenges human rights universalism as being imposed by the west and asks for dialogue, equality, diversity and difference.[16] If we believe that the human rights as developed in the west should be universal vis-à-vis other societies, how is it possible to allow human rights relativism within Europe? This demonstrates that the different manners whereby states may restrict right weakens the precision of state obligations.

5.2.3 Delegation of some functions to a third party

In relation to the human rights institutions which are part of the UN family, a distinction should be drawn between treaty-monitoring bodies composed of experts, such as the Human Rights Committee on the one hand, and the Human Rights Council (HRC) with state representatives as members on the other hand. While the Human Rights Committee in several, but not all, regards is close to a judicial dispute settlement mechanism, the processes of the HRC should be perceived as political bargaining, as explained below.

The membership of the HRC is composed of states. These states are to lesser and greater extent driven by their own interests. Some have questionable human rights records. This creates both a bias in favor of scrutinizing some states more often and an inability or unwillingness to examine other states. The HRC has several tools at its disposal.[17] First, it may conduct universal periodic review of all UN member states.[18] Second, it may respond to specific country situations, including holding special sessions. Special sessions are held at the request of a member of the HRC with the support of one-third of the membership of the HRC. It is not enough to assemble the necessary votes for convening a special session, states must also have a suitable strategy

14 *Şahin v Turkey* (Application no 44774/98), ECtHR, Judgment, 10 November 2005, paras 100, 110, 122 and 154; *SAS v France* (Application no 43835/11), ECtHR, Judgment, 1 July 2014, paras 129, 131, 134, 155 and 157.

15 Benvenisti, 1999, p. 843–845.

16 Mutua, Makau, *Human Rights: A Political and Cultural Critique (Pennsylvania Studies in Human Rights)* (Philadelphia, PA: University of Pensylvania Press, 2002), pp. 5, 18 and 31–38.

17 Schmidt, Markus, 'United Nations' in Moeckli, Daniel, Shah, Sangeeta and Sivakumaran, Sandesh (eds), *International Human Rights Law* (Oxford: Oxford University Press, 2010), pp. 391–432, pp. 392–404.

18 UN General Assembly Resolution 60/251, A/RES/60/251 (2006), para 5(e); Human Rights Council Resolution 5/1 (2007), Annex, section I.

in place to secure the acceptance of their proposed draft resolution.[19] Third, special procedures involving experts with either a thematic or country-specific mandate may be appointed by the HRC. Although the decision to create a mandate may be highly political, the task of carrying out the mandate may be more objective since it is done by a formally independent expert (as opposed to state representatives).[20] Lastly, a complaints procedure based on the previous "1503 procedure" which was created by the UN Economic, Social and Cultural Council, according to which gross violations, rather than individual cases, may be considered by the Council under a confidential procedure.[21]

Early human rights treaties, such as the Genocide Convention[22] and the Refugee Convention[23] did not establish courts or other independent monitoring bodies. The concept of treaty-monitoring bodies was introduced in 1965 with the Convention on the Elimination of All Forms of Racial Discrimination (CERD), an example followed by later UN human rights treaties.

The exact functions of each body differ from treaty to treaty, but basically fall into five categories.[24] First is the consideration of periodic reports by each state party on how it has implemented the treaty.[25] This is the main method of enforcement and monitoring under the major universal treaties. However, the treaty-monitoring bodies cannot impose any real penalties when states fail to comply with reporting requirements, and these bodies possess insufficient resources to give complete and critical consideration to the reports that are made. Hathaway is one of many who calls for revisions aimed at strengthening the self-reporting system.[26] One such revision could be for the treaty-monitoring body to publicly grade on an ordinal scale the human rights records of the state parties, where failure by a party to submit a report would automatically lead to the lowest grade.[27] Second, the treaty-monitoring bodies consider individual complaints of human rights violations against state parties that have accepted—when applicable—the optional protocol or made declarations providing the right of individual complaint.[28] Third,

19 UNGA Resolution 60/251 (2006), para 10; HRC Resolution 5/1 (2007), Annex, sections VI(D) and VII (rules 5 and 6); Schmidt, 2010, p. 397.
20 UNGA Resolution 60/251 (2006), para 6; HRC Resolution 5/1 (2007), Annex, section II.
21 UNGA Resolution 60/251 (2006), para 6; HRC Resolution 5/1 (2007), Annex, section IV.
22 Prevention and Punishment of the Crime of Genocide, established by UNGA Resolution 260 (III), 1948.
23 Convention Relating to the Status of Refugees, adopted 28 July 1951, 189 UNTS 137.
24 Scheinin, Martin, 'Improving Fact-Finding in Treaty-Based Human Rights Mechanisms and the Special Procedures of the United Nations Human Rights Council' in Bergsmo, Morten (ed), *Quality Control in Fact-Finding* (Florence: Torkel Opsahl Academic Epublisher, 2013), pp. 54–72, pp. 56–57.
25 See for example ICCPR, Article 40.
26 Hathaway, 2002, p. 2013.
27 A suggestion made to the author by Judge Krister Thelin, a previous member of the UN Human Rights Committee.
28 For example, Optional Protocol to the International Covenant on Civil and Political Rights, adopted 16 December 1966, 999 UNTS 302, Article 1.

these bodies also consider inter-state complaints in relation to states that have accepted this procedure.[29] Fourth, they may establish inquiry proceedings triggered by reports of serious or systematic human rights violations, often including a country visit by an expert committee. This mechanism has mainly been used under the Convention Against Torture (CAT).[30] Lastly, the treaty-monitoring bodies adopt General Comments which consolidate the findings of the committee and produce a systematic analysis of the requirements of the treaty under a specific article or in relation to particular issues.[31]

The key distinction between human rights commitments based on treaties on the one hand and international customary law on the other hand is that when a state becomes a party to an international human rights treaty, it consents to being scrutinized by the monitoring body of that treaty. This means that the state has delegated some of its sovereignty and there is a degree of accountability, which may differ depending on the treaty and its mechanisms. The regional human rights regimes have stronger monitoring mechanisms through access to courts compared to the UN treaty systems. The treaty-monitoring mechanisms of the UN can only issue recommendations and/or views that are not legally binding.[32]

In the context of individual complaints, NGOs may intervene with *amicus curiae* submissions. The first time that permission was granted for NGO intervention at the ECtHR was in the case *Young, James and Webster v The United Kingdom*.[33] Interventions may also be granted based on the interventionist's connection to the central issue in the case.[34] Even though there is no explicit provision in the American Convention on Human Rights (AmCHR), the Commission and the Court have allowed *amici* interventions. Article 44 of the Rules of Procedure provides broad competence for the Court as regards evidence and information which can be used to permit *amici* interventions.[35] Article 46 of the African Charter on Human and Peoples' Rights (ACHPR) is also drafted in a broad manner which would permit the African commission to permit *amici* interventions. The Rules of Procedure are more explicit and allow the African Commission to accept unsolicited, and to solicit, *amicus curiae* interventions in relation to individual communications.[36] The court's rules contain provisions that can potentially open allow individual and NGO participation in the court's oral proceedings. Rule

29 See for example, ICCPR, Article 41.

30 CAT, Article 20.

31 See for example, ICCPR Article 40, para 4.

32 Başak, International Human Rights Law, 2010, p. 288.

33 *Young, James and Webster v the United Kingdom* (Application no 7601/76; 7806/77), ECtHR, Judgment, 13 August 1981, para 8; See also Lindblom, 2001, pp. 306–307.

34 *Malone v the United Kingdom* (Application no 8691/79), ECtHR, Judgment, 2 August 1984, para 8

35 IACHR Rules of Procedure and Evidence, Article 44; Lindblom, 2001, pp. 306–307.

36 ACmHPR Rules of Procedure, rules 85 and 96(1); Viljoen, Frans and Abebe, Adem Kassie, 'Amicus Curiae Participation Before Regional Human Rights Bodies in Africa', 58 *Journal of African Law* (2014) 22–44, p. 32.

27(3) provides that the court might hear "representatives of parties, witnesses, experts, or such other persons as the Court may decide to hear" during oral proceedings. In addition, the court may "decide to hear as a witness or expert or in any other capacity any person whose evidence, assertions or statements it deems likely to assist it in carrying out its task".[37] Moreover, the court may "ask any person or institution of its choice to obtain information, express an opinion or submit a report to it on any specific point".[38] However, the participation of *amici* before the Court and the Commission has thus far been negligible.[39]

One issue that has been highlighted by feminist scholars is the need to include women as judges, members of treaty monitoring bodies and as decision-makers, in order to ensure that international bodies accommodate women's interests and voices.[40] In August 2014, 17 of 47 (or 36 per cent) judges of the ECtHR were women.[41] In the Inter-American Court of Human Rights (IACtHR), none of the seven judges were women (0 per cent), whereas there were two women judges out of a total of 11 (18 per cent) in the African Court on Human and Peoples' Rights (ACtHPR). This is hardly representative of the gender balance in societies generally.

5.2.4 State acceptance

The International Covenant on Civil and Political Rights (ICCPR) has 168 state parties, which include the major powers such as the US, France, the UK and the Russian Federation, but not China.[42] Fewer states—115 in total—are state parties to the optional protocol granting individuals the right to complain. France and the Russian Federation are members but the US and the UK are not.[43] The International Covenant on Economic, Social and Cultural Rights (ICESCR) has similar figures, with 162 state parties.[44] The US has not ratified this treaty. Even fewer states (just 16) have accepted the optional

37 ACtHPR Rules, rule 45(1).

38 Ibid, rule 45(2).

39 Viljoen and Abebe, 2014, pp. 32, 35 and 41.

40 Chinkin, Wright and Charlesworth, 2005, p. 19.

41 Compared to 38 per cent in September 2002, see Chinkin, Wright and Charlesworth, 2005, p. 20.

42 Chart of signatures and ratifications, International Covenant on Civil and Political Rights, 999 UNTS 171, Status as of 9 October 2014. China ratified the ICCPR on 5 October 1967, however, on 29 September 1972, a communication was received by the Secretary-General from the Minister for Foreign Affairs of the People's Republic of China stating that, *inter alia*, the signature and ratification of, or accession to, any multilateral treaties by The Republic of China "are all illegal and null and void".

43 Chart of signatures and ratifications, Optional Protocol to the International Covenant on Civil and Political Rights, 999 UNTS 171, Status as of 9 October 2014.

44 Chart of signatures and ratifications, International Covenant on Economic, Social and Cultural Rights, 993 UNTS 3, Status as of 10 October 2014.

protocol on the individual complaints procedure.[45] The simple explanation for this is that the protocol was only adopted quite recently. However, ideology and perception on the nature of human rights are also factors in this. A survey of other global human rights treaties would yield similar numbers for state parties. While a significant number of states are parties to global human rights, fewer states accept the individual complaints mechanism that gives these treaty regimes teeth in terms of formal enforcement measures. However, as this chapter demonstrates, there are additional mechanisms that may drive compliance.

The most widely accepted regional regime is the European Convention for the Protection of Human Rights and Fundamental Freedoms (ECHR), where 47 state parties of the Council of Europe accept the individual complaints procedure.[46] Belarus is the only European state outside the Council of Europe regime. Ten states among the 35 member states of the Organization of American States (OAS) have made declarations recognizing the competence of the Inter-American Commission on Human Rights (IACmHR) to receive and examine communications in which a state party alleges that another state party has committed a violation of a human right set forth in the AmCHR.[47] Twenty-two states have recognized the jurisdiction of the IACtHR on all matters relating to the interpretation or application of the AmCHR.[48] Fifty-three states are parties to the ACHPR, South Sudan not being a member.[49] Only seven have declared that they accept the competence of the ACtHPR to receive applications from individuals.[50] While the ECtHR is an effective mechanism, a major problem is that the Court is a victim of its own success. In 2013, the Court received 65,900 new complaints.[51] The large number of complaints impacts considerably on the time it takes for a complaints to be heard. That said, the lower rate of acceptance of the individual mechanism in the American regime and even more in the African regime is a weakness in comparison.

45 Chart of signatures and ratifications, Optional Protocol to the International Covenant on Economic, Social and Cultural Rights, Status as of 10 October 2014.

46 Chart of signatures and ratifications, Statute of the Council of Europe, CETS No: 001, Status as of 11 August 2009; Chart of signatures and ratifications, Convention for the Protection of Human Rights and Fundamental Freedoms, CETS No.: 005, Status as of 10 October 2014.

47 AmCHR, Article 45; Chart of signatures and ratifications, American Convention on Human Rights, Status as of 10 October 2014.

48 AmCHR, Article 62; Chart of signatures and ratifications, American Convention on Human Rights.

49 Chart of signatures and ratifications, African Charter on Human and Peoples' Rights, Status as of 21 February 2013.

50 Protocol to the African Charter on Human and Peoples' Rights on the Establishment of an African Court on Human and Peoples' Rights, adopted 10 June 1998, Article 5; Chart of signatures and ratifications, Protocol to the African Charter on Human and Peoples' Rights on the Establishment of an African Court on Human and Peoples' Rights, Status as of 16 April 2014.

51 European Court of Human Rights, Analysis of statistics 2013.

5.3 Feminist perspective on human rights law

Engle has identified three stages in the development of feminist critiques of human rights law: liberal inclusion feminism (1985–90); feminist critique concerning structural bias (1987–95); and third-world feminism (1992–). The task of feminism during the stage of liberal inclusion was to add women to human rights protections guaranteed under international law. Following this, feminists argued that human rights law was structurally biased in the sense that international law and institutions permitted and even required women's subordination. Third-world feminism studies both mainstream international human rights regimes and its feminist critics. They argue that focusing on structural bias and the male/female divide obscures economic, social and cultural differences between "first-" and "third-world" women. Engle notes that liberal inclusion has succeeded. Structural bias critiques have managed well to set agendas and bring awareness to issues, such as trafficking, female genital mutilation and war-time rape, but have been less successful in responding to attacks from third-world feminists. Third-world feminism has become trapped in the debate between universalism and cultural relativism, where Engle finds a compromise that she calls culturally sensitive universalism.[52]

Otto has outlined the genealogy of the female subjects of international law. There are three main recurring female subjectivities which may overlap: (a) the figure of the wife and mother who needs "protection" both in times of war and peace. She is more an object than a subject of international law; (b) the woman who is "formally equal" with men in the public life sphere; and (c) the "victim" subject who is produced by colonial narratives of gender. All these personas are dependent on the male as the protector, either as the head of the household in peacetime or as warrior in times of war.[53]

5.4 Processes and mechanisms for creating and enforcing human rights law

While international lawyers perceive much of human rights research and compliance problems as hidden in detailed argument and analysis, international relations scholars study general patterns of compliance.[54] To examine compliance is challenging given the complexity of international human rights law in terms of the number of treaties, and the nature of the obligations and enforcement mechanisms, making empirical analysis of state

52 Engle, Karen, 'International Human Rights and Feminsisms: When Discourses Keep Meeting' in Buss, Doris and Manji, Ambreena (eds), *International Law: Modern Feminist Approaches* (Oxford: Hart Publishing, 2005), pp. 47–66, pp. 47–54, 59–65.

53 Otto, Dianne, 'Disconserting "Masculinities": Reinventing the Gendered Subject(s) of International Human Rights Law' in Buss, Doris and Manji, Ambreena (eds), *International Law: Modern Feminist Approaches* (Oxford: Hart Publishing, 2005), pp. 105–129, p. 106.

54 Başak, International Human Rights Law, 2010, p. 289.

compliance difficult. Some rights are digital while others are not. Çali notes that compliance is not always an "either/or" question,[55] in some cases it may be more appropriate to discuss it as a matter of degree and context. Landman notes that measurement of human rights can take the form of: (a) coding country participation in regional and international human rights regimes, coding national constitutions according to their rights provisions; (b) determining how rights are respected in practice, including: qualitative reporting of rights violations, survey data on perceptions of rights conditions, quantitative summaries of rights violations, and abstract scales of rights protection based on normative standards; and (c) individual and aggregate measures that map the outcomes of government policies that have consequences for the enjoyment of rights.[56]

Human rights obligations have been conceptualized as three dimensions: *respect*, *protect* and *fulfil*.[57] Landman shows how these three dimensions combined with the two categories of civil and political rights, and economic, social and cultural rights create a matrix with six fields, which provides a good starting point to operationalize human rights.[58] This type of matrix may be used as a starting point for developing the research design of a project and data collection. An option is to use existing datasets for global comparative analysis which are already available,[59] for example the "torture scale".[60]

The next section considers mechanisms that are relevant for compliance with human rights obligations.

5.4.1 Expressive function of human rights law

The mechanisms of creation and enforcement of international human rights treaties differ from other areas of international law. Notably, the mechanism of reciprocity is less frequently used, if at all. If a state wishes to make another state violating human rights comply with the agreed obligations, it would make no sense and have no effect if the first state would reciprocate by making the same violations against its own population. The violation by a state of the rights of its own inhabitants does not ordinarily infringe on the national interests of other parties to the agreement, so there

55 Başak, International Human Rights Law, 2010, p. 298.

56 Landman, Todd, 'Measuring Human Rights: Principle, Practice, and Policy', 26 *Human Rights Quarterly* (2004) 906–931.

57 Human Rights Committee, General Comment 31, Nature of the General Legal Obligation on States Parties to the Covenant, UN Doc CCPR/C/21/Rev.1/Add.13 (2004), paras 3–5 (respect), para 8 (protect), para 7 (fulfil); Committee on Economic, Social and Cultural Rights, General Comment 12, Right to adequate food (Twentieth session, 1999), UN Doc E/C.12/1999/5 (1999), para 15.

58 Landman, 2009, p. 23.

59 Landman, 2009, p. 32.

60 Hathaway, 2002, pp. 1969–1972, 1977, 1979, 1982–1984, 1995 and 1998.

is no apparently compelling interest to scrutinize the violating behavior and call it to account. The most potent means of enforcement—military intervention and economic sanctions—are rarely used to enforce human rights norms because there is little incentive for individual states to take on such a burden. However, reciprocity may, under certain circumstances, operate if there is a policy of linkage, for example access to economic aid. In cases of human rights violations, aid can be revoked.[61] Considering that mechanisms of reciprocity and coercion appear less effective in the field of human rights, other mechanisms may be more relevant. Processes of persuasion and acculturation (socialization) may better explain why states give expressive reasons for complying with human rights law, to obtain legitimacy through creating and ratifying human rights treaties. Scholars diverge regarding whether states do so rationally or through acculturation processes.[62] There are also different answers as to whether such expressions have any impact.[63] Hathaway argues that the expressive function can work either in unison with, or in opposition to, the instrumental role of the treaty,[64] a point which is revisited later.

Simmons explains that international relations scholars often are pessimistic about the ability of international law to influence human rights practices because they look in the wrong direction. The traditional interstate perspective, with criteria such as international law-making, adjudication and enforcement, indicates that it is a weak legal system. Governments may comply with international agreements only when the treaty does not engage a national interest. Observance of international law should be attributed either to the individual or complementary interests of states, or the distribution of power among them, "Where there is neither community of interests nor balance of power, there is no international law".[65] Realists interpret compliance against states' interest as the result of coercion from more powerful states. The realist conclusion is that human rights treaties have little influence over state behavior because they are not likely to be enforced by other states.[66] Simmons argues that it is difficult to develop a theory of compliance with international human rights treaties purely in the context of international politics.[67] The course of events that affects human rights occurs within the state, which is why local politics is important in this field.

61 Axelrod and Keohane, 1986, pp. 239–241; Henkin, 1979, p. 232; Hathaway, 2002, p. 2007; Goodman and Jinks, 2004, p. 629; Guzman, 2008, p. 45; Simmons, 2009, pp. 123, 125 and 154; Posner, 2009, p. 184; Ginsburg and Shaffer, 2010, p. 770. Compare with Oye, 1986, p. 11.
62 Goodman and Jinks, 2004, p. 631.
63 Simmons, 2009, pp. 57–155; Ginsburg and Shaffer, 2010, p. 770.
64 Hathaway, 2002, pp. 2006–2007.
65 Morgenthau, 1954, p. 252. See earlier, similar statement in Morgenthau, 1940, pp. 274 and 275.
66 Simmons, 2009, pp. 114–116.
67 Simmons, 2009, p. 125.

5.4.2 Diffusion of human rights norms mediated by domestic institutions and domestic actors

As described in sections 5.2.3 and 5.2.4, individuals and non-state actors can, if the concerned state consents, have access to international mechanisms where they can file complaints against states for violations of their human rights. However, the domestic arena has even more potential for enforcing human rights than the international mechanisms.

Henkin explains that the incentive for states to promote and participate in the human rights discourse depends on a state's traditions and commitments. Domestic influences are more relevant in this for the observance of human rights law than other parts of international law.[68] Helfer and Slaughter argue that liberal democratic governments will be more likely to comply with supranational legal judgments than other states because international legal obligations mobilize domestic interest groups that, in turn, pressure the government to comply from within the state.[69]

Most empirical studies on international human rights reach a similar conclusion: that the effectiveness of international law is mediated by domestic institutions and domestic actors. International human rights law largely depends on mechanisms of norm diffusion, and the effect of human rights treaties is typically indirect, depending on the domestic channels used in specific contexts. Ginsburg and Shaffer note that answers to the key question of *whether* improvements in terms of human rights may be associated with, and explained by, international law are typically linked to the existence of certain conditions. A reoccurring theme in literature is that effective human rights protection requires domestic institutions, so that consent to human rights treaties is more likely to improve performance in democracies than in autocracies.[70] Patterns of norm diffusion in relation to human rights may be found in various areas of domestic governance, for example welfare and labor policy[71] and universal suffrage.[72] Risse and Sikkink describe this in terms of international "norms cascade".[73]

68 Henkin, 1979, pp. 237–239.

69 Helfer, Laurence R. and Slaughter, Anne-Marie, 'Toward a Theory of Effective Supranational Adjudication', 107 *Yale Law Journal* (1997) 273–391, pp. 331–335.

70 Ginsburg and Shaffer, 2010, pp. 771–773.

71 Thomas, George M. and Lauderdale, Pat, 'State authority and national welfare programs in the world system context', 3 *Sociological Forum* (1988) 383–399; Abbott, Andrew and DeViney, Stanley, 'The Welfare State as Transnational Event: Evidence from Sequences of Policy Adoption', 16 *Social Science History* (1992) 245–274; Strang, David and Chang, Patricia Mei Yin, 'The International Labor Organization and the welfare state: institutional effects on national welfare spending, 1960–80', 47 *International Organization* (1993) 235–262; summarized by Goodman and Jinks, 2004, p. 649.

72 Ramirez, Francisco O., Soysal, Yasemin and Shanahan, Suzanne, 'The Changing Logic of Political Citizenship: Cross-National Acquisition of Women's Suffrage Rights, 1890 to 1990', 62 *American Sociological Review* (1997) 735–745, pp. 738–743; Goodman and Jinks, 2004, p. 649.

73 Risse and Sikkink, 1999, pp. 21–22.

Simmons suggests three mechanisms that drive compliance and through which human rights treaties can influence domestic politics: (a) influence on national policy agenda; (b) litigation in national courts; and (c) influence on the propensity of groups to mobilize. To elucidate, an internationally negotiated treaty may, first, alter the domestic agenda and empower particular branches of national policy-making. Very few states have the power to design an international human rights treaty that matches exactly their own legislative agenda. The need to consider ratification can therefore rearrange a country's priorities and maybe even its preferences. Second, international legal obligations may form an important part of the body of law on which judicial decisions are based, especially in monist legal systems. It may also have implications in dualist legal systems where the additional step of passing implementing legislation is required. Third, ratified treaties may enhance the likelihood that individuals will mobilize to claim the rights the treaties contain. These three mechanisms interact and reinforce each other. In other words, externally negotiated treaties are potentially a source of influence in local politics.[74] Similarly, Merry has investigated how intermediaries such as community leaders, NGO participants, and social movement activists translate the discourses and practices from the arena of international law and legal institutions to specific situations of suffering and violation.[75] Intermediaries may advance particular claims by using materials from the international plane when instrumentally valuable. The international level becomes, then, not just an arena, but also a repository of materials available for invocation in the domestic sphere.[76] Treaty ratification creates an opportunity for NGOs as "norm entrepreneurs" to begin to provoke interactions aimed at gradual internalization of the norms embodied in the treaty.[77] NGO advocacy is embedded in the system of sovereign states. Since implementation and enforcement of human rights is a state responsibility, NGOs must usually act through, rather than around, states.[78]

Similarly, Hafner-Burton and Tsutsui use quantitative methods to find that states with a greater number of NGOs are more likely to protect the rights of their citizens, controlling for alternative explanations for government compliance with human rights.[79] However, Ginsburg and Shaffer challenge this finding regarding NGO-mobilization as a causal factor in enforcement

74 Simmons, 2009, pp. 114 and 125–155.

75 Merry, Sally Engle, 'Transnational Human Rights and Local Activism: Mapping the Middle', 108 *American Anthropologist* (2006) 38–51, p. 39.

76 Ginsburg and Shaffer, 2010, p. 772.

77 Hathaway, 2002, pp. 2022.

78 Donnelly, Jack, 'Human Rights' in Baylis, John, Smith, Steve and Owens, Patricia (eds), *The Globalization of World Politics* (5th edn, Oxford: Oxford University Press, 2011), pp. 494–509, p. 504.

79 Hafner-Burton, Emilie M. and Tsutsui, Kiyoteru, 'Human Rights in a Globalizing World: The Paradox of Empty Promises', 110 *American Journal of Sociology* (2005) 1373–1411, pp. 1386 and 1398–1399.

of human rights, since it is possible that countries with relatively good or improving human rights records are more likely to allow international NGOs to operate.[80]

Hathaway conducted a study using a large-scale quantitative analysis covering 166 countries over nearly a 40-year period to test the relationship between human rights treaties and countries' human rights practices, controlling for various factors including democracy, gross national product per capita, international war and national war. The analysis concerns five areas of human rights law, namely genocide, torture, fair and public trials, civil liberties and political representation of women.[81] An initial analysis of the relationship between treaty ratification and country ratings indicates that, for the most part, countries that have ratified human rights treaties have better human rights ratings than those that have not ratified. However, non-compliance appears common.[82] Moreover, some of her conclusions are counterintuitive. She finds that treaty ratification is not infrequently associated with worse human rights ratings than otherwise expected. Countries with poor human rights ratings are sometimes more likely to have ratified the relevant treaties than are countries with better ratings. She does, nevertheless, find evidence suggesting that ratification of human rights treaties by fully democratic nations is associated with better human rights practices. This may be explained by the dual nature of international treaties as both instrumental and expressive instruments. Treaties do not only create norms, ratification is also a means for states to express their position in the international community. If positions and not effects are rewarded—due to weak monitoring and compliance mechanisms—states can gain benefits by taking positions that they will not honor. This may explain why ratification of human rights treaties is sometimes associated with worse human rights practices.[83] Hafner-Burton and Tsutsui make a similar finding that governments often ratify human rights treaties as a matter of window dressing, radically decoupling policy from practice and at times exacerbating negative human rights practices.[84] Simmons confronts this phenomenon when she disaggregates the sample of countries so as to exclude both false positives (countries that ratify treaties without intending to comply) and false negatives (countries that credibly enforce human rights guarantees, but do not ratify human rights treaties for domestic institutional reasons). For the middle group of countries in the sample, ratification of human rights instruments is associated with positive improvements in rights protection. Simmons argues that:

80 Ginsburg and Shaffer, 2010, p. 773.
81 Hathaway, 2002, pp. 1939 and 1990.
82 Hathaway, 2002, pp. 1976 and 1999.
83 Hathaway, 2002, pp. 1940–1941, 1978, 2001 and 2009. See also Hafner-Burton, Victor and Lupu, 2012, pp. 88–89.
84 Hafner-Burton and Tsutsui, 2005, pp. 1378, 1383–1386 and 1405.

> [a]t least in the case of civil and political rights, a treaty's greatest impact is likely to be found not in the stable extremes of democracy and autocracy, but in the mass of nations with institutions in flux, where citizens potentially have both the motive and the means to succeed in demanding their rights.[85]

The book by Risse, Ropp and Sikkink, *The Power of Human Rights*, asks a similar question as the studies described above: What are the conditions under which international human rights norms are internalized in domestic practices? The methodology adopted in the book is different, however. The analysis is based on paired cases of countries (as opposed to a large-*n* study) with serious human rights situations from each region of the world. The authors have examined "success stories" of international human rights, such as Chile, South Africa, the Philippines, Poland and the former Czechoslovakia, with more difficult cases of human rights violations in countries such as Guatemala, Kenya, Uganda, Morocco, Tunisia and Indonesia.[86] Using paired cases in the same region follows the logic of MSSD research design whereby different outcomes are compared across similar countries, which allows the isolation of those factors that may account for an outcome. By taking the next step and comparing different states in different regions, one can compare similar outcomes across different countries pursuant to the MDSD research design and identify additional relevant factors.[87] The authors also use process-tracing, documenting change (or lack thereof) in human rights practices, tracing domestic and international normative, and political and institutional developments in an attempt to explain changes.[88] The authors found similar patterns and processes in very different settings. Risse, Ropp and Sikkink develop a five-phase "spiral model" of norms socialization which specifies the causal mechanisms and prevailing logic of action in each phase of the process, generalizable across cases irrespective of cultural, political or economic differences among countries. They challenge approaches that emphasize material structures as the primary determinants of state identities, interests and preferences. As social constructivists, they focus less on economic, military conditions and coercion, and more on norms and ideas.[89] As a result, the spiral model explores the relationship between international human rights norms and actual practices. There is no single statistical test of the spiral in its entirety, quantitative

85 Simmons, 2009, pp. 15, 67–80 and 155; commented by Ginsburg and Shaffer, 2010, p. 772.
86 Risse and Sikkink, 1999, pp. 1–2.
87 Landman, 2009, p. 33–34.
88 Risse and Sikkink, 1999, pp. 8 and 10.
89 Risse and Sikkink, 1999, pp. 3, 4 and 6–8; Risse, Thomas and Ropp, Stephen C., 'International Human Rights Norms and Domestic Change: Conclusions' in Risse, Thomas, Ropp, Stephen C. and Sikkink, Kathryn (eds), *The Power of Human Rights International Norms and Domestic Change* (Cambridge: Cambridge University Press, 1999), pp. 234–278, pp. 236, 238–254.

research may shed light on a few static relationships, capturing one or two "phases" of the model at best.[90]

Risse, Ropp and Sikkink describe norm socialization with three types of social action: (a) *instrumental adaptation* as a response to pressures—both domestic and international, i.e. coercion; (b) *argumentative discourses* involving communication, argumentation and persuasion. Once governments entrap themselves in the human rights discourse, violations of human rights may throw them out of power, as illustrated by the ouster from power of President Marcos in the Philippines and Uganda's Milton Obote; and (c) institutionalization though ratification, changes in domestic laws and domestic mechanisms.[91] This may be compared to Cotterell's three levels of socialization, conformity to rules: (a) as a response to rewards and punishment; (b) because they are rules; and (c) in order to support moral principles as such.[92]

However, even if a correlation may be identified between the adoption of norms as manifested by state ratification of a human rights treaty and a change of state practice, this does not necessarily mean that the norm leads to a change of interests, which in turn changes state practice. Hathaway notes that the observation that countries that ratify treaties generally have better human rights ratings on the whole than those that do not does not mean that ratifying countries have better ratings as a result of ratifying the treaties.[93] Governments may change human rights practices only to gain access to material benefits of foreign aid or to be able to stay in power in the face of domestic opposition. Risse and Sikkink argue that the process of human rights change almost always begins for instrumental or strategic purposes as a response to domestic or transnational pressures. Yet even instrumental adaptation of human rights norms may set into motion a process of identity transformation leading to practices being adopted for instrumental reasons later and maintained for reasons of belief and identity. They use the example of the Reagan administration pro-democracy foreign policy which was initially adopted for instrumental reasons but later became internalized and a question of identity. Another example of change for instrumental reasons includes the Soviet Union and Eastern Europe acceptance of human rights provisions in the Helsinki Act in exchange for Western acceptance of political and territorial status quo in the détente period.[94]

Simmons notes that the spiral model appears to rest on an irrational logic. Governments make tactical concessions that they think may calm international and external criticism. Pursuant to the model, these actions end up entrapping repressive governments. This is a core point on which the model

90 Simmons, 2013, p. 44.

91 Risse and Sikkink, 1999, pp. 11–35; Risse and Ropp, 1999, pp. 255–256.

92 See section 2.4 on the sociology of law. Stein, 1983, pp. 137–139; Finlayson and Zacher, 1983, p. 305; Cotterell, 1992, pp. 141–142.

93 Hathaway, 2002, p. 1989.

94 Risse and Sikkink, 1999, p. 10; Risse and Ropp, 1999, p. 250.

diverges starkly with realist accounts of human rights.[95] As indicated earlier, tactical concessions have been characterized as window dressing[96] or mere expressive gestures.[97] Why do states not foresee the entrapment? Potential answers are that governments miscalculate, are bribed or are going through a process of socialization.[98]

Risse and Sikiink acknowledge that sustained improvements in human rights practices are conditioned by the broader legal and judicial capacities of the country in question. They:

> argue that the enduring implementation of human rights norms requires political systems to establish the rule of law. Stable improvements in human rights conditions require some measure of political transformation ... Enduring human rights changes ... go hand in hand with domestic structural changes.[99]

Simmons elaborates that the spiral model could initially work, but would eventually fail if other institutional changes did not take place in which norms could find domestic traction and eventually be enforced.[100]

According to the realist approach, ideas and norms matter if they are backed by superior economic and/or military power. Risse and Sikkink argue that this approach would, however, need to explain why the US moved from a position before 1973 in which human rights were an inappropriate part of foreign policy to becoming an important part in the 1990s.[101] Risse and Ropp find that "Great Power" pressure is frequently supportive and enabling of domestic human rights change, but seldom crucial, as exemplified with Uganda, Morocco and Guatemala.[102] Risse, Sikkink and Ropp also challenge the modernization theory and the primacy of the domestic domain, i.e. that economic growth determines outcomes in terms of human rights and democracy. The human rights changes in the Philippines, Poland, Czechoslovakia, South Africa and Chile were all preceded by severe economic crisis rather than growth.[103]

5.5 Tension between power and law

The realist assumption for when states comply with human rights requirements is that it is a coincidence, as states do not change their behavior as a

95 Simmons, 2013, p. 47.
96 Hafner-Burton and Tsutsui, 2005, pp. 1378, 1383–1386 and 1405.
97 Hathaway, 2002, pp. 2006–2007.
98 Risse and Sikkink, 1999, p. 27; Simmons, 2013, pp. 48–52.
99 Risse and Sikkink, 1999, pp. 3–4.
100 Simmons, 2013, p. 45.
101 Risse and Sikkink, 1999, p. 35.
102 Risse and Ropp, 1999, p. 268.
103 Risse and Sikkink, 1999, p. 37; Risse and Ropp, 1999, p. 269.

result of human rights norms. There has to be some other factor, for example that the state is coerced by a more powerful state to comply. Hathaway notes that it is difficult for realists to explain why states would be willing to incur the costs of setting up a human rights regime, delegate to that regime the power to control and monitor some aspects of their interactions with their own citizens, commit to comply with treaty requirements, and agree to engage where necessary in sanctioning activity to bring others into compliance.[104] As explained in section 5.4.2, a reoccurring theme in literature is that effective human rights protection requires domestic institutions. In this way, the empirical research is consistent with liberal institutionalism that places the focus on domestic political processes.[105]

The constructivist explanation for state is that states enter into international human rights treaties to signal their adherence to global cultural norms, and in these treaties expressively reflect and convey a global socialization process.[106] Simmons provides quantitative evidence in support of the claim that states ratify international human rights treaties for expressive reasons, highlighting that they are more likely to do so if the treaty regimes reflect values consonant with their own and can be complied with at a reasonable cost.[107] Counter to this, the realist explanation would be that human rights law exists more as a tool of policy against other states. Also, critical law scholars may describe part of the mechanics of international society in the same manner.[108]

104 Hathaway, 2002, p. 1946.

105 Hathaway, 2002, p. 1952.

106 Shaw, Malcolm N., *International Law* (6th edn, Cambridge: Cambridge University Press, 2008), pp. 265–266; Posner, 2009, p. 177 on global legalists; Ginsburg and Shaffer, 2010, p. 759.

107 Simmons, 2009, pp. 12–17, 199, 304–305 and 353–355. Commented by Ginsburg and Shaffer, 2010, p. 759; See also Shaw, 2008, pp. 265–266.

108 Mutua, 2002, pp. 67–70.

6 International criminal justice

6.1 Function of the regime

The purpose of international criminal justice is to end impunity for international crimes (genocide, crimes against humanity, war crimes and—in the future—the crime of aggression), as well as to contribute to the prevention of such crimes.[1] Other relevant interests which may operate as ends in themselves or as constraints to the effort to end impunity are fair trial requirements, victims' participation, reparation to victims, protection of victims and witnesses, truth-seeking and state sovereignty.[2] There has been significant development in relation to gender-related crimes through the practice of the ICTY and the ICTR, which have both recognized that forms of sexual violence can amount to cruel treatment,[3] and outrages on personal dignity[4] as a war crime,[5] breaches of common Article 3 of the Geneva Convention and violations of the laws and customs of war, as well as torture[6] and enslavement[7] as a crime against humanity, and genocide.[8]

International criminal law concerns the individual criminal responsibility of individuals such as political and military leaders and other natural persons (as opposed to the responsibility of states). International criminal law is a

1 Rome Statute, Preamble.

2 Klamberg, 2013, pp. 49–50.

3 *Prosecutor v Tadić* (Case No IT-94-1), ICTY T Ch, Opinion and Judgment, 7 May 1997, paras 194 and 724–726; *Prosecutor v Delalić et al (Čelebići)* (Case No IT-96-21), ICTY T Ch, Judgment, 16 November 1998, para 1066; *Prosecutor v Blaškić* (Case No IT95-14-T), ICTY T Ch, Judgment, 3 March 2000, paras 692, 695 and 700.

4 *Prosecutor v Kunarac et al* (Case No IT-96-23-T and 23/1-T) "Foča", ICTY T Ch II, Judgment, 22 February 2001, para 436.

5 *Prosecutor v Furundžija* (Case IT-95-17/1), ICTY T Ch, Judgement, 10 December 1998, paras 165–189 and 270–275.

6 *Delalić et al*, ICTY T Ch, 16 November 1998, paras 475 and 495–496; *Prosecutor v Furundžija* (Case IT-95-17/1), ICTY A Ch, Judgment, 21 July 2000, para 114.

7 *Kunarac et al*, ICTY T Ch II, 22 February 2001, paras 515–543.

8 *Prosecutor v Jean-Paul Akayesu* (Case No ICTR-96-4-T), ICTR T Ch, Judgement, 2 September 1998, paras 507–509 and 731; *Prosecutor v Clément Kayishema and Obed Ruzindana* (Case No ICTR-95-1-T), ICTR T Ch, Judgment 21 May 1999, paras 95, 114–118, 299, 446 and 532; summarized by Chinkin, Wright and Charlesworth, 2005, p. 23.

broad field which involves numerous issues. This chapter covers two aspects. The first is the criminalized conduct and the degree of precision this has achieved. The second aspect concerns state sovereignty, and the interests and obligations of states vis-à-vis international tribunals and courts.

Even though international criminal law concerns individual criminal responsibility, the role of states is still relevant, mainly for two reasons. First, it is states that create the rules in this area and decide on the design of the mechanisms for adjudication and enforcement. The UN Security Council (which is a body set up by and consisting of states) may use its enforcement powers under Chapter VII of the UN Charter to establish international criminal jurisdictions, as it did with the ICTY and the ICTR.[9] The UN Security Council's decision as to whether to establish such tribunals is subject to the veto power of the permanent members and is thus highly dependent on the distribution of power among states and the interests of the major powers. International criminal jurisdiction may also be created on a consensual basis through treaty, as illustrated by the creation of the ICC. Second, in order for international criminal jurisdiction to be effective, states must be under a legal obligation to cooperate or be subjected to other strong incentives with the same effect. In a national legal system, a prosecutor or a court relies upon a top-down exercise of state authority, while at the international level all investigatory and other enforcement measures require either the consent of the territorial state or a binding decision from an international body such as the UN Security Council—often together with the intervention of other states.[10] In contrast to domestic criminal courts, international tribunals have no enforcement agencies at their disposal. Without the cooperation of the national authorities of states or other entities, such as peace-keeping missions (which are set up by states), they cannot collect evidence or have access to coercive measures.

National courts may also require state cooperation in the exercise of their duties, which can create similar problems, as is experienced at the international level. Examples of this include when documents, witnesses or suspects are outside their jurisdiction in another country, as a national court cannot subject residents abroad to the same powers as residents within their

9 Resolution 827 (1993), UN Doc S/RES/827; Resolution 955 (1994), UN Doc S/RES/955.

10 Cassese, Antonio, 'The Statute of the International Criminal Court: Some Preliminary Reflections', 10 *European Journal of International Law* (1999) 144–171, p. 164; Safferling, Christoph J.M., *Towards an International Criminal Procedure* (Oxford: Oxford University Press, 2001), pp. 64–66; Ciampi, Annalisa, 'Other forms of cooperation' in Cassese, Antonio, Gaeta, Paola and Jones, John R.W.D (eds), *The Rome Statute of the International Criminal Court* (Oxford: Oxford University Press, 2002), pp. 1705–1747, p. 1706; Mathias, Eric and Spencer, J.R., 'The balance of power between the police and the public prosecutor' in Delmas-Marty, M. (ed), *European Criminal Procedures* (Cambridge: Cambridge University Press, 2005), pp. 459–487, p. 459; Cogan, Jacob Katz, 'International Criminal Courts and Fair Trials: Difficulties and Prospects', 27 *Yale Journal of International Law* (2002) 111–140, p. 119; Cryer, Robert et al., *An Introduction to International Criminal Law and Procedure* (2nd edn, Cambridge: Cambridge University Press, 2010), p. 446; Klamberg, 2013, p. 231.

territorial jurisdiction. Whereas this problem only concerns a minority of cases in domestic proceedings, international criminal courts require the assistance of states in relation to every single witness, suspect or document.[11]

6.2 Dimensions of legalization

6.2.1 Degree to which the rules are obligatory

The conduct criminalized in Articles 5–8 of the Rome Statute—genocide, crimes against humanity and war crimes—is reflective of what is prohibited under customary international law. Violations may entail individual responsibility as well as state responsibility. The problem is thus not that some states and their citizens are without obligations, it is rather how to sanction violations, a matter elaborated below and revisited in sections 6.2.3 and 6.4.

As indicated above, this section also focuses on the obligation of states to cooperate with the ICTY, the ICTR and the ICC. The UN Security Council established the *ad hoc* tribunals acting under Chapter VII of the UN Charter and decided that, "all States shall cooperate fully with the tribunals and their organs" in accordance, *inter alia*, with the statutes of the respective tribunal.[12] The UN member states are under an obligation "to accept and carry out the decisions of the Security Council in accordance with the [UN] Charter".[13]

The ICC is a treaty-based body and as such, it is an autonomous body and not a subsidiary organ of the UN Security Council. Thus, in the absence of any explicit decisions of the UN Security Council,[14] the Court does not by default benefit from the enforcement powers under Chapter VII of the UN Charter. The issue of balancing the Court's jurisdiction and the sovereignty of state parties is addressed in Part 9 of the Rome Statute. The Rome Statute distinguishes between states parties and third states. The general obligation to cooperate with the Court in its investigation and prosecution of crimes within the jurisdiction of the Court only applies to states parties. In principle, obligations cannot be imposed on other states not a party to the Rome Statute.[15] However, obligations may be imposed on non-state parties when situations are referred to the Court by the UN Security Council under Chapter VII of the UN Charter.

11 Sluiter, Göran, 'Appearance of Witnesses and Unavailability of Subpoena Powers for the Court' in Bellelli, Roberto (ed), *International Criminal Justice* (Farnham: Ashgate, 2010), pp. 459–472, p. 461. See also Klamberg, 2013, p. 231.

12 Resolution 827 (1993); Resolution 955 (1994).

13 UN Charter, Article 25.

14 The UN Security Council has the power to refer situations to the Court, Rome Statute, Article 13(b).

15 Ciampi, 'Other forms of cooperation', 2002, p. 1609.

6.2.2 Precision of the rules

The outer boundary of the criminalized conduct is set by the principle of legality and expressed in the maxim *nullum crimen sine lege*. From this principle follows, as codified in Article 22 of the Rome Statute, that, "[t]he definition of a crime shall be strictly construed and shall not be extended by analogy. In case of ambiguity, the definition shall be interpreted in favour of the person being investigated, prosecuted or convicted". Even if some conduct amounts to a violation and a crime, it may still be excused under certain circumstances. Mental disease, intoxication, self-defense, duress,[16] mistakes of fact and law,[17] and superior orders[18] are potential grounds for excluding criminal responsibility. The outer boundaries of criminalized behavior, as well as the exceptions, are all subject to interpretation, which creates ambiguity. This ambiguity may to a certain extent be resolved through case law, which means that courts ultimately decide on the exceptions.

Turning, to cooperation, the Statute of the *ad hoc* tribunals states that:

> States shall comply without undue delay with any request for assistance or an order issued by a Trial Chamber, including, but not limited to: a) the identification and location of persons; b) the taking of testimony and the production of evidence; c) the service of documents; d) the arrest or detention of persons; e) the surrender or the transfer of the accused to the International Tribunal.[19]

Further, the obligation to cooperate, "being based on a Security Council binding resolution made under Chapter VII of the UN Charter, by virtue of Article 103 of the UN Charter takes precedence over customary and treaty obligations concerning personal immunities",[20] which normally protects heads of state and state officials. This is a clear limitation of the principle of state sovereignty. However, loopholes have been created in this broad obligation to cooperate for national security information[21] and material provided to the tribunals on a confidential basis.[22]

16 Rome Statute, Article 31.

17 Rome Statute, Article 32.

18 Rome Statute, Article 33.

19 Statute of the International Criminal Tribunal for the Former Yugoslavia adopted 25 May 1993 by Resolution 827 as amended until 7 July 2009, Article 29; Statute of the International Criminal Tribunal for Rwanda adopted 8 November 1994 by resolution 955 as amended until 16 December 2009, Article 28.

20 Gaeta, Paola, 'Official Capacity and Immunities' in Cassese, Antonio, Gaeta, Paola and Jones, John R.W.D (eds), *The Rome Statute of the International Criminal Court* (Oxford: Oxford University Press, 2002), pp. 975–1002, p. 989; Cryer et al., 2010, pp. 545 and 549–550.

21 ICTY Rules of Procedure and Evidence (RPE) as amended 8 December 2010, rule 54 *bis* (e); MICT Rules of Procedure and Evidence (RPE) 8 June 2012, rule 56(e). There is no corresponding ICTR rule.

22 ICTY RPE, rule 70(b); ICTR RPE as amended 9 February 2010, rule 70(b); MICT RPE, rule 76(b).

The Rome Statute provides similar specificity on the obligations, including: the arrest and surrender of persons to the Court; the identification and whereabouts of persons or the location of items; the taking of evidence; the questioning of any person being investigated or prosecuted; the service of documents; facilitating the voluntary appearance of persons as witnesses or experts before the Court; the temporary transfer of persons; the examination of places or sites, including the exhumation and examination of grave sites; the execution of searches and seizures; the provision of records and documents, including official records and documents; the protection of victims and witnesses and the preservation of evidence; the identification, tracing and freezing or seizure of proceeds, property and assets and instrumentalities of crimes for the purpose of eventual forfeiture; and any other type of assistance which is not prohibited by the law of the requested state.[23] Similarly, immunities offer no protection to heads of state and state officials of a state party,[24] a proposition more debatable in relation to heads of state and state officials of a non-state party.[25] As with the ICTY and the ICTR, a state party may deny a request for assistance only if the request concerns the production of any documents or disclosure of evidence which relates to its national security.[26]

6.2.3 Delegation of some functions to a third party

As indicated in section 1.2.1.3, delegation concerns the question of who interprets and enforces the obligation of states. It is shown below that the power of interpreting whether a state is failing to comply has been delegated to the *ad hoc* tribunals and the ICC, but the power to bring enforcement action against non-complying states remains with other states and, when applicable, the UN Security Council.

Although the *ad hoc* tribunals and the ICC cannot take enforcement measures by themselves, states can still be subject to measures taken by other States or sanctions imposed by the UN or other intergovernmental organizations.[27] The leading case in relation to the *ad hoc* tribunals concerned *Blaškić* regarding the Croatian government's refusal to cooperate with the ICTY. The Appeals Chamber stated the following:

23 Rome Statute, Articles 58, 59, 89, 92 and 93.

24 Rome Statute, Article 27.

25 Compare Schabas, William A., *The International Criminal Court – A Commentary on the Rome Statute* (Oxford: Oxford University Press, 2010), p. 451 with Kreß, Claus, 'The International Criminal Court and Immunities under International Law for States Not Party to the Court's Statute' in Bergsmo, Morten and Yan, Ling (eds), *State Sovereignty and International Criminal Law* (Beijing: Torkel Opsahl Academic EPublisher, 2012), pp. 223–265.

26 Rome Statute, Articles 72 and 93(4).

27 Knoops, Geert-Jan Alexander, *Theory and Practice of International and Internationalized Criminal Proceedings* (The Hague: Kluwer Law International, 2005), p. 312.

> However, it is self-evident that the International Tribunal, in order to bring to trial persons living under the jurisdiction of sovereign States, not being endowed with enforcement agents of its own, must rely upon the cooperation of States. The International Tribunal must turn to States if it is effectively to investigate crimes, collect evidence, summon witnesses and have indictees arrested and surrendered to the International Tribunal. The drafters of the Statute realistically took account of this in imposing upon all States the obligation to lend cooperation and judicial assistance to the International Tribunal. This obligation is laid down in Article 29 and restated in paragraph 4 of Security Council resolution 827 (1993) … The exceptional legal basis of Article 29 accounts for the novel and indeed unique power granted to the International Tribunal to issue orders to sovereign States (under customary international law, States, as a matter of principle, cannot be "ordered" either by other States or by international bodies).

It is clear that in the area of enforcement, the *ad hoc* tribunals are still dependent upon States and the UN Security Council. In *Blaškić*, the Appeals Chamber pointed out that UN member states and the UN Security Council can take individual or collective action in seeking compliance by any other member state with a binding order of the International Tribunal, and "[i]t is primarily for its parent body, the Security Council, to impose sanctions, if any, against a recalcitrant State".[28] In the view of the *Blaškić* Appeals Chamber, such a collective action "(i) may only be taken after a judicial finding has been made by the International Tribunal; and (ii) may take various forms, such as a political or moral condemnation, or a collective request to cease the breach, or economic or diplomatic sanctions".[29]

The power of a tribunal to make a judicial finding regarding non-compliance may be reported by the President of the Tribunal to the UN Security Council. A chamber, a judge and the prosecutor may initiate such proceedings.[30] The prosecutor may also communicate concerns of a state's failure to comply to the UN Security Council directly.[31] Is the regime efficient, do states comply? The example of Croatia illustrates that in cases of state non-compliance, the efficiency of tribunals is dependent on states. Eventually, Croatia's policy changed and it started to cooperate with the

28 *Prosecutor v Blaškić* (Case No IT-95-14-A), ICTY A Ch, Judgment on the Request of the Republic of Croatia for Review of the Decision of the Trial Chamber II of 18 July 1997, 29 October 1997, para 26.

29 Ibid, para. 33.

30 Ibid, para. 36.

31 Mundis, Daryl, 'Reporting non-compliance' in May, Richard et al. (eds), *Essays on ICTY Procedure and Evidence: In Honour of Gabrielle Kirk McDonald* (The Hague: Kluwer Law International, 2001), pp. 421–438, pp. 436–438; May and Wierda, 2002, p. 59; see also Klamberg, 2013, pp. 258–259.

ICTY.[32] This was, arguably, the result of pressure by the EU, Croatia's economic and political interest to cooperate with, and integrate into, the EU and, to a lesser extent, for isolated idealistic reasons. This illustrates that in cases of non-compliance, the efficiency of tribunals is dependent on other states acting individually or collectively (e.g. through the EU).

In a procedure similar to that of the *ad hoc* tribunals, where a state party of the ICC fails to comply with a request to cooperate by the Court, the Court has the power to make a judicial finding and refer the matter to the Assembly of States Parties, or to the UN Security Council where the Council refers the matter to the Court.[33] Sluiter describes this as a "vertical" feature of the cooperation regime.[34] It is unclear whether the Assembly of States Parties can take any action beyond making the finding of non-compliance.[35] Non-state parties may cooperate with the Court through referring a situation to the Court for investigation themselves, a process known as self-referral. Once a state has entered an *ad hoc* arrangement or an agreement with the Court, problems or failures are handled through the same channels as would be a problem with a state party.[36] The obligations under the Rome Statute will, arguably, also apply to non-state parties in relation to situations referred to the Court by the UN Security Council resolution under Chapter VII of the UN Charter, as illustrated by the Prosecutors' investigations in relation to the situation in Darfur (Sudan).[37]

6.2.4 State acceptance

As indicated above, all UN member states have an obligation cooperate fully with the *ad hoc* tribunals and their organs. This practically universal obligation is limited by the fact that the jurisdiction of the tribunals is limited to international crimes committed on the territories of former Yugoslavia (the ICTY) or Rwanda (the ICTR).

This may be contrasted with the ICC, which potentially may exercise jurisdiction over alleged international crimes committed in any state. The

32 Cogan, 2002, pp. 123–124.

33 Rome Statute, Article 87(7); see also Articles 112(2)(f) and 119; Sluiter, 2002, p. 71; Kreß, Claus and Prost, Kimberly, 'Article 87 – Request for cooperation: general provisions' in Triffterer, Otto (ed), *Commentary on the Rome Statute of the International Criminal Court* (2nd edn, München, Oxford and Baden-Baden: C.H. Beck/Hart/Nomos, 2008), pp. 1517–1531, pp. 1528–1531, paras 32–39.

34 Sluiter, 2002, p. 88.

35 Wartanian, Annie, 'The ICC Prosecutor's Battlefield: Combating Atrocities while Fighting for States' Cooperation: Lessons from the U.N. Tribunals Applied to the Case of Uganda', 36 *Georgetown Journal of International Law* (2005) 1289–1316, pp. 1289–1316 and 1298.

36 Rome Statute, Article 87(5); see also Article 112(2)(f); Kreß and Prost, Article 87, 2008, pp. 1525–1526, paras 24–27.

37 Rome Statute, Article 13(b); Sixth Report of the Prosecutor of the International Criminal Court, to the UN Security Council pursuant to UNSC 1593 (2005), 2007; Kreß and Prost, Article 87, 2008, p. 1525, para 26. See also Klamberg, 2013, pp. 259–260.

word "potentially" is crucial because as the ICC's jurisdiction is primarily based on state consent, it may only exercise jurisdiction in relation to alleged international crimes committed on the territory of a state party or by a national of a state party.[38] Germany advanced during the negotiations of the Rome Statute the proposal that the Court should have universal jurisdiction over acts committed in all states, regardless of their accession to the Rome Statute. This and similar proposals met the resistance of several states, including major powers such as China, Russia and the US, which were successful in limiting the jurisdiction of the Court.[39] This shows how major powers can influence the content and scope of a treaty even if it is highly unlikely that they will ratify the treaty. In this particular case, state sovereignty (and power) prevailed over universality. An exception to the requirement on consent is the provision which allows the UN Security Council under Chapter VII of the UN Charter to refer situations to the Court,[40] including situations which involve non-state parties. This power has been used in relation to the situation in Darfur (Sudan) and Libya.[41] Such decisions are subject to the veto power of the permanent five members of the UN Security Council (P-5), meaning that Council referrals should be analyzed, at least in part, with an eye on the distribution of power between states and alliances the non-permanent members have formed with the permanent members. As such, the actual scope of the ICC primarily concerns the 122 state parties, but the major powers (Russia, China and the US), states with are currently involved conflicts (Syria, Somalia, Yemen, Pakistan and Israel) and states with serious human rights situations (Eritrea and North Korea) are absent. This, arguably, weakens the scope of the regime, but does not make it irrelevant. The Court is exercising jurisdiction over nine situations (Uganda, Democratic Republic of the Congo (DRC), Central African Republic (CAR I and II), Darfur in Sudan, Kenya, Libya, Côte d'Ivoire and Mali). It could be argued that the list of situations investigated reflects the distribution of power among states. But this is only partly true, as the situations in Uganda, the DRC, the CAR and Côte d'Ivoire have all been triggered by their own governments through self-referrals. The influence of power is more evident in the choice of states that have been subjected to UN Security Council referrals: Sudan and Libya may be compared with the on-going conflict in Syria, where there is at present no referral. The non-referral of Syria is probably best explained by the state's economic and military ties to Russia, the latter with veto power in the UN Security Council.

38 Rome Statute, Article 12(2).

39 Wilmshurst, Elizabeth, 'Jurisdiction of the Court' in Lee, Roy S. (ed), *The International Criminal Court: the Making of the Rome Statute: Issues, Negotiations and Results* (The Hague: Kluwer Law International, 1999), pp. 127–141, pp. 132–139.

40 Rome Statute, Article 13(b).

41 Resolution 1593 (2005), UN Doc S/RES/1593; Resolution 1970 (2011), UN Doc S/RES/1970.

6.3 Feminist perspective on international criminal justice

A key area of concern from a feminist perspective is international crimes involving sexual violence, where the majority of victims are women. Rape during war was publicly addressed in an international context during World War I in relation to rapes committed by German soldiers against Belgian women. After World War II, the international prosecution of war criminals did not include prosecution for the crime of rape. There has been notable progress at the ICTY and the ICTR in the prosecution of wartime rape and sexual violence, but there is still a significant impunity gap.[42]

Feminist theory not only provides a perspective on international criminal justice, it has also affected the functioning of this regime. As indicated above, the progressive development of international humanitarian law and international criminal law has involved increased recognition of the distinct harms which women may disproportionally experience. For example, the ICTY and the ICTR have elaborated upon rape as a war crime and an element of genocide in cases such as *Akayesu*.[43] Sexual violence, which has most often been directed against women, has been addressed explicitly in the Rome Statute.[44] A gender perspective is not only relevant for the scope of the criminal behavior prosecuted, however, it also involves questions relating to victims and witness protection. The protection of victims and witnesses aims to minimize risks to their security, avoid incursions on their dignity and reduce trauma associated with giving evidence. The *ad hoc* tribunals are under an obligation to provide such protection. However, protective measures concerning victims and witnesses are frequently in conflict with, if not diametrically opposed to, the right of the accused to a fair trial.[45] The concerns at the *ad hoc* tribunals for the protection of victims and witnesses and the need to strike a balance with the objective of a fair trial served as a precedent for the Rome Statute, which incorporates similar provisions.[46]

Moreover, some common law systems have rules that aim at protecting victims and witnesses, and shielding the jury from considering irrelevant matters that would affect their fair assessment of the evidence in sexual assault cases. For example, rule 412(a) of the US Federal Rules of Evidence provides as a general rule that evidence offered to prove any alleged

42 Nikolic-Ristanovic, Vesna, 'Sexual Violence, International Law and Restorative Justice' in Buss, Doris and Manji, Ambreena (eds), *International Law: Modern Feminist Approaches* (Oxford: Hart Publishing, 2005), pp. 273–293, p. 273.

43 *Akayesu*, ICTR T Ch, 2 September 1998, paras 507–509 and 731, see also Tadić, ICTY T Ch, 7 May 1997, paras 194 and 724–726; see also *Furundžija*, ICTY T Ch, 10 December 1998, paras 165–189 and 270–275; *Kunarac et al*, ICTY T Ch II, 22 February 2001, para 436; Adamson and Sriram, 2010, pp. 42–43.

44 Rome Statute, Articles 7(1)(g), 8(2)(b)(xxii) and 8(2)(e)(vi).

45 ICTY Statute, Article 22; ICTR Statute, Article 21; Statute of the International Residual Mechanism for Criminal Tribunals adopted 22 December 2010 by Resolution 1966, Article 20; ICTY RPE, rules 69 and 75; ICTR RPE, rules 69 and 75; MICT RPE, rules 75 and 86.

46 Rome Statute, Article 68(1); see also Klamberg, 2013, p. 63.

victim's sexual predisposition is inadmissible. In cases of sexual assault, rule 96(ii) of the ICTY and ICTR Rules of Procedure and Evidence and rule 118(ii) of the Mechanism for International Criminal Tribunal (MICT)[47] Rules of Procedure and Evidence prohibit consent as a defense to rape being raised if the victim has been subjected to or threatened with or has had reason to fear violence, duress, detention or psychological oppression. If an accused person raises the argument, rule 96(iii) of the ICTY and ICTR Rules of Procedure and Evidence and rule 118(iii) of the MICT Rules of Procedure and Evidence require an *in camera* hearing to evaluate whether the evidence is relevant and credible. This is a higher admissibility standard than rule 89(C) of the ICTY and ICTR Rules of Procedure and Evidence, which narrows the presumption for admissibility.[48] Rule 96(iv) of the ICTY and ICTR Rules of Procedure and Evidence and rule 118(iv) of the MICT Rules of Procedure and Evidence provide that in cases of sexual assault, prior sexual conduct of the victim shall not be admitted in evidence. In *Delalić*, the Trial Chamber stated that:

> the prime objective of this provision is to adequately protect the victims from harassment, embarrassment and humiliation by the presentation of evidence which relates to past sexual conduct ... the value, if any, of information about the prior sexual conduct of a witness in the context of trials of this nature was nullified by the potential danger of further causing distress and emotional damage to the witnesses.[49]

The Trial Chamber also found that rule 96(iv) "is an exclusionary rule which totally forbids the introduction of evidence concerning prior sexual conduct in sexual assault cases and there can be no waiver of its imperative application".[50] Rule 71 of the ICC Rules of Procedure and Evidence provides that subject to Article 69, paragraph 4 of the Rome Statute, "a Chamber shall not admit evidence of the prior or subsequent sexual conduct of a victim or witness". The phrase "subject to article 69, paragraph 4" indicates that the rule is not absolute. The rule restricts or fetters a Chamber's discretion, or guides it towards a particular result. This flexibility in rare and exceptional cases is attached with a guarantee in rule 70(D) against character assassination of the victim or witness. Rule 72 provides a screening procedure when there

47 The MICT was established by the UN Security Council through Resolution 1966 (2010), UN Doc S/RES/1966 to carry out a number of essential functions of the ICTR and the ICTY after the completion of their respective mandates.

48 Sellers, Patricia Viseur et al., 'Rule 89(C) and (D): At Odds or Overlapping with Rule 96 and Rule 95' in May, Richard (ed), *Essays on ICTY Procedure and Evidence: In Honour of Gabrielle Kirk McDonald* (The Hague: Kluwer Law International, 2001), pp. 275–290, p. 287.

49 *Prosecutor v Delalić et al (Čelebići)*, (Case No IT-96-21), ICTY T Ch, Decision on the Prosecution's Motion for the Redaction of the Public Record, 5 June 1997, para 48.

50 Ibid, para 58.

is an intention to introduce or elicit evidence that the victim consented to an alleged crime of sexual violence.[51]

The account above demonstrates that progress has been achieved within international criminal justice, both in relation to prosecution of offenders and protection of witness and victims of sexual violence. Yet, as Nikolic-Ristanovic argues, criminal trials are not the only mechanism to acknowledge women's sufferings. Other means may be necessary for such acknowledgement and to address other concerns, such as healing and empowerment through truth telling. The use of truth and reconciliation commissions is one such alternative mechanism.[52]

6.4 Processes and mechanisms for creating and enforcing international criminal justice

There is a partial overlap between international criminal law and human rights law in the sense that some violations of human rights obligations are also international crimes. To clarify, an act of torture may both involve state responsibility under the CAT and individual criminal responsibility as a crime against humanity under the Rome Statute. The main difference is the addressee, being the state under human rights law and the individual under international criminal law. The same reasoning applies to international humanitarian law on the one hand and international criminal law on the other hand, as there may also be an overlap between these two bodies of law, but the main difference is the addressee. The mechanisms for enforcing international criminal justice vis-à-vis the individual is, arguably, different from that of enforcing responsibility against the state, as they have to be mediated either through a state or an international institution. Mechanisms such as reciprocity, coercion, persuasion and socialization have different meanings and apply differently vis-à-vis a state compared to an individual. When discussing individual criminal responsibility, other mechanisms are applicable at an individual level, such as retribution and deterrence. Some processes may, arguably, be relevant in both contexts, for example, socialization. They seek the same aim, i.e. to prevent and sanction violations of certain international norms. The difference is that the mechanism of enforcement are in different dimensions. While the mechanisms of creating and enforcing state responsibility are horizontal matters between states, the creation and enforcement of international criminal law is vertical, where states and organizations are legislators and enforcement is against individuals. This means that mechanisms that seek to include states in the creation and enforcement of international criminal law must be distinguished from mechanisms directed against individuals.

51 Piragoff, Donald, 'Evidence' in Lee, Roy S. (ed), *The International Criminal Court – Elements of Crimes and Rules of Procedure and Evidence* (Ardsley, NY: Transnational Publishers, 2001), pp. 349–401, pp. 384–391.

52 Nikolic-Ristanovic, 2005, pp. 290–291.

Since international criminal justice concerns individual criminal responsibility, non-state actors are clear addressees; members of these groups may investigated and prosecuted. Crimes against humanity may be conducted not only by states by also as part of an organizational policy,[53] i.e. a non-state actor. The Pre-Trial Chamber in the *Situation in Kenya* has determined "that organizations not linked to a State may, for the purposes of the Statute, elaborate and carry out a policy to commit an attack against a civilian population".[54] War crimes may be committed in non-international armed conflicts,[55] i.e. a conflict between a state and one or several state actor(s). The responsibility for crimes is not limited to state actors. International criminal justice is clearly designed with non-state actors in mind.

6.4.1 Coercing, socializing and entrapping states

Since there is an overlap between human rights law and international criminal law, the same mechanisms discussed previously[56] would also be relevant here. Under the same logic, effective support for international criminal justice requires domestic institutions. Compliance is thus more likely in democracies than in autocracies. Domestic interest groups in democracies may pressure the government to join the ICC Statute and the state may comply. In relation to more autocratic states, governments may ratify the ICC Statute for tactical concessions that they think may calm international and external criticism.[57] Pursuant to the spiral model, these actions end up entrapping repressive governments and their leaders. However, as Simmons and Danner note, conclusive evidence on governments' motives for joining the ICC is very hard to come by.[58]

Simmons's and Danner's hypothesis is that states which have been involved in civil wars within the past five years are more likely to support the Court, *conditional* on these states' inability credibly to hold perpetrators accountable through domestic institutions.[59] This hypothesis was based on commitment theory, which suggests that some governments *rationally* use the ICC to tie their own hands as they make tentative steps towards conflict

53 Rome Statute, Article 7(2)(a).

54 *Situation in Kenya* (No ICC-01/09), ICC PT Ch II, Decision Pursuant to Article 15 of the Rome Statute on the Authorization of an Investigation into the Situation in the Republic of Kenya, 31 March 2010, paras 60–62; repeated in *Prosecutor v Muthaura et al* (Case no ICC-02/09-01/11), ICC PT Ch II, Decision on the Confirmation of Charges Pursuant to Article 61(7)(a) and (b) of the Rome Statute, 23 January 2012, para 112.

55 Rome Statute, Article 8(2)(c)–(f).

56 See section 5.4.2 on diffusion of human rights norms mediated by domestic institutions and domestic actors.

57 Compare Risse and Sikkink, 1999, p. 10; Risse and Ropp, 1999, p. 250.

58 Simmons, Beth A. and Danner, Allison 'Credible Commitments and the International Criminal Court' (unpublished manuscript) (2008), p. 16.

59 Ibid, pp. 18–20.

resolution.[60] Controlling for alternative theories, Simmons and Danner found that patterns of ratification of the Rome Statute provide strong support for the credible commitments theory. Democracies with no recent history of civil war are quite likely to join the ICC. A finding that may appear surprising, but expected by credible commitment theory, is that non-democracies with recent civil war experience are as, or even more likely, to quickly ratify the Statute. By contrast, democracies with a recent history of civil war are far less likely to ratify the Rome Statute. A currently democratic country that has experienced civil war within the past five years is almost 80 per cent less likely to ratify the Rome Statute than is a non-democratic country without a recent past of civil violence. In other words, states with the least democratic and worst reputations for respecting the rule of law and with a recent past of civil violence were the most likely to ratify the Rome Statute. The fact that non-democratic countries with recent civil wars tend to be among the most likely countries to ratify the Rome Statute provides evidence of behavior consistent with credible commitment theory.[61]

6.4.2 Obtaining state cooperation

Snyder and Vinjamuri argue that recent international criminal tribunals have failed to deter subsequent abuses in the former Yugoslavia and Central Africa because tribunals, including the ICC, have often been unable to gain the active cooperation of powerful actors and states where abuses occur. Thus, they find it questionable whether the strategy of prosecuting international crimes will succeed in the long run, unless it is implemented in a more pragmatic way.[62] Goldsmith similarly argues that the ICC is unlikely to punish leaders responsible for international crimes because the Court has no inherent enforcement powers. It depends completely on member states to arrest and transfer defendants. The efficacy of prosecutions depends on the uncertain resolve of states to use military or economic force to extricate the oppressive leader from their country.[63]

To what extent has military and economic force, i.e. coercive mechanisms, been used and to what extent have such measures been effective? In Resolution 827 (1993), the UN Security Council established the ICTY with an explicit obligation for the states to cooperate with the Tribunal. The Tribunal initially had significant difficulties to gain cooperation from states whose officials and leaders were under investigation and prosecution.[64]

60 Ibid, p. 4.

61 Ibid, pp. 21–22, 24–27 and 31–32.

62 Snyder, Jack and Vinjamuri, Leslie, 'Trials and Errors: Principles and Pragmatism in Strategies of International Justice', 28 *International Security* (2003/2004) 5–44, pp. 1–2.

63 Goldsmith, Jack, 'The Self-Defeating International Criminal Court', 70 *University of Chicago Law Review* (2003) 89–104, p. 92; Posner, 2009, p. 204.

64 See for example *Blaškić*, ICTY A Ch, 29 October 1997; Annual Report of the International Tribunal for the Prosecution of Persons Responsible for Serious Violations of International

The ICC has met similar challenges.[65] After issuing findings, the ICTY has reported states to the UN Security Council for non-compliance. The UN Security Council has adopted resolutions ordering the states concerned to cooperate.[66] This has been coupled with economic and political pressure from the EU, which made co-operation with the ICTY "[a] basic condition for any progress in the development of the relations … between the E.U. and the countries of the region".[67] The UN Security Council also authorized the member states acting through or in cooperation to establish a multinational implementation force to assist the ICTY.[68] This economic, political and military pressure combined with domestic events in the states concerned contributed to increased cooperation with the ICTY.[69] Posner argues that it was not the ICTY's demands that led to the apprehension, transfer and jurisdiction over Slobodan Milošević, rather, it was the military, economic and diplomatic pressure on Serbia.[70]

The question on the relative weight of these factors may be worthwhile to research further. Case-specific research designs may be suitable for such inquires in order to take into account contextual factors. It remains to be seen if this can be generalized.

6.4.3 International criminal justice and deterrence

There has been limited empirical work on whether or not international criminal justice deters others from committing such crimes.[71] Ku and Nzelibe utilize economic models of deterrence to analyze whether a potential

Humanitarian Law Committed in the Territory of the Former Yugoslavia Since 1991, 1998, paras 96–98 and 123–124.

65 Sixth Report of the Prosecutor of the ICC, 2007.

66 Resolution 1207 (1998), UN Doc S/RES/1207.

67 *ICTY Press Release, CC/PIO/223-E, 3 July 1997*: The new president of the European Union, the Grand Duchy of Luxembourg, will make co-operation with the ICTY "A basic condition for any progress in the development of the relations (…) between the E.U. and the countries of the region".

68 Dayton Agreement, Annex 1A—Agreement on the Military Aspects of the Peace Settlement; Resolution 1031 (1995), UN Doc S/ RES/1031, 1995 (IFOR), para 14; Resolution 1088 (1996), UN Doc S/RES/1088, 1996 (SFOR), para 19; see also Ciampi, Annalisa, 'The obligation to cooperate' in Cassese, Antonio, Gaeta, Paola and Jones, John R.W.D (eds), *The Rome Statute of the International Criminal Court* (Oxford: Oxford University Press, 2002), pp. 1607–1638, pp. 1618–1619.

69 Western Balkans Project, "Croatian President Stjepan Mesic addressed the nation concerning the opening of talks on accession to the EU", 10 March 2005, available at www.westernbalkans.info/htmls/save_pdf2.php?id=598 (accessed 9 December 2014).

70 Posner, 2009, p. 199.

71 Ku, Julian and Nzelibe, Jide, 'Do International Criminal Tribunals Deter or Exacerbate Humanitarian Atrocities?', 84 *Washington University Law Quarterly* (2006) 777–833, p. 790; Cronin-Furman, 2013, p. 2 note 4. See summary of Jo, Hyeran and Simmons, Beth A., 'Can the International Criminal Court Deter Atrocity? An Analysis of Violence against Civilians in Civil Wars' (2015, forthcoming), pp. 4–6.

perpetrator of humanitarian atrocities would likely be deterred by the risk of future prosecution by an international criminal tribunal or court. Two factors are central to the reduction of crime after taking into account a particular individual's preference for risk—certainty and severity of punishment. Their conclusion is that the likely pool of defendants will be composed of individuals in weak states who have been forced from political power by local or foreign forces. Prosecution at the international level will often serve as a weaker substitute, rather than a complement, to pre-existing sanctions. In certain circumstances, they argue, international courts might actually exacerbate humanitarian atrocities by prosecuting individuals whose political cooperation is critical to successful peace negotiations in weak or failed states. They also contend that even when there is support for international courts by powerful countries like the US, it is still very likely that international courts will play a marginal, if not counterproductive, role in deterring humanitarian atrocities in the weak or failing states where such atrocities are most likely to be committed.[72]

Ku and Nzelibe suggest an alternative approach to their study which would have been to measure the correlation between the prosecution of certain crimes and the change in the levels of such crimes, an approach that is commonly used in empirical assessments of the prosecution of domestic crimes.[73]

Ku's and Nzelibe's assumptions may be challenged. They compare the low number of ICTR prosecutions with the much larger number of offenders prosecuted at the domestic level in Rwanda, in support of the conclusion that the ICTR has a low deterrent effect.[74] This ignores the fact that the ICTR was deliberately constructed with a shared burden of work, where high-level defendants were prosecuted at the ICTR and medium-/low-level defendants at the domestic level.

Gilligan reaches a different conclusion compared to Ku and Nzelibe. The assumption is too often that foreign military or economic intervention is the only way human rights abusers may be brought to justice, but of course that is not the case. The atrocity-committing leaders of today may lose power tomorrow and become fugitives. He analyzes the deterrent effect of the ICC within the context of a game-theoretic model. Despite the lack of an international police force to enforce its indictments, the ICC may still deter leaders from committing atrocities at the margin because it offers potential asylum-granting states the option of refraining from offering asylum to leaders who commit atrocities. Gilligan makes the assumption that potential asylum-granting states comply with requests for cooperation (such as transfer of suspects to an international court) not to avoid punishment from the regime's other members because, by assumption, there are no such punishments. Instead, potential asylum-granting states simply comply because it is costless

72 Ku and Nzelibe, 2006, pp. 780–781, 783, 785, 792, 807 and 817–819.
73 Ku and Nzelibe, 2006, p. 791.
74 Ku and Nzelibe, 2006, p. 808.

to do so when the political survival of the leader targeted for prosecution is low.[75]

Cronin-Furman has surveyed the theory of criminal deterrence in order to assemble a specified set of expectations about how deterrence might be expected to operate in the international arena. Deterrence theory is based on a strong rational actor assumption, which holds that "a person commits an offense if the expected utility to him exceeds the utility he could get by using his time and other resources at other activities". Cronin-Furman holds that given the requirements of deterrence, the ICC is the only institution in the existing international criminal justice system capable of producing any deterrent effect and that it is likely do so only under a narrow set of conditions. Earlier tribunals such as the International Military Tribunal in Nurnberg focused on retribution. While references to deterrence is missing in the statutes of the *ad hoc* tribunals, the Rome Statute's Preamble provides that the ICC was established, among other goals, "to put an end to impunity for the perpetrators of these crimes and thus to contribute to the prevention of such crimes". Based on the logic underlying the commission of international crimes, she determines that commanders who permit or fail to punish their subordinates for violations (as opposed to commanders who explicitly order the commission of crimes for tactical reasons) are more likely to be deterred by an adequately high risk of prosecution. The reason is that the group of commanders who are at risk of being held criminally accountable for their failure to stop mass atrocity do not derive as substantial a benefit from that failure as do the commanders who order them. In order for the ICC to have a deterrent effect, it must be the case that potential perpetrators believe the new regime of the ICC may apply to them, that no stronger deterrent influences already operate as disincentives to the commission of the crime and that the incentives to offend are not so strong that they outweigh the risk of punishment. Given a high enough likelihood of facing prosecution and punishment, the first set of potential perpetrators may be deterred by the threat of ICC trials.[76]

Regardless if it is Ku and Nzelibe or Cronin-Fruman who are correct, their studies have some limitations. International courts may be perceived as part of a greater effort to deter international crimes. Action is also taken at the domestic level, a level that interacts with international rules and institutions. This may be difficult to measure but not impossible, as illustrated in the following example.[77]

Jo and Simmons argue that the ICC can potentially deter violence against civilians through the threat of prosecution, as well as through social mechanisms. They find conditional evidence that extensions of ICC jurisdiction

75 Gilligan, Michael J., 'Is Enforcement Necessary for Effectiveness? A Model of the International Criminal Regime', 60 *International Organization* (2006) 935–967, pp. 937–938, 943 and 950–953.

76 Cronin-Furman, 2013, pp. 435–437, 439, 442, 444–447 and 454.

77 See also Ku and Nzelibe, 2006, pp. 793–797 on the availability of extra-legal or informal sanctions.

and extensions of its authority are associated with reduced violence against civilians. This is conditional, as social deterrence depends on the existence of groups or networks having the ability to apply costly social pressure.[78]

Kim and Sikkink use a data set on domestic and international human rights prosecutions in 100 transitional countries to explore whether prosecuting human rights violations can decrease repression.[79] The finding that the prosecution of human rights violations is a causal factor can be challenged, as it is possible that countries with relatively low or decreasing human rights repressions are more likely to allow prosecutions. Further, their study focuses on domestic trials, which may have limited applicability for the efficiency of international investigations and prosecutions.

Snyder and Vinjamuri challenge the view that changes in behavior follow the adoption of new beliefs about appropriate standards of behavior. They review the empirical claims of different approaches to international justice and evaluate them in a survey of 32 cases of civil wars between 1989 and 2003.[80] They argue, in contrast, that the prevailing pattern of political power and institutions shapes behavior in ways that are difficult to change simply through normative persuasion. They challenge the deterrent effect of the ICC, since deterrence depends on the predictable ability to enforce the law coercively, which often falls short in countries where abuses take place. When enforcement power is weak, pragmatic bargaining may be an indispensable tool in getting perpetrators to relinquish power and desist in their abuses. They argue that social constructivist theory of normative change, however, fundamentally misunderstands how norms gain social force. As a result, legalist tactics for enforcing international criminal justice can backfire when institutional and social preconditions for the rule of law are lacking. Instead, if norms are to shape behavior and outcomes, they must gain the support of a dominant political coalition in the social milieu in which they are to be applied. The coalition must establish and sustain the institutions that will monitor and sanction compliance with the norms. To this end, as a bridge between lawlessness and norm-governed social relations, pragmatic bargaining is more efficient where amnesty is one possible tool.[81]

As already indicated, one has to distinguish between the behavior of individuals and states, as different mechanisms may operate differently towards states compared with individuals. Morrow analyzes when states follow the international laws of war, focusing on reciprocity as the primary mechanism which explains states compliance. He notes that reciprocity is typically thought of as a state response to the actions of another state. However, reciprocity on the laws of war also occurs at the level of individuals on the battlefield. He distinguishes

78 Jo and Simmons, 2015, forthcoming.

79 Kim, Hunjoon and Sikkink, Kathryn, 'Explaining the Deterrence Effect of Human Rights Prosecutions for Transitional Countries', 54 *International Studies Quarterly* (2010) 939–963, p. 953.

80 Snyder and Vinjamuri, 2003/2004, pp. 17–18.

81 Snyder and Vinjamuri, 2003/2004, pp. 11–14 and 39–44.

between issues such as the use of chemical weapons, where control over violations is centralized, making it difficult for individuals to commit violations on their own, and treatment of civilians, where every soldier has the ability to commit violations on their own. The latter example entails an agency problem in the control of individual soldiers, below the state level. The distortion created by the agency problem depends, *inter alia*, on military training and control. Consequently, states should respond more strongly to centralized violations than those that are the result of individual violations.[82] When taking into account ratification as well as regime type, Morrow finds that ratification has little effect on non-democratic countries, whereas it induces restraint in democracies. Democracies that have not ratified the relevant treaty have the worst record of compliance, followed by non-democratic countries regardless of ratification status. Democracies that have ratified have the best compliance record. At the same time, joint ratification does not appear to prevent democracies from retaliating against opponents whose violations rise to the level of non-compliance. Democracies take their legal obligations more seriously than other states, yet are still willing to respond to violations in kind, following the logics of reciprocity.[83] To summarize, Morrow finds that the ratification of treaties does not affect the behavior of non-democratic countries, but it does affect that of democracies. This finding is consistent with work regarding the role of domestic institutions in explaining variation in compliance with human rights treaties,[84] as discussed above.[85]

Valentino, Huth and Croco found no evidence that treaty ratification influences the behavior of democracies in their study, however. They compare three theories to explain variation in the intentional killing of civilian populations: (a) states that have ratified international treaties that restrict the killing of non-combatants will intentionally kill fewer numbers of enemy non-combatants during war than other states (the laws of war); (b) the nature of states' domestic political regimes is the main determinant of their conduct during war (domestic politics); and (c) deep ethnic, religious or cultural differences between combatants tend to "barbarize" warfare, transforming combat from a strictly military clash between contending armies into the wholesale slaughter of enemy civilians (identify conflicts). They utilize a data set on civilian and military fatalities covering all interstate wars from 1900 to 2003 and control for the balance of capabilities between the opposing sides and population size. The results of their empirical analyses indicate that the laws of war do not provide strong protection for civilians in times of war. The data revealed that the signatories to the Hague Conventions of 1907 or the Geneva Conventions of 1949 did not kill fewer civilians than

82 Morrow, James D., 'When Do States Follow the Laws of War?', 101 *American Political Science Review* (2007) 559–572, p. 561.

83 Ibid, p. 567.

84 Ginsburg and Shaffer, 2010, p. 776

85 Section 5.4.2 on the diffusion of human rights norms mediated by domestic institutions and domestic actors.

non-signatories. Further, they found no evidence to support the hypothesis that leaders in states with strong democratic norms kill fewer numbers of civilians in war than do leaders in other kinds of states. Nor did they find support for theories that focus on racial and religious identities as a prime cause of civilian targeting.[86] Instead, they offer their own explanation:

> the decision to target civilians is based less upon international laws or the individual characteristics of the states involved in the war and more on the incentives to target civilians created by the risks, threats, and opportunities associated with the particular conflict … the killing of noncombatants during war is often a calculated military strategy designed to achieve victory by coercing the adversary or by undermining the war-related productive capacity of his civilian population.[87]

In other words, strategic incentives overwhelmed any pressure to exercise restraint attributable to treaties such as the Hague Conventions of 1907 or the Geneva Conventions of 1949.[88]

Morrow has examined the influence of treaties on treatment of prisoners of war based on rational choice and game theory. His assumption is that the laws of war rely on reciprocity for enforcement. Treaties on treatment of prisoners of war are pre-war agreements to avoid certain strategies and can be upheld during war when reciprocity and audience costs make both sides unwilling to be the first to use a banned strategy.[89] There are at least two difficulties with this. First, it is noted in section 1.3.1 on reciprocity that for efficient enforcement, states must be able to distinguish between cooperation and defection. States cannot observe in detail whether another state is complying with the standards of prisoners of war treatment because prisoners of war are in the hands of the other side. Second, as mentioned above, there is an agency problem in the control of individual soldiers.[90] One example is how Canadian soldiers mistreated captured German soldiers after the Dieppe raid in 1942 by tying their hands in violation of the rules. The prisoners were freed and the German soldiers reciprocated in kind towards commonwealth soldiers, which in turn was counter-sanctioned by the British against German soldiers. In conclusion, Morrow finds that as a consequence of reciprocity, states refrain from violating prisoner of war treaties in times of war.[91]

86 Valentino, Benjamin, Huth, Paul and Croco, Sarah, 'Covenants without the Sword: International Law and the Protection of Civilians in Times of War', 58 *World Politics* (2006) 339–377, pp. 339–350, 368–369.
87 Ibid, pp. 340, 350–357, 370–372.
88 Ginsburg and Shaffer, 2010, p. 776.
89 Morrow, 2001, p. 973. See also Klabbers, 2004, p. 35: "the practitioner at a Ministry of Defence contemplating whether or not to treat prisoners of war decently would enhance the quality of her decisions if she were to have an understanding of such things as game theory and reciprocity".
90 Morrow, 2001, p. 975.
91 Morrow, 2001, p. 982. Commented by Gilligan, 2006, p. 941.

Morrow's account of how reciprocity operates within the field of international humanitarian law and international criminal law may come in conflict with is prescribed by the law in these fields. Article 1 of the 1949 Geneva Conventions provides that the state parties "undertake to respect and to ensure respect for the present Convention in all circumstances", which suggests that the principle of reciprocity is rejected. Reprisals could in limited situations be a defence for war crimes. The ICTY Trial Chamber in *Martić* stated the following:

> belligerent reprisals are acts resorted to by one belligerent which would otherwise be unlawful, but which are rendered lawful by the fact that they are taken in response to a violation of that law committed by the other belligerent. Reprisals are therefore drastic and exceptional measures employed by one belligerent for the sole purpose of seeking compliance with the law of armed conflict by the opposite party. It follows that reprisals, in order to be considered lawful, are subject to strict conditions ... Reprisals may be used only as a last resort and only when all other means have proven to be ineffective. This limitation entails that reprisals may be exercised only after a prior and formal warning has been given, which has failed to put an end to the violations committed by the adversary. In addition, reprisals may only be taken after a decision to this effect has been made at the highest political or military level. A further requirement is that the measures taken must be proportionate to the initial violation of the law of armed conflict of the opposite party.[92]

The Appeals Chamber upheld the Trial Chamber findings.[93] In other words, there is some room for the principle of reciprocity to operate a crude form of law enforcement in the field of international criminal justice.[94]

In summary, empirical research suggests that efficient strategies in deterring international crime must take into account the agency problem, the importance of domestic groups and networks and how to prevent states from granting transfer for travel and/or asylum vis-à-vis suspected perpetrators. However, the empirical studies surveyed above make somewhat conflicting findings. Thus there is a need for additional research in this area.

6.5 Tension between power and law

Deitelhoff notes that the establishment of the ICC is not easily accommodated within international relations theories that rely either on realism and

92 *Prosecutor v Martić* (Case No IT-95-11) "RSK", ICTY T Ch I, Judgment, 12 June 2007, paras 465–467.

93 *Prosecutor v Martić* (Case No IT-95-11-A), ICTY A Ch, Judgment, 8 October 2008, paras 263–269.

94 Cryer et al., 2010, p. 422.

power structures or on liberal rational-choice-based theories of legalization and institutional design. Power-based approaches can explain the selective establishment of the *ad hoc* tribunals and the initial interest of the major powers in the establishment of the ICC, but they cannot fully account for the final institutional design of the ICC. Turning to rational-based theories and cost-benefit analysis, it is easy to understand why Western powers with functioning national judicial systems and a low probability of involvement supported the ICC. It is more difficult to understand the support of developing countries that were plagued by military uprisings and failing state structures, which could risk their heads of state being investigated and prosecuted. Rather, theories based on discourse and persuasion may better explain why states supported the ICC. Discourse theory views the creation of legal norms as the result of rational discourses which transform actors' preferences based on the better argument. Deitelhoff tests and confirms this explanation by conducting a qualitative content analysis of the ILC report of 1994 and all summaries of state speeches within negotiations as recorded by UN press releases and summary minutes from 1994 to 1998 relating to establishing the ICC.[95] In other words, persuasion during the negotiations caused states' interests to change and was the driving force for cooperation, rather than narrow calculations of state interest.[96]

Equally important to explaining how the ICC came into existence—or perhaps even more so—is how well it will function. Posner predicts that the ideal of legalism behind international courts will run aground on the realities of power. States can starve the funds of a legalistic institution, ignore it or work around it because the institution treats all states as equal, although they are not. He perceives this as the likely fate of the ICC.[97] Simmons and Danner are more optimistic when they argue that "the existence of the Court significantly raises the expected costs of committing atrocities compared to the status quo of impunity".[98] Nevertheless, the issue of cooperation will be crucial. When characterizing the cooperation regime, it may either be described as decentralized (horizontal) or centralized (vertical).[99] The centralized relationship involves far-reaching obligations for states vis-à-vis the Court, together with a lack of reciprocity and the final say in disputes referred to the requesting side (the international tribunal/Court).[100] However, the powers of international tribunals and courts are limited to interpretation, and in the absence of an explicit provision they lack power to take enforcement

95 Deitelhoff, Nicole, 'The Discursive Process of Legalization: Charting Islands of Persuasion in the ICC Case', 63 *International Organization* (2009) 33–65, pp. 33–34, 40, 42–45 and 48.

96 Hafner-Burton, Victor and Lupu, 2012, p. 58, footnote 50 and p. 86.

97 Posner, 2009, p. 203.

98 Simmons and Danner, 2008, pp. 9–10.

99 May and Wierda, 2002, p. 54; Cryer et al., 2010, pp. 509–510. Compare with Waltz dichotomy of the national and the international realms, Waltz, 1979, p. 113.

100 *Blaškić*, ICTY A Ch, 29 October 1997, para 68: "It will be for the Judge to appraise the grounds offered for withholding the documents"; Sluiter, 2002, pp. 83–87.

measures. Further, consideration should be given in this to the fact that the ICC is treaty-based and its statute is only binding on state parties, whereas the UN *ad hoc* tribunals are set up by the UN Security Council with the use of it enforcement powers under Chapter VII of the UN Charter which binds all states. Based on this, it is argued that the *ad hoc* tribunals represent a more centralized cooperation model, while the ICC is a more decentralized model. The power of prosecutors and judges to initiate proceedings, issue decisions and make findings on state cooperation and non-compliance, arguably, make them into "supervisors" and makes the international criminal justice regime an example of "supranational dispute settlement".[101] This is a feature that strengthens the regime.

101 Tallberg, 1999, p. 9; Tallberg and McCall Smith, 2012, p. 5. See section 1.2.1.3 on delegation.

7 Use of force

7.1 Function of the regime

The regime on the use of force as manifested in the UN Charter is described a system of collective security. The case for collective security rests on the claim that regulated, institutionalized balancing predicated on the notion of all against one provides more stability than unregulated, self-help balancing predicated on the notion of each for his own. The advantages of collective security fall into two categories: (a) it provides for more effective power balancing against aggressors; and (b) it promotes trust and cooperation.[1] Stability in the field of security has spill-over effects in other fields, in that it may promote the orderly development of trading relations, and an open and interdependent economic order.[2] Interestingly, international relations scholars appear to use international law and international organizations as partly interchangeable concepts in the context of use of force.[3] The law on the use of force may also be described as a way of managing mutual expectations amongst states, namely if a state attacks another state it should expect the other state to defend itself either alone or collectively. Moreover, if attacks occur against a civilian population, states know that the UN Security Council might choose to intervene. Lastly, the denial of authorization of the use of force by the UN Security Council may cause costs in the domestic as

1 Kupchan, Charles A. and Kupchan, Clifford A., 'The Promise of Collective Security', 20 *International Security* (1995) 52–61, pp. 52 and 54–59. They use a wide definition of collective security including all those that operate in a regulated, norm-governed environment and are predicated on the logic of all against one, not each for his own. This would include concerts, "an arrangement in which great powers that have no incentive to challenge each other militarily agree on a set of rules to coordinate their actions with each other, as well as with the minor powers in the system, often in the establishment of spheres of influence." (compare ibid., p. 53 with Mearsheimer, 1994, p. 35).

2 Art, Robert J. and Waltz, Kenneth, 'The Fungiblity of Force' in Art, Robert J. (ed), *The Use of Force: Military Power and International Politics* (6th edn, Lanham, MD, Boulder, CO, New York, NY, Toronto and Oxford: Rowman & Littlefield Publishers, 2004), pp. 3–22, pp. 14–16.

3 Russett, Bruce, Oneal, John R. and Davis, David, 'The Third Leg of the Kantian Tripod for Peace: International Organizations and Militarized Disputes, 1950–85', 52 *International Organization* (1998) 441–467, p. 441; Oneal, Russett and Berbaum, 2003, p. 372.

well as the international arena that states need to take into account before using force.[4]

7.2 Dimensions of legalization

7.2.1 Degree to which rules are obligatory

The UN Charter provides the essentials of the regime on use of force which binds the organization and its members. Article 2(4) provides the cornerstone of this regime: the prohibition on the threat or use of force in international relations. Moreover, it follows from Article 2(6) that UN members shall ensure that non-member states comply with the prohibition against the use of force.[5]

This prohibition is also a part of international customary international law, which binds all states, regardless of whether or not they are members of the UN. The ICJ stated in the 1986 *Nicaragua* decision, "that both the Charter and the customary international law flow from a common fundamental principle outlawing the use of force in international relations".[6] The ICJ considered that the adoption by states of the Declaration on Friendly Relations (General Assembly Resolution 2625(1970)) afforded an indication of their *opinio juris* as to customary international law on this question.[7]

The ILC in the course of its work on the codification of the law of treaties expressed the view that "the law of the Charter concerning the prohibition of the use of force in itself constitutes a conspicuous example of a rule in international law having the character of *jus cogens* [an unconditionally binding rule or peremptory norm]".[8] The ICJ took note of this view but did not directly rule on the matter.[9] Regardless, if the prohibition on the use of force has the status of *jus cogens*, the rule is obligatory for all states as custom.

Article 51 of the UN Charter reserves the right of individual or collective self-defense, which is described as "the inherent right". The ICJ recognized in the 1986 *Nicaragua* decision that this formulation refers to "pre-existing customary international law", which means that it is a right of all states.[10]

4 Rodley, Nigel and Başak, Çali, 'Use of Force in International Law' in Başak, Çali (ed), *International Law for International Relations* (Oxford: Oxford University Press, 2010), pp. 213–233, p. 229.

5 Henkin, 1979, p. 137.

6 *Military and Paramilitary Activities in and against Nicaragua* (Nicaragua v United States of America), ICJ, Judgment of 27 June 1986, para 181.

7 Ibid, para. 191.

8 *Yearbook of the International Law Commission (1966)*, Volume II, UN Doc A/CN.4/SER.A/1966/Add.l (1966), p. 247.

9 *Nicaragua Case*, ICJ, Judgment of 27 June 1986, para 190. See comment by Shelton, 2010, p. 150, and Bring, Mahmoudi and Wrange, 2011, p. 16.

10 *Nicaragua Case*, ICJ, Judgment of 27 June 1986, para 181.

7.2.2 Precision of rules

The prohibition on the use of force is a key principle in the UN system of collective peace and security. Article 2(4) of the UN Charter provides the following (emphasis added):

> All Members shall refrain in their international relations from the threat or use of *force* against the *territorial integrity* or *political independence* of any state, or in any other manner inconsistent with the *Purposes of the United Nations*.

There are two explicit exceptions: (a) self-defense (Article 51); and (b) action by the UN Security Council in order to maintain or restore international peace and security (Articles 39, 42 and 43). Mahmoudi argues that there is a third explicit exception, namely enforcement action by regional organizations authorized by the UN Security Council,[11] but this is, arguably, already covered by the second exception listed above. While the text on this matter at a first glance may appear completely precise, it is not watertight.[12] This is illustrated below by studying the concepts of humanitarian intervention, self-defense against non-state actors and anticipatory and preventive self-defense.

The question of humanitarian intervention arises when the life and physical safety of a considerable number of people in a country are in jeopardy and the government of that country seems unwilling or unable to help them,[13] it may even be responsible for the atrocities. The scope of Chapter VII of the UN Charter has been broadened with a flexible interpretation of the concept "threat to international peace and security". The UN Security Council has, with reference to international peace and security, included the persecution of minorities with "spill over" security risks for neighboring countries (Resolution 688 on Northern Iraq), humanitarian crises in failed states (Resolution 794 on Somalia), humanitarian/democratic crises in almost failed states (Resolution 940 on Haiti),[14] and gross and systematic violation of human rights (Resolution 1973 on Libya). More controversial is humanitarian intervention in the absence of UN Security Council authorization, such as the Kosovo intervention 1999 and, to some extent, Iraq.[15] In the aftermath of the Kosovo intervention, the International Commission on Intervention and State Sovereignty (ICISS) introduced the concept of Responsibility to Protect (R2P).

11 Mahmoudi, Said, 'International Use of Force: Quo Vadis?', 15 *Juridisk Tidsskrift* (2003) 341–358, p. 342.

12 Beckman, Olof, *Armed Intervention: Pursuing Legitimacy and the Pragmatic Use of Legal Argument* (Lund: Lund University, 2005), p. 61.

13 Ibid, p. 14.

14 Bring, Ove, 'From Suez to Kosovo: A Dynamic View of Chapters VI to VIII of the UN Charter' in Bring, Ove (ed), *Internationell våldsanvändning och folkrätt* (Stockholm: Norstedts juridik, 2006), pp. 45–67, p. 57.

15 Other legal grounds were also invoked to legitimize the use of force against Iraq. The argument of humanitarian intervention also appears to be an *ex post facto* justification.

In its report, ICISS kept the door open for military intervention without UN Security Council authorization.[16]

The formulation on the prohibition on the use of force in Article 2(4) may be interpreted either narrowly or extensively. It is possible to argue that an armed humanitarian intervention is compatible with Article 2(4) even in the absence of UN Security Council authorization as long as the intervention does not threaten the territorial integrity or political independence of a state.[17] However, if one instead emphasizes the purposes of the UN as formulated in the Preamble and Article 1 of the UN Charter, humanitarian intervention is only permissible when based on UN Security Council authorization.[18] This ambiguity is reflected in the definition of the crime of aggression as agreed upon in Kampala 2010 where only a "manifest violation of the Charter of the United Nations" is criminalized. The word "manifest" was inserted to exclude humanitarian interventions from the jurisdiction of the ICC.[19] There is less ambiguity if one considers the outcome document of the UN 2005 World Summit, which stresses that collective action should be taken through the UN Security Council in accordance with the UN Charter.[20] This was a rejection of the more far-reaching ICISS proposal on military intervention. How should the 2005 outcome document be reconciled with the 2010 Kampala agreement? The rules on inter-state use of force in the UN Charter has a different addressee—states—compared to the Kampala agreement which deals with individual criminal responsibility. The prohibition for states to use of force is stricter than the scope of behavior that may entail individual criminal responsibility.

The second controversy concerns self-defense against non-state actors. There is no requirement in Article 51 of the UN Charter on self-defense that the armed attack is from a state. This raises the question against whom may a state use self-defense. Before the terror attacks of 9/11, the assumption was that for the purposes of Article 51 an armed attack meant the attack by a state against another state. The requirement that the attacker has to be a state was (and maybe still is) a part of international customary law which complements

16 Report of the International Commission on Intervention and State Sovereignty 'Responsibility to Protect', December 2001, pp. XII–XII: "[t]here is no better or more appropriate body than the United Nations Security Council to authorize military intervention for human protection purposes … Security Council should take into account that if it fails to discharge its responsibility to protect … concerned states may not rule out other means to meet the gravity and urgency of that situation."

17 Henkin, 1979, p. 145 on Operation Entebbe, 1976; D'Amato, Anthony, 'The Invasion of Panama Was a Lawful Response to Tyranny', 84 *American Journal of International Law* (1990) 516–524, p. 520; Reisman, Michael W., 'Sovereignty and Human Rights in Contemporary International Law', 84 *American Journal of International Law* (1990) 866–876, pp. 873–874.

18 Henkin, 1979, p. 145; Beckman, 2005, p. 61; Crawford, 2012, pp. 752–754 and 755–757.

19 Wrange, Pål, *Aggressionsbrottet och Internationella brottmålsdomstolen* (Stockholm: Totalförsvarets folkrättsråd, Försvarsdepartementet, 2011), p. 68.

20 UN General Assembly Resolution 60/1, A/RES/60/1 (2005) 2005 World Summit Outcome, paras 138–139.

Article 51. The US's response to the 9/11 attacks can be justified in two different ways. First, it could be argued that the widespread acceptance of other states towards the US's actions reflected a change in customary international law, meaning that international law now accepts the use of force as a response to large-scale terrorist acts (i.e. non-state actor). A second, less radical, approach supported by statements made by the US is that the *de facto* government of Afghanistan at the time of the attacks was complicit and responsible for the attacks. This would mean that the traditional interpretation of Article 51 to a large extent is intact. At the same time, such an interpretation would, arguably, exclude the use of force outside the territory of Afghanistan under the slogan of "war against terrorism" argued by the US.[21] There is also a third position, namely that the US should have sought prior authorization for the use of force by the UN Security Council and, in the absence of such authorization, the actions of the US against Afghanistan did not meet the requirement of self-defense.[22]

Turning to anticipatory and preventive self-defense, this refers to the use of force against a state before that state has carried out an armed attack. There is a long-standing controversy as to whether the UN Charter definitely excludes the possibility of anticipatory self-defense. The restrictive approach is that, on its face, the text of Article 51 is incompatible with anticipatory actions. The permissive approach is based on the argument that Article 51 reflects customary international law which was formed in the nineteenth century and, in particular, as a result of the correspondence exchanged by the US and Britain in the period from 1838 to 1842. The exchange concerned the seizure and destruction in 1837 in American territory by the British armed forces of a vessel (the *Caroline*) used by persons assisting an armed rebellion in Canada. In protesting against the incident, the US Secretary of State, Daniel Webster, required the British government to show the existence of "necessity of self-defense, instant, overwhelming, leaving no choice of means, and no moment of deliberation". Lord Ashburton (for the British government) in his response did not dispute Webster's statement of principle and, as such, it is argued to be customary international law. However, this contention has been challenged. The reference to 1838–42 as the critical date for customary international law said to be lie behind the UN Charter drafted in 1945 may be anachronistic. In relation to the modern era, Henkin argues for narrowing the possibility of anticipatory self-defense down to the small and special exception for the case of a surprise nuclear attack. It should not be used for more likely situations between states generally.[23] Two examples where the principles of *Caroline* case have been invoked are the six-day-war between Israel and its neighbors

21 Compare with Bring, Mahmoudi and Wrange, 2011, pp. 166–167; Crawford, 2012, pp. 771–774.

22 Mahmoudi, 2003, p. 349; Mahmoudi, Said, 'Self-Defence and International Terrorism', 48 *Scandinavian Studies in Law* (2006) 203–214, p. 206.

23 Henkin, 1979, pp. 141–144.

and Israel's attack 1981 against Osirak (an Iraqi nuclear reactor). The legality of both operations has been subject to debate. Even more controversial is the doctrine of preventive self-defense against states that are seen as potential adversaries. This doctrine is applicable in the absence of any proof an attack or even an imminent attack. This doctrine, arguably, lacks legal basis but has at least two historic precedents: (a) the attack on Serbia by Austria Hungary in 1914; and (b) the US military operations against Iraq 2003.[24]

These three examples may all be analyzed with a feminist perspective, in that women are sometimes paraded as the objects of the conduct "uncivilized" states, justifying military action by the "civilized". Chinkin, Wright and Charlesworth note that such military action rarely considers the views of women themselves, particularly those women who are not members of urban literate elites.[25]

Based on the three abovementioned examples, the rules on the use of force, arguably, may be subject to interpretation. States have used this ambiguity to pursue their interests. Thus, the question of who has power to interpret the rules becomes relevant, an issue for the next section.

7.2.3 Delegation of some functions to a third party

States have, to various extents, delegated monitoring, adjudication and enforcement in cases of conflict and/or disputes on the use of force to two bodies: the UN Security Council and the ICJ. In the future, a third body may become relevant. The ICC may assume jurisdiction over the crime of aggression from 2017, pursuant to the Kampala 2010 agreement.[26]

7.2.3.1 UN Charter and the UN Security Council

Chapter VII of the UN Charter is an attempt to overcome the weakness of a decentralized system of international law enforcement. Although the Chapter is a long step toward the establishment of a centralized law-enforcement agency, Morgenthau argues that it is subject to three important qualifications and exceptions which limit, and under certain conditions, even nullify, the centralization of law enforcement.[27] In other words, the precision of the rules is low.

First, consider the aim of the UN to create a collective security regime. The UN Security Council has the power to "determine the existence of any threat to the peace, breach of the peace, or act of aggression and shall ... decide what measures shall be taken in accordance with Articles 41 and 42, to maintain

24 Bring, Mahmoudi and Wrange, 2011, pp. 165–166; Crawford, 2012, pp. 750–752.

25 Chinkin, Wright and Charlesworth, 2005, p. 33.

26 Review Conference of the Rome Statute, Resolution RC/Res.6 adopted at the 13th Plenary Meeting, 11 June 2010, annex I, Articles 15 *bis* (3) and 15 *ter* (3); Wrange, 2011.

27 Morgenthau, 1954, p. 279.

or restore international peace and security".[28] All UN members shall "accept and carry out the decisions of the Security Council in accordance with the ... Charter".[29] Article 43 provides that the member states are under an obligation to "make available to the Security Council ... armed forces, assistance, and facilities ... necessary for the purpose of maintaining international peace and security". This means that the UN Security Council may adopt authoritative and binding enforcement decisions. The use of coercion is essential to a collective security system.[30] However, these obligations are to be discharged by agreements between member states and the UN Security Council. Considering that the enforcement regime is based on voluntary agreements, a decentralized element is reintroduced, as a state may limit its military contribution or withhold an agreement altogether. The mechanism in Chapter VII for collective action can be put into existence and operate only under the condition that individual states agree individually to allow it to exist and operate.[31, 32] A unified force under the direct command and disposal of the UN Security Council as envisaged in Article 43 has never materialized.[33]

Second, Article 51 recognizes the pre-existing and "inherent right of individual or collective self-defense if an armed attack occurs against a Member of the United Nations". Individual self-defense as a right to meet an attack with corresponding force is an exception to centralized law enforcement. Morgenthau notes that collective self-defense at the time of its introduction was a newcomer to legal terminology (and, potentially, a contradiction in terms). However, the use of a new term does not necessarily make the enforcement mechanism centralized. Instead, Morgenthau argues that it may be perceived as a reaffirmation of the traditional principle in international law that it is for the injured state to enforce international law against the lawbreaker (i.e. self-help), and that the injured state can rely upon the voluntary cooperation of other states to make international law prevail.[34] Based on this perspective, states have failed to establish an international police system and the UN and its member states have not developed and maintained machinery for peaceful settlement of disputes (making self-help unnecessary and undesirable).[35] Schmitt goes even further and argues that the renunciation of war as a matter of "national policy" in the 1928 Kellogg-Briand Pact (the precursor to Articles 2(4) and 51 of the UN Charter) was deeply deceptive. In practice, the declaration was accompanied by specific reservation concerning war in self-defense—reservations that were, according to Schmitt, no

28 UN Charter, Article 39.
29 UN Charter, Article 25.
30 Mearsheimer, 1994, p. 34; see also Ruggie, John Gerard, 'The False Premise of Realism', 20 *International Security* (1995) 62–70, p. 63.
31 Morgenthau, 1954, p. 280.
32 UN Charter, Article 43.
33 Bring, Mahmoudi and Wrange, 2011, p. 186.
34 Morgenthau, 1954, p. 281.
35 Henkin, 1979, p. 138.

mere exceptions to the norm of peacefulness but "give the norm its concrete content ... in dubious cases". As sovereignty meant the right to determine whether the enemy had attacked (or would attack unless deterred), and what was needed to counter the foreseeable attack, no change occurred in political reality.[36] According to Schmitt's concept of the sovereign, the powerful states will be the ones "who decide on the exception".[37]

Third, the exercise of veto power reintroduces into the system of law enforcement of the UN the principle of decentralization by making the operation of the system dependent upon the will of each of the P-5. The veto eliminates any possibility of centralized measures of law enforcement against any of the P-5. Such measures will, arguably, also only apply to small and medium powers in rare and extraordinary circumstances because of the alignments that small and medium states may have with any of the P-5.[38] The veto also eliminates, for all practical purposes, the possibility of collective self-defense to the centralized enforcement system of Chapter VII. Article 51 not only recognizes the "inherent right of individual or collective self-defense", but also creates an expectation that the UN Security Council has a role in such situations:

> Measures taken by Members in the exercise of this right of self-defense shall be immediately reported to the Security Council and shall not in any way affect the authority and responsibility of the Security Council under the present Charter to take at any time such action as it deems necessary in order to maintain or restore international peace and security.[39]

It is difficult to envisage a case of collective resistance to aggression by a number of states in which not at least one of the P-5 is involved in one or the other side.[40] Boyle is more optimistic, but when he evaluates the UN Security Council's role in the (absence of) adjudication and resolution of the 1976 Entebbe incident, his conclusion is that this example is "symptomatic of deficiencies" of the "current evolutionary stage of international law and organisations".[41] Henkin appears to have the same view in the sense that they both believe that the UN is relevant; it can undo and deter violations that might come into its cognizance. However, it represents a primitive system: the UN is legislator, as well as judge and executive, but its judgments are

36 Schmitt, 1932, pp. 50–51; Koskenniemi, 2001, p. 433.
37 Schmitt, 1922/1934, pp. 5–7; Koskenniemi, 2001, p. 428.
38 UN Charter, Article 27(3); Morgenthau, 1954, pp. 282–283.
39 UN Charter, Article 51 not only recognizes the "inherent right of individual or collective self-defence" but also creates an expectation that the UN Security Council has a role in such situations: "Measures taken by Members in the exercise of this right of self-defence shall be immediately reported to the Security Council and shall not in any way affect the authority and responsibility of the Security Council under the present Charter to take at any time such action as it deems necessary in order to maintain or restore international peace and security."
40 Morgenthau, 1954, p. 284.
41 Boyle, 1985, p. 121.

political, not juridical.[42] With the end of the Cold War, the antagonistic relationship between the major powers arguably has retracted (but certainly has not disappeared nor become irrelevant), which in turn has increased the opportunity for the UN Security Council to act. The prime example is Resolution 678 (1990), where the UN Security Council authorized UN member states to use all necessary means (including the use of force) in order to compel Iraq to leave Kuwait.

7.2.3.2 International Court of Justice

Access to the ICJ is limited and its jurisdiction is based on consent, which weakens its potential for dispute settlement.[43] None of the major powers, including the US, Russia or China, consents to the optional clause included in the Court's Statute recognizing the compulsory jurisdiction of the Court.[44] There are very few ICJ cases on the use of force. Following the ICJ's decision in the *Nicaragua* case in which it determined that the US violated the principle of non-intervention and the prohibition on the use of force, the US withdrew its acceptance under the optional clause (Article 36(2)).[45] The ICJ had jurisdiction in the *Democratic Republic of the Congo v Uganda* case as both countries had accepted the optional clause, which resulted in the ruling that Uganda, by *inter alia* engaging in military activities against the DRC on the latter's territory, violated the prohibition of the use of force and the principle of non-intervention.[46] The ICJ has also issued an advisory opinion on the legal consequences of the construction of a wall in the occupied Palestinian territory, where the Court had reasons to discuss the use of force against non-state actors.[47] These judgments and the advisory opinion are rare exceptions which show the limited role of the ICJ in this area.

The potential future role of the ICC will, arguably, be limited as its jurisdiction in relation to the crime of aggression primarily will be based on consent subject to significant limitations. The Court may exercise jurisdiction over a crime of aggression arising from an act of aggression committed by a state party. State parties may opt out from the Court's jurisdiction by a declaration to that effect. In relation to a non-state party, the Court shall not exercise its jurisdiction over the crime of aggression when committed by that state's nationals or on its territory. The UN Security Council may extend the jurisdiction of the Court to crimes of aggression committed by nationals of a

42 Henkin, 1979, pp. 168 and 185.

43 ICJ Statute, Article 36.

44 ICJ, Declarations Recognizing the Jurisdiction of the Court as Compulsory (last visit 7 May 2013).

45 *Nicaragua Case*, ICJ, Judgment of 27 June 1986, para 292.

46 *Armed Activities on the Territory of the Congo* (Democratic Republic of the Congo v Uganda), ICJ, Judgment of 19 December 2005, paras 1 and 345.

47 *Legal Consequences of the Construction of a Wall in the Occupied Palestinian Territory*, ICJ, Advisory Opinion of 9 July 2004.

non-state party or on the territory of such states, but such extension is subject to the veto power of the P-5. As such, it is highly unlikely that the ICC will exercise jurisdiction over crimes of aggression committed by nationals of a non-state party or on the territory of such states.[48] It could, arguably, only happen when none of the P-5 perceive that their (or their allies') vital interests are threatened.

To summarize, the two (in the future potentially three) dispute settlement mechanisms are subject to the consent of the individual states affected, and non-cooperative states may only be subjected to the powers of the UN Security Council (i.e. abstain from using the veto) when the P-5 finds it suitable. This makes the degree of delegation weak.

7.2.4 State acceptance

All states are members of the UN and, as such, are state parties to its Charter, with a few exceptions: the Republic of China (Taiwan) and the two permanent non-member states, the Holy See and Palestine. Considering that the substantial rules of the UN Charter on the prohibition of the threat or use of force and self-defense are part of customary international law, the obligations in this regime are binding for all states, regardless of UN membership. However, only 69 states have accepted the optional clause in the Court's Statute recognizing the jurisdiction of the ICJ as compulsory. Even if the ICC would assume jurisdiction over the crime of aggression by 2017, such jurisdiction would be limited to state parties, at present 122 states. However, the major powers such as the US, Russia or China are not parties to the ICC Statute and showed great reluctance to be subjected (or to subject their citizens) to this mechanism.

7.3 Feminist perspective on use of force

With a feminist perspective, the meaning of security is broadened to include the experiences of women and the effects of structural inequalities in terms of gender. It adopts gender as a category of analysis. Feminist scholarship has revealed unequal gender relations and social practices that support war and shows that war is a social construct dependent on myths of protection and subordination of women.[49] A key document that confronts gender subordination is UN Security Council Resolution 1325 on women, peace and security, adopted on 31 October 2000. This Resolution expresses concern that civilians, particularly women and children, account for the vast majority of those adversely affected by armed conflict, including as refugees and

48 Resolution Rc/Res.6, annex I, Articles 15 *bis* (4) and (5) and 15 *ter*.

49 Tickner, Ann L., 'What is Your Research Program? Some Feminist Answers to International Relations' Methodological Questions', 49 *International Studies Quarterly* (2005) 1–21, pp. 4 and 6; Amnéus, 2008; pp. 64–65.

internally displaced persons, and increasingly are targeted by combatants and armed elements. It recognizes the consequent impact this has on durable peace and reconciliation. The Resolution reaffirms the role of women in the prevention and resolution of conflicts and in peace-building, and stresses the importance of their equal participation and full involvement in all efforts for the maintenance and promotion of peace and security, as well as the need to increase their role in decision making with regard to conflict prevention and resolution. It also reaffirms the need to implement fully international humanitarian and human rights law which protects the rights of women and girls during and after conflicts. The Resolution can be summarized as three "Ps": protection (of the rights of women and girls during and after conflicts); participation (women's active and meaningful participation in all peace processes, as well as their representation in formal and informal decision making at all levels); and prevention (development of effective gender-sensitive early warning mechanisms and institutions, and strengthening of efforts to prevent violence against women, including various forms of gender-based violence).[50] The Resolution addresses enforcement measures under Article 41 of the UN Charter, where it is stated that the UN Security Council shall consider such measures' "potential impact on the civilian population, bearing in mind the special needs of women and girls, in order to consider appropriate humanitarian exemptions".[51] However, the Resolution lacks any specific reference and considerations on enforcement measures taken under Article 42. Amnéus argues the general provisions on the role, participation and considerations in relation to women and gender are not only relevant for peacekeeping, but also for peace-enforcement measures.[52]

The UN Security Council reaffirmed in Resolution 1820 its commitment to the continuing and full implementation of Resolution 1325 (and other relevant Resolutions). It stressed that sexual violence, when used or commissioned as a tactic of war in order to deliberately target civilians or as a part of a widespread or systematic attack against civilian populations, can significantly exacerbate situations of armed conflict and may impede the restoration of international peace and security. Although the UN Security Council affirmed that effective steps to prevent and respond to such acts of sexual violence can significantly contribute to the maintenance of international peace and security, it did not explicitly define or limit what these steps could consist of. These could include Chapter VII measures, which is supported by operative paragraph 5 of the Resolution that mentions "targeted and graduated response", which could include non-military measures under Article 41 as well as military measures under Article 42.[53]

50 Report of the Secretary-General on women and peace and security, 12 September 2007, UN Doc S/2007/567, para. 42.

51 Resolution 1325 (2000), UN Doc S/RES/1325, operative para 14.

52 Amnéus, 2008, pp. 229–230.

53 Amnéus, 2008, p. 233.

Feminism in this context is not only a perspective, but also a program of action, namely that social justice, including gender justice, is necessary for achieving peace. Sustainable peace and security requires the full and equal participation of women. Amnéus has incorporated gender perspectives when discussing human security, the concept of the responsibility to protect and humanitarian intervention. She notes that women's groups and feminist researchers have developed mixed gender positions on responsibility to protect, ranging from reluctance to accept any new norm on the use of force to embracing the doctrine despite its lack of gender analysis. For those supporting the doctrine, a key point is that it should take into account the provisions of UN Security Council Resolution 1325 and subsequent resolutions on women, peace and security. To be concrete, this could include gender training for peace operations and the inclusion of women in intervention forces and as civilian personnel. Not only rape, but also other forms of abuse of women and girls should be included in the threshold of when to intervene.[54]

7.4 Processes and mechanisms for creating and enforcing the law on the use of force

International anarchy makes cooperation among sovereign states difficult. This may create the impression that international law is irrelevant when comes to preventing the use of force between states. However, when the international system is perceived as a state of anarchy, the central question is, arguably, not, "Why do wars occur?", but rather, "Why do wars not occur more often?". Jervis argues that states are restrained (to use force) only externally, by what others are doing, or by anticipation of what others will do if they act against the others' interests. This pattern characterizes the balance of power.[55] This would lead to rather pessimistic prospects for how effective international law is in terms of influence on states' behavior.

Various processes and mechanisms may be relevant for the use of force. International organizations have functions that range from capabilities for enforcing rules by military action (coercion), through facilitating the rational pursuit of self-interest in ways that also serve existing mutual interests (reciprocity), to "teaching" a set of norms that may sharply revise actors' preferences and sense of their self-interest (persuasion and socialization).[56] These functions may, to various degrees, explain a causal relationship linking international organizations to peace. Considering coercion, the UN may, in theory,

54 Amnéus, 2008, pp. 20, 60–65, 71, 220 and 222.

55 Jervis, Robert, 'From Balance to Concert: A Study of International Security Cooperation' in Oye, Kenneth A. (ed), *Cooperation Under Anarchy* (Princeton, NJ: Princeton University Press, 1986), pp. 58–79, pp. 58–59.

56 Finnemore, Martha, 'International Organizations as Teachers of Norms: The United Nations Educational, Scientific, and Cultural Organization and Science Policy', 47 *International Organization* (1993) 565–597, pp. 593–594. As commented by Russett, Oneal and Davis, 1998, p. 444.

as a collective security organization act on the principle of unified action of all against any state, including a member that commits an act of aggression, threat or breach of the peace. Alliances such as the North Atlantic Treaty Organization (NATO) are typically directed against other states; but they may, through different mechanisms, including overt military coercion, suppress violent conflict among their members.[57] In addition, not all processes require UN action or authorization. States relying on reciprocity may both prevent conflict and shorten the duration of conflicts. Transparency is one factor relevant for the principle of reciprocity that can prevent defection from cooperative behavior. Transparency may be achieved through agreements that provide guidelines for determining whether or not an actor is cooperating.[58] International organizations may contribute to peaceful conflict management not only through the provision of information (i.e. transparency), but also by lowering transaction costs[59] and socialization.[60] Norms and rules may facilitate arms control and delegitimize the use of force.[61]

Sanctioning problems is not unique for enforcing the law on the use of force and repressing aggression. However, sanctioning tends to be more difficult in relation to the use of force compared to other fields of international law, due to high costs of punishing the aggressor.[62] It is a serious challenge to measure what, if any, extent international law influences the use of force. Henkin argues that the "UN's greatest influence for peace cannot be measured nor proven". However, he still has the ambition to describe how nations behave and holds that, "it is not wholly an assertion of faith to insist that the existence of the organization reaffirmed the norm of the Charter and enhanced its deterrent influence … A nation could initiate the use of force only with full awareness that it would have to answer in this world forum".[63] Henkin builds his case in two parts with a focus on inter-state conflicts, in which he stresses that when the UN Charter was adopted, states had no intention to prohibit civil war or revolution.[64]

The first part is a general observation with a series of scattered observations. He notes that since World War II there have been only very few violations against prohibition against the use of force: the Arab-Israeli hostilities in 1956, 1967 and 1973; India-Pakistan in 1965; the Soviet Union's invasion of Czechoslovakia in 1968; the Ogaden war in 1977–78 (Ethiopia-Somalia);

57 Russett, Oneal and Davis, 1998, p. 445.
58 Jervis, 1986, pp. 73–76.
59 Keohane, 1983, p. 150–151; Keohane and Martin, 1995, p. 42; Goldstein et al., 2001, p. 13; Ginsburg and Shaffer, 2010, p. 754.
60 Shannon, Megan, 'Preventing War and Providing the Peace? International Organizations and the Management of Territorial Disputes', 26 *Conflict Management and Peace Science* (2009) 144–163, p. 147.
61 Russett, Oneal and Davis, 1998, p. 446.
62 Compare Axelrod and Keohane, 1986, p. 236.
63 Henkin, 1979, p. 167.
64 Henkin, 1979, pp. 155–157.

and the war between Vietnam-Cambodia-China in 1978–79. There has not been full and sustained hostilities or state-to-state aggression even in circumstances in which in the past might have been expected. Moreover, in the period since World War II there have not been analogous conquests and wars that followed World War I, such as the Japanese conquest of Manchuria, Italy's aggression in Ethiopia, Hitler's invasion of Poland, Japan's attack on Pearl Harbour and the Gran Chaco war. In reaching this conclusion, Henkin puts the Vietnam war and Korea war in a basket separate from interstate war. Korea was in some respects an "internal war" and Vietnam is difficult to characterize. He notes that the significant fact is not that threats and disputes involving violence occurred in situations, such as Greece-Turkey over Cyprus, Indonesia's colonialism in Malaysia, and border disputes between India-China and India-Pakistan. More important is that these conflicts did not become "all-out" war, and were soon terminated. He argues that the war over Kashmir in 1965 represented the first war after the adoption of the UN Charter, the kind of war the UN was designed to prevent. It was quickly terminated under pressure from the UN. The UN made important contributions to peace in the Israel-Middle East conflict. From this, it can be determined that a new level of evolution and foundation of international order has been established. The norm against war between states has been largely respected. Non-international armed conflict is something else.[65]

It is true that the number of international armed conflicts have decreased since World War II.[66] However, it does not follow that this is the result of the adoption of the UN Charter outlawing the threat or use of force. Correlation is not the same as causation. There may be other causes, such as alliance building, the threat of mutually assured destruction in case of direct war between the major powers that possess nuclear weapons, economic interdependence and/or the increased number of democratically governed states. Henkin's findings on this first level, arguably, run the risk of being subjective and anecdotal. He provides examples that both support and counter his hypothesis, and his classifications of the Vietnam and Korea wars can be contested.

A potential remedy, which Henkin attempts to provide in his second part is more in-depth case studies of the Suez crisis of 1956, the abduction of Eichmann in 1960 (did not involve the use of force in its strict sense), the Cuban missile crisis of 1962 and the developments in Indochina/Vietnam in 1954–73.[67] Henkin does not set out his explicit methodology, but he does investigate the chain of events, an approach similar to process-tracing. He also checks his claim with counterfactual reasoning.[68] Boyle goes even

65 Henkin, 1979, pp. 146–147 and 171–172.

66 Sarkees, Meredith Reid, Wayman, Frank Whelon and Singer, J. David, 'Inter-State, Intra-State, and Extra-State Wars: A Comprehensive Look at Their Distribution over Time, 1816–1997', 47 *International Studies Quarterly* (2003) 49–70, pp. 51–52.

67 Henkin, 1979, pp. 241–312.

68 Henkin, 1979, see * on p. 254.

further in his enquiry in relation to the 1976 Entebbe incident.[69] Chayes examines the legal aspects of the 1962 Cuban missile crisis in relation to three interrelated decisions taken by the US: (a) the choice of the blockade, or "quarantine, as against harsher or milder responses"; (b) the decision to seek an Organization of American States (OAS) authorizing resolution; and (c) the manner and method of approach to the UN. He notes that the meetings of the Executive Committee of the National Security Council were not dominated by debates on the finer points of law. Nevertheless, the factual record shows that decision-makers made a considerable effort to integrate legal factors into their deliberations. Chayes challenges the view that law is a set of fixed, self-defining categories of permissible and prohibited conduct, a conception invalid even as to domestic law. International law is indeterminate.[70] Bowie has made a similar inquiry into the Suez Crises of 1956.[71] Song and Tønnesson have examined the impact of the UNCLOS on conflict behavior and management in the South China Sea during four periods: in negotiations leading to the treaty (1973–82); from its signing to the entry into force (1982–94); from then until the China-ASEAN Declaration on the Conduct of Parties in the South China Sea (1995–2002); and from the setting of a timeline for outer limits of continental shelf submissions to the events following the 2009 submissions (2003–13).[72] The study is similar to the enquires of Henkin, Boyle and Chayes, going through the chain of events examining how law and institutions established to uphold law restrain states. All these are examples of in-depth studies on the influence of international law on conflict, peace and the use of force. The next sections examine alternative enquires that rely more on quantitative methods. The focus is on aspects on the enforcement of the law on the use of force: conflict prevention and shortening the duration of conflicts.

7.4.1 Conflict prevention

Political scientists have traditionally concentrated on the effects of joint democracy and economic interdependence on the effects of peace. Both of these elements have a statistically significant and substantively important independent effect on reducing the frequency of militarized disputes between dyads (pairs) of states, even after holding constant the influence of other theoretically relevant variables, such as alliance ties, relative power, proximity,

69 Boyle, 1985.

70 Chayes, Abram, *The Cuban Missile Crisis: International Crises and the Role of Law* (Lanham: University Press of America, 1987 (originally published 1974)), pp. 6–7 and 100–101.

71 Bowie, Robert R., *Suez 1956: International Crises and the Role of Law* (London: Oxford University Press, 1974).

72 Song, Yann-huei and Tønnesson, Stein, 'The Impact of the Law of the Sea Convention on Conflict and Conflict Management in the South China Sea', 44 *Ocean Development & International Law* (2013) 235–269.

wealth and economic growth.[73] Russett, Oneal and Davis have examined whether dense networks of IGO membership make an additional contribution to the avoidance of serious militarized disputes, separate from, or in interaction with, joint democracy and economic interdependence. They point out that previous research indicates that numerous IGOs are set up during the peaceful periods immediately following major wars; hence, one would see a correlation between IGOs and peace, but not necessarily a causal relationship linking IGOs to peace.[74]

Russett, Oneal and Davis use probit analysis, a form of multiple regression appropriate to a dichotomized rather than continuous dependent variable (in this context, the presence or absence of a militarized dispute). They limited their study to the period 1950–85, and to neighboring pairs of states that contain at least one state defined as a major power (Britain, China, France, the Soviet Union and the US). This excludes pairs that, in the majority of cases, had no reasonable opportunity to engage in armed conflict because they were too weak militarily and had few serious interests at stake. They took account of other explanatory factors such as joint democracy, economic interdependence, economic growth, joint membership of a military alliance and proximity. They found that virtually all variables are significant as hypothesized. They found preliminary support for the hypothesis that the absence of militarized disputes between two states has a causal effect on their subsequent readiness to join IGOs together and to remain in such organizations. This suggests that there is a virtuous circle of reciprocity between IGOs and peace.[75] There are some limitations with the first study of Russett, Oneal and Davis, for example, it is limited to the Cold War. The same hypothesis could be tested in relation to the era before World War II and post-Cold War. Accordingly, Oneal, Russett and Berbaum expanded in a subsequent study the scope of the original study to the period 1886–1992 for all pairs for which data was available. They conducted tests in the spirit of Granger's test of causality.[76] Granger proposed that a variable X might be a cause of Y if past values of X can be used to predict Y more accurately than using past values of Y alone.[77] They checked for other explanatory factors such as democracy, trade and economic interdependence, joint IGO membership, military capability, membership

73 Oneal, John R. et al., 'The Liberal Peace: Interdependence, Democracy, and International Conflict, 1950–1985', 33 *Journal of Peace Research* (1996) 11–28; Oneal, John R. and Russett, Bruce, 'The Classical Liberals Were Right: Democracy, Interdependence, and Conflict, 1950–1985', 41 *International Studies Quarterly* (1997) 267–294; Russett, Oneal and Davis, 1998, p. 442.

74 Vasquez, John A., *The War Puzzle* (Cambridge: Cambridge University Press, 1993), pp. 269ff; Jacobson, Harold K., Reisinger, William M. and Mathers, Todd, 'National Entanglements in International Organizations', 80 *American Political Science Review* (1986) 141–159, pp. 156–157; Russett, Oneal and Davis, 1998, p. 42,

75 Russett, Oneal and Davis, 1998, pp. 449–462.

76 Oneal, Russett and Berbaum, 2003, pp. 372 and 375.

77 Granger, C.W.J., 'Investigating Causal Relations by Econometric Models and Cross-spectral Methods', 37 *Econometrica* (1969) 424–438.

of the same alliance, contiguity and distance.[78] Among other findings, joint memberships in IGOs showed to be more closely associated with peace here than in the previous research. The effect of sharing common memberships in international organizations for avoiding disputes is equal to that of trade.[79] There is, however, further research that partly questions the robustness of this linkage between IGOs and peace.[80]

Other scholars have examined which specific IGOs are more likely to prevent conflict. Boehmer, Gartzke and Nordstrom have found that IGOs that vary in institutional structure, mandate and member cohesion vary in their impact on interstate conflict prevention.[81] They suggest a bargaining theory, midway between realism and liberalism. The theory suggests that war often results from incentives to bluff where there is uncertainty relating to the other side's interests or power. Thus, IGOs can promote peace by revealing confidential information about competing states. This requires extensive institutional structures and/or support from member states (especially the major powers). The theory also suggests that IGOs which possess or develop consensus and cohesion are more likely to be successful in promoting peace.[82]

Shannon has focused on the process by which international organizations broker peace. Previous research used the absence or presence of a dispute as a dependent variable, which masks some of the political processes by which international organization members procure peace. In order to uncover the influence of international organizations on conflict management, Shannon looked for cooperation among unlikely practitioners—territorial rivals. She finds that organizations with interventionist capabilities encourage disputing members to attempt peaceful conflict resolution.[83]

Axelrod argues that the foundation of cooperation is not trust, but the durability of the relationship. If the major powers can be certain that they will be interacting with each other year after year, cooperation will have a better chance to evolve and deepen.[84] This suggests that the legal framework should be designed to preserve the existing distribution of power among states, for example the privileged status of the P-5.

Two contributing causes why security dilemmas emerge and provide the dynamics for starting an armed conflict is lack of information and problems

78 Oneal, Russett and Berbaum, 2003, pp. 376–379.

79 Oneal, Russett and Berbaum, 2003, pp. 379 and 381.

80 Boehmer et al., 2004, p. 5; Pevehouse, Jon and Russett, Bruce, 'Democratic International Governmental Organizations Promote Peace', 60 *International Organization* (2006) 969–1000, pp. 969–970.

81 Boehmer et al., 2004, pp. 2 and 29.

82 Boehmer et al., 2004, pp. 7–14. Other similar studies on economic interdependence: Bearce, David H. and Omori, Sawa 'How Do Commercial Institutions Promote Peace?', 42 *Journal of Peace Research* (2005) 659–678; Haftel, Yoram Z., 'Designing for Peace: Regional Integration Arrangements, Institutional Variation, and Militarized Interstate Disputes', 61 *International Organization* (2007) 217–237.

83 Shannon, 2009, pp. 145 and 148.

84 Axelrod, 1984, pp. 182 and 187–188.

between the parties of committing to peace (commitment problems).[85] Third parties, such as the UN, may alleviate these problems through at least four different means: (a) diplomatic engagement; (b) intimidation, including calls for compliance or condemnation; (c) assurance through observation teams and/or peace-keepers; or (d) peace enforcement following UN Security Council authorization. Beardsley argues that the choice of means may affect the outcome, ranging from compromise, stalemate and one-sided victory. [86]

The UN may use diplomatic engagement such as the use of good offices, fact-finding or mediation, typically executed by the Secretary-General, special representatives or *ad hoc* commissions. The focus of such involvement typically involves improving the information environment among the sides so that they can more quickly come to understand each other's concerns and reach a resolution. Empirical studies show that diplomatic engagement in the form of mediation can improve the ability of the actors to either reach a new arrangement or to back down from military hostilities.[87]

Turning to security dilemmas involving commitment problems, the UN may, through sending an observer group or promising a peacekeeping force, allow the parties to a dispute feel more comfortable with a peaceful bargain.[88] When other means have been exhausted the UN Security Council may, under Chapter VII of the UN Charter, authorize the use of force. Military force may be a means to prevent the parties from future defections when implementing a settlement.[89] While an understanding of information and commitment problems and relevant action will prevent, dampen or shorten armed conflicts, it will not change the fact that some policies aimed at increasing

85 Jervis, Robert, *Perception and Misperception in International Politics* (Princetion, NJ: Princeton University Press, 1976), p. 67.

86 Beardsley, Kyle, 'UN intervention and the duration of international crises', 49 *Journal of Peace Research* (2012) 335–349, p. 338.

87 Ibid, p. 338; see also Walter, Barbara F., *Committing to peace : the successful settlement of civil wars* (Princeton, NJ: Princeton University Press, 2002), pp. 13–14, 15, 82–83, 89 and 152–153; Wilkenfeld, Jonathan, *Mediating International Crises* (New York, NY: Routledge, 2005); Beardsley, Kyle, 'Agreement without peace? International mediation and time inconsistency problems', 52 *American Journal of Political Science* (2008) 723–740; Beardsley, Kyle, *The Mediation Dilemma* (Ithaca, NY: Cornell University Press, 2011).

88 Beardsley, 2012, p. 338. Beardsley notes that, "[o]ther empirical studies confirm that the use of peacekeeping and security guarantees can help resolve critical barriers to successful bargaining such as commitment problems and related security dilemmas: Doyle, Michael W. and Sambanis, Nicholas, 'International peacebuilding: A theoretical and quantitative analysis', 94 *American Political Science Review* (2000) 779–801; Doyle, Michael W. and Sambanis, Nicholas, *Making War and Building Peace: United Nations Peace Operations* (Princeton, NJ: Princeton University Press, 2006); Fortna, Virginia P., 'Inside and out: Peacekeeping and the duration of peace after civil and interstate wars', 5 *International Studies Review* (2003) 97–114; Gilligan, Michael J. and Sergenti, Ernest, 'Evaluating UN peacekeeping with matching methods to improve causal inference' (unpublished manuscript) Department of Politics, New York University (2006); Walter, 2002, pp. 80, 98–99, 105.

89 Beardsley, 2012, p. 338.

a state's security will threaten the security of other states.[90] For more long-term results, the parties to a dispute need to identify a new distribution of the goods or issues in question, which is mutually preferable to conflict and credibly commit to that via some sort of compromise settlement. Beardsley uses competing-risks models, controlling for: (a) whether or not one of the sides of the crisis dyad is a member of the P-5, because research shows that P-5 involvement can substantially decrease UN involvement in international crises; and (b) whether or not regional security organizations were involved in the crisis, since regional involvement can be a substitute for UN involvement. The result is that UN military involvement does well to decrease the risk of one side achieving victory, while diplomatic engagement increases the ability of the belligerents to reach a compromise in the long run. Assurance and intimidation alone are weaker as crisis management mechanisms.[91]

The quantitative research surveyed above lends some support to the conclusion that international institutions may prevent armed conflicts. However, it appears difficult to isolate the specific significance of the provisions of the UN Charter that prohibit the use of force. Even though the number of interstate conflicts has decreased since the norm prohibiting the use of force between states was established and codified in the UN Charter, it does not follow that there is causal relationship. It is impossible to create an experiment environment with an international system without the UN tested against a system with the UN. A more reasonable approach is to view the UN and its Charter as a part of a greater normative framework which seeks to prevent the use of force. The relevance of international institutions and norms can only be examined indirectly in the manner of the surveyed research above. As indicated earlier,[92] quantitative methods that show correlation between a treaty norm and state behavior do not necessarily prove a causal relationship. However, they can eliminate many alternative explanations that initially appear to be more powerful explanations.[93]

7.4.2 Conflict duration

Much of the debate on the use of force concerns whether international law and institutions can prevent armed conflicts. While international law aims to prevent conflict, it also strives to shorten the duration of disputes. Based on empirical analyses of militarized interstate dispute duration (1950–2000), Shannon, Morey and Boehmke find that increasing shared participation in international organizations reduces the length of disputes, even after accounting for selection of international conflict. They studied the duration of conflict dyads and explored a broad class of Militarized Interstate Disputes, not

90 Jervis, 1976, p. 76.
91 Beardsley, 2012, pp. 336 and 343–347.
92 Section 1.4.3 on correlation and causality.
93 Simmons, 2009, p. 199.

limiting themselves to the definition of war, which requires 1,000 deaths, commonly used in peace and conflict studies.[94]

They suggest that in an anarchic world where states are free to determine their own policies, organizations may not have the power to single-handedly prevent conflict between members. However, international organizations have the incentive and ability to change the bargaining environment so that members settle disputes more quickly. International organizations may shorten disputes by helping parties to a conflict to overcome commitment problems. Commitment problems are a bargaining obstacle that provokes lengthy conflicts between states. Such problems occur when disputants have an incentive to break an agreement they might reach to end a conflict. Commitment barriers may take various forms, including the distribution of power between states. Institutions may use a variety of mechanisms to address commitment problems, including calling for a ceasefire, making parties to the conflict aware that the international community may be considering further, more punitive measures to stop the conflict,[95] i.e. a mechanism of coercion; or mitigating commitment problems by bringing the states together to negotiate, and by enforcing and guaranteeing agreements. Strong enforcement mechanisms and continued pressure from third parties, including international organizations, help to uphold ceasefires; and the threat and imposition of sanctions on states which fail to reach agreements and continue fighting may also be used.[96]

The study by Shannon, Morey and Boehmke has its strength in establishing a correlation between increasing shared participation in international organizations and the reduction in the length of disputes. However, this does not automatically mean that one is the cause of the other. There may be a third factor that correlates and explains both participation in international organizations and the reduced length of disputes. They test an alternative explanation to the hypothesis that international organizations mitigate commitment problems, namely that international organizations may reduce information asymmetries (or a combination of the two functions). Information-providing organizations have well-established bureaucracies with extensive amounts of data about their members' capabilities. They find that joint membership in information providing organizations has no discernable impact upon conflict duration.[97] They also control for other potentially explanatory variables, namely: (a) whether both states are democracies; (b) geographic distance between the disputing states; and (c) the distribution of power, i.e. the relative balance of military capability between dyad members. They find it surprising that joint democracy has no significance on the duration of the conflict. While

94 Shannon, Megan, Morey, Daniel and Boehmke, Frederick J., 'The Influence of International Organizations on Militarized Dispute Initiation and Duration', 54 *International Studies Quarterly* (2010) 1123–1141, pp. 1123 and 1128.

95 Ibid, pp. 1123–1124.

96 Ibid, p. 1126.

97 Ibid, pp. 1128–1129 and 1135.

geographic distance and power imbalances work to keep states out of conflict, they appear to play no role in the duration once a Militarized Interstate Dispute has begun.[98] Shannon, Morey and Boehmke note that while we expect international organizations to shorten disputes, not all scholars applaud institutions and third parties in the same manner.[99] Regan studied conflicts from 1944 to 1999 with and without interventions. The study is based on a hazard model which takes into account when the intervention is made. This allows the explanatory variables to vary as a function of time within a particular case. The conclusion is that interventions—whether military or economic—do not act as effective tools of conflict management. Instead, intervention alone greatly increases the expected duration of a conflict. Also, surprisingly, Regan finds that neutral interventions are strongly associated with longer conflicts than are biased interventions.[100] Similarly, Weener and Yuen studied 48 cases of ceasefires in international wars ending between 1946 and 1997 analyzing the duration of peace after each ceasefire using hazard analysis. They find that ceasefires that come about as a consequence of third-party pressure are significantly more likely to fail if the ceasefire agreement has little to do with the military balance of the belligerents and the expectations of how the conflict would have played out in the absence of a third-party intervention. In other words, third parties may increase the duration of fighting if they prematurely interrupt disputes where one side has a significant advantage. Commitment problems persist in these conflicts because the stronger combatant realizes it has more to gain from continued fighting than from settling.[101]

Greig and Diehl have studied all enduring rivalries between states in the period 1946–96 in order to examine whether the presence of UN peacekeeping forces enhances or inhibits mediation and negotiation attempts to reach a peace agreement (as distinct from a ceasefire agreement).[102] They note that previous research suggests that traditional peacekeeping is generally successful in maintaining ceasefires.[103] However, some theoretical logics may warrant pessimism. Rational choice theory suggests that armed conflict is the result of information problems. When bargaining breaks down, an armed conflict will provide the belligerent parties with information on each other's capabilities and resolve. Peacekeepers prevent the transmission of information necessary for the parties to settle. However, mediators may be able to

98 Ibid, pp. 1130–1131 and 1134.

99 Ibid, p. 1125.

100 Regan, Patrick M., 'Third-party Interventions and the Duration of Intrastate Conflicts', 46 *Journal of Conflict Resolution* (2002) 55–73, pp. 56, 64 and 71–72.

101 Werner, Suzann and Yuen, Amy, 'Making and Keeping Peace', 59 *International Organization* (2005) 261–292, pp. 271–273 and 287–290; Shannon, Morey and Boehmke, 2000, p. 1125.

102 Greig, J. Michael and Diehl, Paul F., 'The Peacekeeping-Peacemaking Dilemma', 49 *International Studies Quarterly* (2005) 621–645, p. 622.

103 Diehl, Paul F., *International peacekeeping* (Baltimore, MD: Johns Hopkins, 1993), pp. 33–40 and 167–175; Fortna, Virginia P., *Peace Time: Cease-Fire Agreements and the Durability of Peace* (Princeton, NJ: Princeton University Press, 2004), pp. 189–193 and 209–210.

provide the necessary information. Thus any potential negative effects of peacekeeping may be compensated by mediation. Greig and Diehl control for other variables, including if the peacekeeping mission has failed to keep a ceasefire, timing of diplomatic attempts, intensity, outcomes and duration of conflict, the distribution of power between disputants, the occurrence of political shifts that influence the prospects for mediation success, and the characteristics of the mediator and the negotiators. They find that UN peacekeeping missions are often prematurely deployed to enforce ceasefires. These UN missions may inadvertently lengthen conflicts by rendering the parties to the dispute complacent to settle.[104]

Section 1.3.1 on reciprocity notes that one way to promote cooperation is to make interactions more frequent and break down the issues into small pieces,[105] which is also relevant for shortening the duration of conflicts. For example, Henry Kissinger arranged for the Israeli disengagement from the Sinai after 1973 to proceed in stages that were coordinated with Egyptian moves leading to normal relationships with Israel.[106]

A related issue is whether states contribute to peacekeeping for self-interest or the urgency for intervention (such as the need to promote peace, and prevent human suffering). This is difficult to examine, not least because a state may call an intervention peacekeeping, but may have ulterior motives. Rost and Greig have developed a theoretical framework that ties together four sets of influences on a third-party state's decision about whether to intervene in a non-international armed conflict: (a) state interests; (b) the urgency for intervention; (c) the risks of peacekeeping; and (d) the opportunities for success. In identifying whether state interest is at hand, they look at whether the two states involved are adjoining, whether there is a defense-pact, a colonial relationship, similar religious and ethnic groups and economic exchanges. Turning to the urgency of intervention, they examine data on forced displacement, the occurrence of genocide, the intensity of fighting in terms of battle-deaths and the duration of the non-international armed conflict. Their finding challenges the conventional wisdom that peacekeeping is only used for "easy cases"; instead, they find that states are often drawn to conflicts that show the greatest need for intervention and those posing the greatest challenges. State interests were also shown to exert powerful influence upon the choice of when and where states deploy peacekeepers. Political, social and economic ties each increase the likelihood of a state becoming involved in peacekeeping. In contrast, neighboring states are not significantly more likely to deploy peacekeepers, even when the conflict produces large numbers of refugees. State interests seem to drive weaker states' peacekeeping decisions more than the decisions of the major powers. Rost and Grieg see two potential

104 Greig and Diehl, 2005, pp. 626–627 and 633–643; Shannon, Morey and Boehmke, 2000, p. 1125. See also Diehl, 1993, p. 175.

105 Axelrod, 1984, pp. 129–132.

106 Axelrod, 1984, pp. 129–132.

explanations: first, non-major powers have fewer resources, which may restrict them to intervene only when their interests are at stake. Second, major powers can, to a greater extent, control international organizations and allies to provide peacekeeping in conflicts in which they have an interest. Major power peacekeeping is strongly driven by conflicts that show the greatest capacity to spread, those producing the highest numbers of battle-deaths and involving a large number of warring parties. Weaker states' peacekeeping, while influenced less by the intensity of fighting, is more strongly encouraged by concern about consequences for civilians, encouraging them to intervene in long-running, ethnically rooted civil wars that produce large numbers of refugees. In this respect, both major and non-major powers choose tough cases for peacekeeping, intervening where it is needed the most.[107]

7.4.3 Non-governmental organization involvement

NGOs may be a factor relevant for inter-state use of force to the extent that state policies are dependent on domestic debates and processes. It is more difficult to determine how NGOs may interact and influence states at the international level. Further, the majority of NGOs deal with issues that do not fall into the traditional understanding of matters of international peace and security, the domain of the UN Security Council. NGOs may obtain formal accreditation at the UN from the Economic and Social Council. From this, they enjoy privileged status within the framework of the General Assembly, but are not represented at the UN Security Council. However, the UN Security Council has, since the end of the Cold War, undergone a transformation and broadened its mandate to include matters that previously were understood as economic and social categories. NGOs are now to a larger extent included in consultations with members of the UN Security Council.[108] UN Security Council Resolution 1325 (2000) on women, peace and security is an example of how NGOs have been successful in providing input into UN Security Council deliberations and policy-making.[109]

7.5 Tension between power and law

The conditions for the formation and maintenance of a strong regime that regulates and in general prohibits the use of force is that states, especially the major powers, must be reasonably satisfied: (a) with the status quo; and (b) that gains are greater without resort to the use of threat of unlimited war as compared with the risks and costs of less constrained competition. States

107 Rost, Nicolas and Greig, J. Michael, 'Taking matters into their own hands: An analysis of the determinants of state-conducted peacekeeping in civil wars', 48 *Journal of Peace Research* (2011) 171–184; pp. 172–173, 176–177, 179–180 and 182.

108 Niemetz, 2014, p. 69.

109 Niemetz, 2014, pp. 69–70.

must share values on mutual security and cooperation and believe that other states do the same.[110] A realist would challenge these assumptions, namely they would challenge that states trust each other in an anarchic world where states have military power and uncertain intentions.[111] Waltz argues that, "[i]n international politics force serves, not only as the *ultima ratio*, but indeed as the first and constant one".[112] Mearsheimer presents a similar stance that:

> the causes of war and peace are mainly a function of the balance of power, and institutions largely mirror the distribution of power in the system. In short, the balance of power is the independent variable that explains war; institutions are merely an intervening variable in the process ... realism treats war as an inevitable, and indeed sometimes necessary, form of state activity ... war is an extension of politics by other means. Realists are very cautious in their prescriptions about the use of force: wars should not be fought for idealistic purposes, but instead for balance-of-power reasons.[113]

Realism claims to be purely descriptive and ideologically neutral. This claim of neutrality and instrumental perception on the use of force is not only at odds with liberal institutionalism and theories on collective security, which have the explicit and implicit assumption that peaceful means are preferable,[114] it is also contrary to the school of hard legal positivism, which claims to be descriptive and non-idealistic. Hard legal positivists argue that states have agreed that disputes primarily should be settled peacefully, rather than through forceful means, and thus that peace is an end in and of itself.[115] It is noted that even Morgenthau argues that, "the preservation of peace has become the prime concern of all nations",[116] a possible example of the implicit idealism in Morgenthau's realism.[117]

The function of a regime on the use of force is to reinforce peaceful patterns of behavior, and values on mutual security and cooperation. The regime must allow sanction against states that do not share these values and which seek

110 Jervis, 1983, p. 176.

111 Mearsheimer, 1994, pp. 14 and 28–37.

112 Waltz, 1979, p. 113. See also Art, 2004, pp. 5–6.

113 Mearsheimer, 1994, pp. 13 and 48.

114 Mearsheimer, 1994, p. 14 and p. 48 footnote 182: "Realism is not a normative theory, however, and it provides no criteria for moral judgment. Instead, realism merely seeks to explain how the world works."

115 Weil, 1983, pp. 420 and 423: "At a time when international society needs more than ever a normative order capable of ensuring the peaceful coexistence, and cooperation in diversity, of equal and equally sovereign entities, the waning of voluntarism in favor of the ascendancy of some, neutrality in favor of ideology, positivity in favor of ill-defined values might well destabilize the whole international normative system and turn it into an instrument that can no longer serve its purpose."

116 Morgenthau, 1954, p. 20.

117 Scheuerman, 2008, p. 56.

to change the status quo by the use or threat of force. Such enforcement can either be done through a centralized system of collective security or be of a more decentralized nature based on self-help. Even if the regime on the use of force belongs to the latter category, it would not necessarily mean war in perpetuity because medium and small states may compensate their lack of power by joining alliances or bandwagoning with a stronger, adversarial power.[118] As explained earlier, there are few examples of disputes on the use of force settled by the ICJ, but these are examples of "interstate dispute settlement" using the terminology of Tallberg and McCall Smith, having been initiated by states.[119] This feature, and the fact that disputes may only be settled by the ICJ with the consent of states, weaken the regime.

Rules may still have relevance in a decentralized system if they represent a common understanding of states of what is acceptable behavior. Even if an aggressive state is not sanctioned for its behavior in terms of a military reaction from other states, other means of sanctioning are possible. Examples include severance of diplomatic relations, trade relations technology transfers and other exchanges.[120] Some have argued that the norms on the use of force lack any significance, illustrated by examples such as the Soviet/Warsaw Pact interventions in Hungary in 1956 and Czechoslovakia in 1968, which did not cause a military response from the US or NATO. However, the two interventions, arguably, led to a lower long-term economic and technological exchange between the West and East compared to a situation where the interventions had not happened, mainly to the detriment of Warsaw Pact bloc. Moreover, if one assumes that foreign policy is influenced by, and interacts with, domestic factors, the perceived aggression of a state may cause political difficulties at the domestic level in that state. The Iraq war of 2003 is such an example. Thus, perceived violations of the rules on the use of force may have consequences even for major powers. Boyles argues that during an international crisis, states rarely, if ever, sacrifice their vital national interests for considerations of international law or vice versa. This is because in situations of apparent conflict between the two, government decision-makers commence to define or redefine their vital national interests to include considerations of international law. Conversely, they define or redefine international law to take account of their vital national interests.[121] This is an interesting argument because it means that even if a state in the eyes of other states departs from international law, the rules will have a constraining effect.

If a regime on the use of force and its rules has an effect on state behavior, what rules should be included? For example, should the regime permit the use of force in anticipatory or preventive self-defense? In relation to this question

118 Waltz, 1979, p. 17.

119 Tallberg and McCall Smith, 2012, p. 5, who also describe the ICJ as interstate dispute settlement. See section 1.2.1.3 on delegation.

120 Arend, 1999, pp. 30–32.

121 Boyle, 1985, p. 79.

of what the law ought to be, international relations scholars have different tools than legal scholars. One of the most important ideas in international relations is that the system is not entirely stable because insecure states—while not being aggressors—may, through measures intended to increase their own security, decrease the security of other states.[122] Reciprocity is the key component of game theory[123] and thus also relevant for the security dilemma theory and the law on the use of force.[124] The key to maintain compliant behavior when it comes to the use of force is the ability and willingness to devote resources far out of proportion to the stakes of the current issue in order to maintain the perception that rules will be enforced in the current dispute and future disputes.[125]

The security dilemma theory and the broader spiral model constitute a valuable theory on war and peace via interaction. They capture general dynamics leading to the outbreak of war and the maintenance of peace—that is, by reversing or alleviating the security dilemma.[126] Let us consider the nuclear arms race during the Cold War or the tensions between Israel and Iran and the controversial doctrine of preventive self-defense explained in section 7.2.2. If preventive self-defense is permissible, all states involved could make a reasonable argument that they have the legal right to strike the opposing state first as a measure of self-defense, with no requirement that there has to be an instant and overwhelming threat from the opposing party. This would, arguably, negate the attempts and function of the regime to create order (the assumption in section 7.1). In this way, international relations theory can be used to motivate the design of a regime and its specific rules. Shiping notes that security dilemma theory and the broader spiral model have been (and, arguably, should be) deployed for prescribing policies for some of the most pressing challenges in international politics, including managing arms races, designing a lasting peace to ethnic conflicts, and avoiding a possible conflict between a rising China and the US as the reigning hegemon.[127] Such use of the security dilemma theory and the broader spiral model should, arguably, not be limited to designing policies, but it should also be used in the design of legal institutions and when describing the rationale behind norms. A realist would probably be skeptical towards such attempts, while a liberal would argue that regimes may alleviate the security dilemma.[128] The constructivist

122 Herz, John, 'Idealist Internationalism and the Security Dilemma', 2 *World Politics* (1950) 157–180, p. 157; Jervis, 1976, p. 76; Jervis, 1978, pp. 169 and 186; Ullman, Richard H., 'Redefining Security', 8 *International Security* (1983) 129–153, pp. 132–133.

123 Axelrod, 1984, pp. 3–20.

124 Axelrod, 1984, p. 4.

125 Compare with Axelrod, 1984, p. 155.

126 Shiping, Tang, 'The Security Dilemma: A Conceptual Analysis', 18 *Security Studies* (2009) 587–623, p. 588.

127 Ibid, pp. 588–589.

128 Doyle, Michael W., 'Kant, Liberal Legacies, and Foreign Affairs', 12 *Philosophy & Public Affairs* (1983) 205–235, pp. 205–235 and 230–232.

may perceive the security dilemma as one of the channels through which reshaping identity can remake anarchy.[129]

Those who view international law as devoid of non-instrumental significance or prescriptive worth argue that the instances when states have adhered to the UN Charter are better explained by the low cost of compliance, rather than state-internalization of international law. Even if one perceives the law on the use of force as merely rhetoric, international law serves to limit the range of legal and political arguments politicians, diplomats and legal experts use. International law also offers a framework of evaluating state conduct. Even when states use a force in a manner which is widely regarded as illegal, they use international law arguments as a means of legitimizing their action and thus it represents a limit.[130] For example, in relation to the US-led invasion of Iraq in 2003, the US and UK governments made elaborate arguments based on self-defense and the validity of decade-old UN resolutions.[131] Similarly, Russia went to great length in its illegal annexation of Crimea in 2014 to argue that the "green men" taking control of various buildings were "local self-defense forces" and not Russian troops,[132] contradicted by various international observers and later by President Putin himself.[133] Although these two examples may expose a disregard for international law, they also illustrate that even in the act of violation, states still relate to international law, which in turn sets boundaries on how to use force.

129 Wendt, 1992, pp. 407 and 416–417; Shiping, 2009, p. 588.

130 Rodley and Başak, 2010, pp. 230–231.

131 'A case for war – Lord Goldsmith's published advice on the legal basis for the use of force against Iraq' *The Guardian* (17 March 2003), available at www.theguardian.com/world/2003/mar/17/iraq2 (accessed 26 October 2014).

132 'Russia says cannot order Crimean "self-defense" units back to base' *Reuters* (5 March 2014), available at www.reuters.com/article/2014/03/05/us-ukraine-crisis-lavrov-spain-idUSBREA240NF20140305 (accessed 26 October 2014). 'Crimea crisis: Russian President Putin's speech annotated' *BBC* (19 March 2014), available at www.bbc.com/news/world-europe-26652058 (accessed 26 October 2014).

133 'Putin admits Russian forces were deployed to Crimea' *Reuters* (17 April 2014), available at http://uk.reuters.com/article/2014/04/17/russia-putin-crimea-idUKL6N0N921H20140417 (accessed 26 October 2014); 'Putin acknowledges Russian military serviceman were in Crimea' *Russia Today* (17 April 2014), available at http://rt.com/news/crimea-defense-russian-soldiers-108/ (accessed 26 October 2014).

8 Reconciling international law and international relations

8.1 Function of regimes

The assumption has been that regimes (and international law) exist as a response to social needs, also expressed as function, interests or objectives. Interstate cooperation is more likely to occur if states have significant common interest and common values. The main objectives of the surveyed regimes vary from liberalization of trade, environmental protection, human rights, ending impunity for international crimes to international order through peace. All of the regimes have rules with a broad support, manifested through treaties with many state parties, customary international law (which is based on state practice and the *opinio juris* of states) or both. Other objectives may, under certain circumstances, reinforce or restrain the effect of these regimes. State sovereignty, for example, plays a role in all of the surveyed regimes. It follows from state sovereignty that states are free to define the terms upon which they allow access to their market for foreign goods, a potential restraint on liberalization of trade.[1] The assumption in international environmental law is that states have the sovereign right to exploit their own resources pursuant to their own environmental policies, which may collide with international environmental concerns. Sovereignty and human rights are normally portrayed as fundamentally opposed. However, the state is also the primary guardian of human rights. Turning to the cooperation of states with international criminal tribunals and courts, loopholes have been created for national security information, potentially acting as a restraint to the objective of ending impunity.[2] Lastly, the concept of self-defense is closely intertwined with the concept of state sovereignty, they are mutually reinforcing.

Considering that states appear to share certain values, one may speak of a community or a society of states.[3] However, cooperation and community does not equal total harmony. Harmony requires complete identity of interests,

1 Zamora, 1989, p. 34; Langlet, 2009, p. 217. See section 3.2.1 on the degree to which World Trade Organization rules are obligatory.
2 ICTY RPE, rule 54 *bis* (e); MICT RPE, rule 56(e). See section 6.2.2 on the precision of the rules.
3 Compare with Bull, 1977, pp. 5–6.

while cooperation takes place in situations that contain a mix of conflicting and complementary interests.[4]

This book approaches the relevance of international law on state behavior in two ways. The first approach is to measure legalization in different dimensions (obligation, precision, delegation and state acceptance), which may appear somewhat formalistic. The second approach where different mechanisms are examined partly overlaps with first when it comes to delegation. These findings are summarized below.

8.2 Degree of legalization

The surveyed regimes expose different variations in the dimensions of obligation, precision, delegation and state acceptance.

The obligations within all of the five regimes are subject to exceptions. A key question is who decides whether it is the general rules or the exceptions that are applicable in a given situation and how such decisions are enforced. Schmitt's definition of the sovereign is "he who decides on the exception".[5] In a decentralized system based on self-help, this is the state. When questions on interpretation and enforcement are delegated to a central institution (e.g. a court), that institution assumes the relevant powers that are normally associated with the state in this area. The difference between the surveyed regimes is thus not obligation, precision and the existence of exceptions, but rather who decides on the obligations and exceptions. This insight is crucial in understanding legalization of regimes.

As indicated in section 1.2.1.5, Abbott and others argue that the WTO and the ICC correspond to situations of the near ideal type of full legalization. They do not explicitly mention the regime on the use of force, but they do mention situations of anarchy where international relations scholars tend to place such matters. This study made two amendments to the typology suggested by Abbott and others: (a) obligation should be perceived as binary dimension and not as a continuum use of an additional criterion; and (b) a fourth dimension was added, namely acceptance of states.[6] One consequence is that the assessment of the ICC should be changed. Considering its consent-based nature and the absence of the major powers, it is a weaker regime compared to the finding of Abbott and others and, as such, should be notated as (o, P, D, a).[7] If it is considered that the criminal acts under the jurisdiction of the Court are of customary nature, this designation could be changed to (O), but in relation to state cooperation which primarily concerns state parties, it should be designed as (o). By comparison, the WTO lacks a prosecutorial

4 Axelrod and Keohane, 1986, p. 226.

5 Schmitt, 1922/1934, pp. 5–7; Koskenniemi, 2001, p. 428.

6 Jervis, 1978, pp. 194 and 199–209; Jervis, 1983, pp. 173–176; Abbott et al., 2001, p. 20. See sections 1.2 on how to compare legal regimes, 1.2.1.1 on obligations and 1.2.1.4 on acceptance of states.

7 For notations, see section 1.2.1.5 on variations of international legalization.

entity and, as such, it has a weaker dispute settlement mechanism. However, this is compensated by its broad membership, including the major powers. The broad membership also compensates for the fact that the rules are only treaty based and not supported by customary international law, giving it a grade of (o, P, d, A). International environmental protection consists of several sub-regimes with various degrees of legalization. UNCLOS is strong in its broad membership, while the Kyoto Protocol is weaker because major polluters, such as China and the US, are under no obligation to cut emissions. In China's case, this is because it was classed as a developing country when the Protocol was drafted, and the US is not a state party. Environmental concerns are often balanced against other interests, which makes the obligations less precise. UNCLOS contains mechanisms for dispute settlement, but they remain to be proven efficient. In other environmental areas, international dispute settlement and enforcement is even weaker. Although participation is broad, the composite regime is graded (o, p, d, A). Considering that the core human rights are not only subject to wide codification and ratification in treaties, but also have the status of international customary law, the regime on human rights is strong in obligation. The main challenge with human rights law is not the high level of state acceptance, which is manifested in the wide ratification of various treaties, but that it becomes weaker in precision, as there are several ways of making exceptions and imposing limits. The level of delegation varies, where some regional regimes, in particular in Europe, are strong. The human rights regime is thus graded (O, p, d, A). The regime on the use of force is strong in obligation and state acceptance, but weak in precision and delegation (O, p, -, A). It is for the P-5 to control the UN Security Council and the body is highly politicized. The basic principle that makes decentralization inevitable when it comes to the use of force is to be found in the principle of sovereignty.[8] A realist would argue that, "the most basic motive driving states is survival … each state in the international system aims to guarantee its own survival",[9] and is unwilling to delegate this to others. The weak dispute settlement mechanism in the regime on the use of force does not mean that the states inevitably are bound for armed conflict. Norms may still be relevant, as states seek to legitimize their actions through legal norms, which drive them into norm-abiding behavior. The principle of reciprocity works in the same direction.

To summarize, the WTO regime is, arguably, the least politicized and most legalized of the five regimes surveyed, followed in descending order by the regimes on international criminal justice, human rights, environmental protection, while the regime on the use of force is the most politicized. This corresponds well with the assumption in sections 2.1.1 and 2.3 that technical areas are, to a greater extent, legalized, while areas of high politics are less legalized. However, reviewing criteria such as obligation, precision,

8 Morgenthau, 1954, p. 286.
9 Mearsheimer, 1994, pp. 10 and 11.

delegation and state acceptance does not necessarily give us the correct picture. The abovementioned criteria do not fully account for mechanisms such as reciprocity and socialization. In this way, a better explanation may be found as to why states appear to comply with the law even when it comes to areas which are highly politicized.

8.3 Uncovering mechanisms for the creation and enforcement of international law

This book examines how international law may be relevant and influences the course of international relations focusing on the operation of five regimes. Based on this analysis, some observations can be made in relation to mechanisms of creating and enforcing international law. There are clear reasons why different regimes need to be designed differently. The principle of reciprocity operates well or at least to some degree in certain areas, such as trade and the use of force. It works less well in relation to human rights law because a violation by a state of the rights of its own inhabitants does not ordinarily infringe on the national interests of other parties to the agreement. The principle of reciprocity is equally weak in relation to problems concerning international public goods because states cannot isolate their actions toward one state from another, for example in restraining the size of fishing catches in the high seas or air pollution. Institutions may provide a means to facilitate discrimination.[10] Under certain conditions, the principle of reciprocity may operate as a crude form of law enforcement in the field of international criminal justice.[11] However, reciprocity may, to some extent, apply if human rights, international criminal justice and environmental protection are linked to other areas, for example trade or economic aid.

Where the principle of reciprocity is weak in certain areas, other mechanisms may be necessary in order to promote compliance and change state behavior. This becomes obvious in relation to environmental protection, human rights and international criminal justice, where domestic institutions and NGOs have a key role. The spiral model of Risse, Ropp and Sikkink explains how even oppressive governments may entrap themselves in the human rights discourse by engaging in discourses involving communication, argumentation and persuasion.[12] Entrapment in the human rights discourse may appear irrational. Explanations for this irrational behavior include that governments miscalculate, are bribed or are under socialization.[13] States consenting to international criminal justice institutions, such as the ICC, may also appear irrational and this behavior can be explained in the same way. However, such behavior may still be rational. Simmons and Danner

10 Snidal, 1986, pp. 53–54. See section 1.3.1 on reciprocity.
11 Cryer et al., 2010, p. 422.
12 Risse and Sikkink, 1999, pp. 11–35; Risse and Ropp, 1999, pp. 255–256.
13 Risse and Sikkink, 1999, p. 27; Simmons, 2013, pp. 48–52.

suggest and find evidence that some governments rationally use the ICC to tie their own hands as they make tentative steps toward conflict resolution.[14] Moreover, processes of persuasion and socialization may better explain why states, for expressive reasons in order to obtain legitimacy, create and ratify treaties on human rights, international criminal justice and environmental protection. This may either be a rational process or through socialization.[15] If power to influence is seen solely in material and economic terms, the role of NGOs is weak. However, if power includes possession of status, information and communication skills, NGOs may, to a greater extent, mobilize support for their values and exercise influence over governments. The ability of international NGOs to exercise influence will vary according to the regime and issues involved in a given policy problem.[16]

8.4 Asymmetrical distribution of power

Based on the above, it is argued that variations in the degree of legalization between different regimes concern, to a lesser extent, whether states have consented to legal obligations but, rather, on who has the power to interpret and enforce the obligations (i.e. delegation). The design of the dispute settlement mechanism, the distribution of power of states and expression of common interest of the surveyed regimes represent shared values or a collective identity.[17]

Asymmetrical distribution of power among states is reflected in all five regimes to varying degrees. When it comes to trade, this asymmetrical distribution is manifested in how the rules are adopted and, to some degree, how they are implemented. Wealthy states have the power and capacity to impose trade sanctions and to withstand them, to withhold MFN status or not to care whether the status is granted.[18] The regime design for the "Area" symbolizes an effort to compensate for the asymmetrical distribution of power, more specifically economical and technical resources. The Kyoto Protocol, to some degree, attempts to compensate for asymmetries by imposing different levels of obligations on states, but it also exposes weaknesses, most notably by the fact that China and the US, the biggest polluters, have no obligations to reduce their emissions. The debate between universalism and cultural relativism in relation to human rights law may also be perceived as a consequence of asymmetrical distribution of power where the West seeks to impose its values and interests on the developing world. Turning to international criminal

14 Simmons and Danner, 2008, p. 4.

15 Compare with Goodman and Jinks, 2004, p. 631.

16 Willetts, Peter, 'Transnational actors and international organizations in global politics' in Baylis, John, Smith, Steve and Oqwens, Patricia (eds), *The Globalization of World Politics* (5th edn, Oxford: Oxford University Press, 2011), pp. 326–342, p. 339.

17 Tallberg and McCall Smith, 2012, p. 18–20. Compare with Keohane et al., 2001, p. 74, who use three dimensions: independence, access and embeddedness.

18 Byers, 1999, p. 5.

justice, the situations investigated by the ICC may illustrate that the distribution of power plays a role in the operation of this regime.[19] It is highly unlikely that any citizens of the US, Russia or China will be subject to the Court's jurisdiction. The mentioned powers may also veto any UN Security Council referral of a situation in a non-state party to the Court. As Byers argues, "[p]ower derived from military strength gives some States the option of using force to impose their will, and the ability to resist the efforts of others to impose theirs".[20] However, as suggested earlier, "'anarchy' as employed by realists has nothing to do with conflict; rather it is an ordering principle, which says that the system comprises independent political units (states) that have no central authority above them".[21] To say that the international system is anarchic does not imply that it entirely lacks organization.[22]

8.5 International relations as the sociology of international law

This book argues that international relations—to the extent it considers the impact and relevance of legal rules—is the sociology of international law. By engaging in interdisciplinary collaboration, international law scholars may better explain whether and to what extent international law influences state behavior. This is important in order to clarify how the horizontal order of international law works differently from the vertical order of domestic systems. Even in domestic systems with powerful governments, not all rules are enforced in each and every instance. However, to be an effective legal system, a majority of the objects governed must comply with the rules.[23] As Henkin argues, although there is no international "government", there is an international "society".[24] Interdisciplinary collaboration may also be a means to manage and distinguish between *de lege lata*—what the law is—from *de lege ferenda*—what the law should be. Legal scholars engage themselves in analysis both in relation to *de lege lata* and *de lege ferenda*. While lawyers have the tools to establish what the law is, it is not obvious that legal training in isolation offers systematic and appropriate means of suggesting what the law should be. In relation to the latter, other social sciences such as economics, international relations and history may offer more suitable tools and perspectives.

As a legal scholar, some caution is warranted against using methods from other fields in social science. This book examines to what extent international law can influence state behavior and treats this as a matter that can be tested with empirical methods. Several of the inquiries described in the book involve quantitative methods and correlations between different variables.

19 See section 6.2.4 on state acceptance.
20 Byers, 1999, p. 5.
21 Mearsheimer, 1994, p. 10.
22 Axelrod and Keohane, 1986, p. 226.
23 Axelrod, 1984, p. 155.
24 Henkin, 1979, p. 14.

Quantitative methods that show correlation between treaty commitment and state behavior do not necessarily prove a causal relationship. However, they can eliminate many alternative explanations that initially appear to be more powerful explanations. Quantitative methods may also be used to identify interesting individual cases which can be studied more in-depth in order to uncover causal mechanisms.

It is possible to reconcile international law scholarship and international relations. The mainstream academic approaches of the two disciplines have, by tradition, either emphasized politics, power or law. To argue that international relations may function as the sociology of international law may appear provocative. However, as Goldstein and others argue, law is embedded in politics, and affected by political interests, power and institutions. International law cannot be understood in isolation from politics. Conversely, law and legalization affect political processes and political outcomes. The relationship between law and politics is reciprocal, mediated by institutions.[25] The primary object of study is the same as that analyzed in international relations, namely states and their relationships. It is the methods and aims that differ. While legal scholars focus on the prescriptive and technical, the concern of international relations is, rather, explanatory and descriptive. They should not been seen as two competitive narratives but, rather, as complementary.[26]

25 Goldstein et al., 2001, p. 3; Hafner-Burton, Victor and Lupu, 2012, p. 48. See also Klabbers, 1996, p. 170.

26 Dunoff and Pollack, 2013, pp. 4–5.

Bibliography

Abbott, Andrew and DeViney, Stanley, 'The Welfare State as Transnational Event: Evidence from Sequences of Policy Adoption', 16 *Social Science History* (1992) 245–274.

Abbott, Kenneth W. et al., 'The Concept of Legalization' in Goldstein, Judith L. et al. (eds), *Legalization and World Politics* (Cambridge, MA and London: MIT Press, 2001), pp. 17–35.

Abbott, Kenneth W. and Snidal, Duncan, 'Hard and Soft Law' in Goldstein, Judith L. et al. (eds), *Legalization and World Politics* (Cambridge, MA and London: MIT Press, 2001), pp. 37–72.

Adamson, Fiona B. and Sriram, Chandra Lekha, 'Perspectives in International Law in International Relations' in Başak, Çali (ed), *International Law for International Relations* (Oxford: Oxford University Press, 2010), pp. 25–45.

Ahmedi, Idris, *The Remaking of American Strategy toward Iran and Iraq: Outline of a Theory of Foreign Policy Change* (Stockholm: Stockholm University, 2013).

Allee, Todd L. and Scalera, Jamie E., 'The Divergent Effects of Joining International Organizations: Trade Gains and the Rigors of WTO Accession', 66 *International Organization* (2012) 243–276.

Amnéus, Diana, *Responsibility to Protect by Military Means – Emerging Norms on Humanitarian Intervention?* (Stockholm: Stockholm University, 2008).

Arend, Anthony C., *Legal Rules and International Society* (New York, NY and Oxford: Oxford University Press, 1999).

Armstrong, David, Farrell, Theo and Lambert, Hélène, *International Law and International Relations* (2nd edn, Cambridge: Cambridge University Press, 2012).

Art, Robert J. and Waltz, Kenneth, 'The Fungiblity of Force' in Art, Robert J. (ed), *The Use of Force: Military Power and International Politics* (6th edn, Lanham, MD, Boulder, CO, New York, NY, Toronto and Oxford: Rowman & Littlefield Publishers, 2004), pp. 3–22.

Aust, Anthony, *Handbook of International Law* (Cambridge: Cambridge University Press, 2005).

Axelrod, Robert, *The Evolution of Cooperation* (New York, NY: Basic Books, 1984).

Axelrod, Robert and Keohane, Robert O., 'Achieving Cooperation Under Anarchy: Strategies and Institutions' in Oye, Kenneth A. (ed), *Cooperation Under Anarchy* (Princeton, NJ: Princeton University Press, 1986), pp. 226–254.

Barrett, Scott, 'Economic Theory of Environmental Law' in Bodansky, Daniel, Brunnée, Jutta and Hey, Ellen (eds), *The Oxford Handbook of International Environmental Law* (Oxford: Oxford University Press, 2007), pp. 231–261.

Başak, Çali, 'International Human Rights Law' in Başak, Çali (ed), *International Law for International Relations* (Oxford: Oxford University Press, 2010), pp. 281–305.
Başak, Çali, 'International Law for International Relations: Foundations for Interdisciplinary Study' in Başak, Çali (ed), *International Law for International Relations* (Oxford: Oxford University Press, 2010), pp. 3–24.
Beach, Derek and Brun Pedersen, Rasmus, *Process-Tracing Methods. Foundations and Guidelines* (Ann Arbor, MI: The University of Michigan Press, 2013).
Bearce, David H. and Omori, Sawa 'How Do Commercial Institutions Promote Peace?', 42 *Journal of Peace Research* (2005) 659–678.
Beardsley, Kyle, 'Agreement Without Peace? International Mediation and Time Inconsistency Problems', 52 *American Journal of Political Science* (2008) 723–740.
Beardsley, Kyle, *The Mediation Dilemma* (Ithaca, NY: Cornell University Press, 2011).
Beardsley, Kyle, 'UN Intervention and the Duration of International Crises', 49 *Journal of Peace Research* (2012) 335–349.
Beckman, Olof, *Armed Intervention: Pursuing Legitimacy and the Pragmatic Use of Legal Argument* (Lund: Lund University, 2005).
Benvenisti, Eyal, 'Margin of Appreciation, Consensus, and Universal Standards', 31 *International Law and Politics* (1999) 843–854.
Bergström, Sture et al., *Juridikens termer* (9th edn, Stockholm: Liber, 2002).
Bernauer, Thomas, 'The Effect of International Environmental Institutions: How We Might Learn More', 49 *International Organization* (1995) 351–377.
Berry, John W., 'Acculturation' in Grusec, Joan E. and Hastings, Paul D. (eds), *Handbook of Socialization: Theory and Research* (New York, NY: The Guildford Press, 2007), pp. 543–560.
Beveridge, Fiona, 'Feminist Perspectives in International Economic Law' in Buss, Doris and Manji, Ambreena (eds), *International Law: Modern Feminist Approaches* (Oxford: Hart Publishing, 2005), pp. 174–201.
Beyerlin, Ulrich, 'Different Types of Norms in International Environmental Law: Policies, Principles and Rules' in Bodansky, Daniel, Brunnée, Jutta and Hey, Ellen (eds), *The Oxford Handbook of International Environmental Law* (Oxford: Oxford University Press, 2007), pp. 425–448.
Boehmer, Charles, Gartzke, Erik and Nordstrom, Timothy, 'Do Intergovernmental Organizations Promote Peace?', 57 *World Politics* (2004) 1–38.
Bohlander, Michael, 'The Influence of Academic Research on the Jurisprudence of the International Criminal Tribunal for the Former Yugoslavia – A first overview', 3 *The Global Community Yearbook of International Law and Jurisprudence* (2003) 195–209.
Bowie, Robert R., *Suez 1956: International Crises and the Role of Law* (London: Oxford University Press, 1974).
Bown, Chad P., 'Participation in WTO Dispute Settlement: Complainants, Interested Parties, and Free Riders', 19 *World Bank Economic Review* (2005) 287–310.
Boyle, Francis Anthony, *World Politics and International Law* (Durham, NC: Duke University Press, 1985).
Braithwaite, John and Drahos, Peter, *Global Business Regulation* (Cambridge: Cambridge University Press, 2000).
Bring, Ove, 'From Suez to Kosovo: A Dynamic View of Chapters VI to VIII of the UN Charter' in Bring, Ove (ed), *Internationell våldsanvändning och folkrätt* (Stockholm: Norstedts juridik, 2006), pp. 45–67.

Bring, Ove, Mahmoudi, Said and Wrange, Pål, *Sverige och folkrätten* (4th edn, Stockholm: Norstedts Juridik AB, 2011).

Brunnée, Jutta, 'Common Areas, Common Heritage, and Common Concern' in Bodansky, Daniel, Brunnée, Jutta and Hey, Ellen (eds), *The Oxford Handbook of International Environmental Law* (Oxford: Oxford University Press, 2007), pp. 550–573.

Bull, Hedley, *The Anarchical Society: A Study of Order in World Politics* (London: Macmillan, 1977).

Busch, Marc and Reinhardt, Eric, 'Bargaining in the Shadow of the Law: Early Settlement in GATT/WTO Disputes', 24 *Fordham International Law Journal* (2000) 158–172.

Busch, Marc, Reinhardt, Eric and Shaffer, Gregory, 'Does Legal Capacity Matter? A Survey of WTO Members', 8 *World Trade Review* (2009) 559–577.

Buss, Doris and Manji, Ambreena, 'Introduction' in Buss, Doris and Manji, Ambreena (eds), *International Law: Modern Feminist Approaches* (Oxford: Hart Publishing, 2005), pp. 1–16.

Buzan, Barry, 'From International System to International Society: Structural Realism and Regime Theory Meet the English School', 47 *International Organization* (1993) 327–352.

Byers, Michael, *Custom, Power and the Power of Rules: International Relations and Customary International Law* (Cambridge: Cambridge University Press, 1999).

Cappelletti, Mauro, *The Judicial Process in Comparative Perspective* (Oxford: Clarendon Press, 1989).

Cassese, Antonio, 'The Statute of the International Criminal Court: Some Preliminary Reflections', 10 *European Journal of International Law* (1999) 144–171.

Chandler, David, 'The Revival of Carl Schmitt in International Relations: The Last Refuge of Critical Theorists?', 37 *Journal of International Studies* (2008) 27–48.

Charney, Jonathan I., 'Is International Law Threatened by Multiple International Tribunals?', 271 *Recueil des Cours* (1998).

Chaumont, Charles M., 'La Signification du Principe de Spécialité des Organisations Internationales' in Rolin, Henri (ed), *Mélanges offerts à Henri Rolin Problèmes de droit de gens* (Paris: A. Pedone, 1964), pp. 55–66.

Chayes, Abram, *The Cuban Missile Crisis: International Crises and the Role of Law* (Lanham. MD: University Press of America, 1987 (originally published 1974)).

Chinkin, Christine, 'Sources' in Moeckli, Daniel, Shah, Sangeeta and Sivakumaran, Sandesh (eds), *International Human Rights Law* (Oxford: Oxford University Press, 2010), pp. 103–123.

Chinkin, Christine, Wright, Shelley and Charlesworth, Hilary, 'Feminist Approaches to International Law: Reflections from Another Century' in Buss, Doris and Manji, Ambreena (eds), *International Law: Modern Feminist Approaches* (Oxford: Hart Publishing, 2005), pp. 17–46.

Churchill, Robin and Lowe, Vaughan, *The Law of the Sea* (Manchester: Manchester University Press, 1999).

Ciampi, Annalisa, 'The Obligation to Cooperate' in Cassese, Antonio, Gaeta, Paola and Jones, John R.W.D (eds), *The Rome Statute of the International Criminal Court* (Oxford: Oxford University Press, 2002), pp. 1607–1638.

Ciampi, Annalisa, 'Other Forms of Cooperation' in Cassese, Antonio, Gaeta, Paola and Jones, John R.W.D (eds), *The Rome Statute of the International Criminal Court* (Oxford: Oxford University Press, 2002), pp. 1705–1747.

Clapham, Andrew, *Human Rights Obligations of Non-State Actors* (Oxford: Oxford University Press, 2006).

Cogan, Jacob Katz, 'International Criminal Courts and Fair Trials: Difficulties and Prospects', 27 *Yale Journal of International Law* (2002) 111–140.

Conybeare, John, 'Trade Wars: A Comparative Study of Angla-Hanse, Franco-Italian, and Hawley-Smoot Conflicts' in Oye, Kenneth A. (ed), *Cooperation Under Anarchy* (Princeton, NJ: Princeton University Press, 1986), pp. 147–172.

Cotterrell, Roger, *The Sociology of Law: An Introduction* (2nd edn, London, Dublin and Edinburgh: Butterworths, 1992).

Crawford, James, *Brownlie's Principles of Public International Law* (8th edn, Oxford: Oxford University Press, 2012).

Cronin-Furman, Kate, 'Managing Expectations: International Criminal Trials and the Prospects for Deterrence of Mass Atrocity', 7 *International Journal of Transitional Justice* (2013) 434–454.

Cryer, Robert et al., *An Introduction to International Criminal Law and Procedure* (2nd edn, Cambridge: Cambridge University Press, 2010).

Curzon, G. and Curzon, V., 'The Management of Trade Relations in the GATT' in Shonfield, A. (ed), *International Economic Relations of the Western World 1959–1971* (London: Oxford University Press, 1976), pp. 143–244.

D'Amato, Anthony, 'The Invasion of Panama Was a Lawful Response to Tyranny', 84 *American Journal of International Law* (1990) 516–524.

Damaška, Mirjan R., *The Faces of Justice and State Authority* (New Haven, CT and London: Yale University Press, 1986).

Danish, Kyle W., 'International Relations Theory' in Bodansky, Daniel, Brunnée, Jutta and Hey, Ellen (eds), *The Oxford Handbook of International Environmental Law* (Oxford: Oxford University Press, 2007), pp. 205–230.

Daujotas, Rimantas, 'Defining the Extent of NGO's Participation in the WTO', 3 *Organizational Forms ejournal* (2011).

Dawidowicz, Martin, 'Public Law Enforcement Without Public Law Safeguards? An Analysis of State Practice on Third-Party Countermeasures and Their Relationship to the UN Security Council', 77 *British Yearbook of International Law* (2006) 333–418.

Deitelhoff, Nicole, 'The Discursive Process of Legalization: Charting Islands of Persuasion in the ICC Case', 63 *International Organization* (2009) 33–65.

Diehl, Paul F., *International Peacekeeping* (Baltimore, MD: Johns Hopkins, 1993).

Donnelly, Jack, 'Human Rights' in Baylis, John, Smith, Steve and Owens, Patricia (eds), *The Globalization of World Politics* (5th edn, Oxford: Oxford University Press, 2011), pp. 494–509.

Downs, George W., Rocke, David M. and Barsoom, Peter N., 'Is the Good News about. Compliance Good News about Cooperation?', 50 *International Organization* (1996) 379–406.

Doyle, Michael W., 'Kant, Liberal Legacies, and Foreign Affairs', 12 *Philosophy & Public Affairs* (1983) 205–235.

Doyle, Michael W. and Sambanis, Nicholas, 'International Peacebuilding: A Theoretical and Quantitative Analysis', 94 *American Political Science Review* (2000) 779–801.

Doyle, Michael W. and Sambanis, Nicholas, *Making War and Building Peace: United Nations Peace Operations* (Princeton, NJ: Princeton University Press, 2006).

Dunoff, Jeffrey L. and Pollack, Mark A., 'What Can International Relations Learn from International Law?' *Temple University Legal Studies Research Paper No 2012–14* (2013).

Dutta, Pushan, Mihova, Ilian and Van Zandtb, Timothy 'The Effect of WTO on the Extensive and the Intensive Margins of Trade', 91 *Journal of International Economics* (2013) 204–219.

Ebbesson, Jonas, 'Public Participation' in Bodansky, Daniel, Brunnée, Jutta and Hey, Ellen (eds), *The Oxford Handbook of International Environmental Law* (Oxford: Oxford University Press, 2007), pp. 681–703.

Eide, Asbjörn, 'International Law, Dominance, and the Use of Force', 11 *Journal of Peace Research* (1974) 1–20.

Engle, Karen, 'International Human Rights and Feminsisms: When Discourses Keep Meeting' in Buss, Doris and Manji, Ambreena (eds), *International Law: Modern Feminist Approaches* (Oxford: Hart Publishing, 2005), pp. 47–66.

Esty, Daniel C., 'Non-Governmental organizations at the World Trade Organization: Cooperation, Competition or Exclusion', 1 *Journal of International Economic Law* (1998) 123–147.

Falk, Richard A., 'New Approaches to the Study of International Law', 61 *American Journal of International Law* (1967) 477–495.

Finlayson, Jock A. and Zacher, Mark W., 'The GATT and the Regulation of Trade Barriers: Regime Dynamics and Functions' in Krasner, Stephen D. (ed), *International Regimes* (Ithaca, NY and London: Cornell University Press, 1983), pp. 273–314.

Finnemore, Martha, 'International Organizations as Teachers of Norms: The United Nations Educational, Scientific, and Cultural Organization and Science Policy', 47 *International Organization* (1993) 565–597.

Fogdestam Agius, Maria, *Interaction and Delimitation of International Legal Orders* (Uppsala: Uppsala universitet 2013).

Footer, Mary, *An Institutional and Normative Analysis of the World Trade Organization* (Leiden and Boston, MA: Martinus Nijhoff, 2005).

Forsythe, David P., 'Human Rights Studies: On the Danges of Legalistic Asssumption' in Coomans, Fons, Grünfeld, Fred. and Kamminga, Menno T. (eds), *Methods of Human Rights Research* (Antwerp and Oxford: Intersentia, 2009), pp. 59–76.

Fortna, Virginia P., 'Inside and Out: Peacekeeping and the Duration of Peace after Civil and Interstate Wars', 5 *International Studies Review* (2003) 97–114.

Fortna, Virginia P., *Peace Time: Cease-Fire Agreements and the Durability of Peace* (Princeton, NJ: Princeton University Press, 2004).

Freestone, David and Salman, Salman M.A., 'Ocean and Freshwater Resources' in Bodansky, Daniel, Brunnée, Jutta and Hey, Ellen (eds), *The Oxford Handbook of International Environmental Law* (Oxford: Oxford University Press, 2007), pp. 337–361.

Gaeta, Paola, 'Official Capacity and Immunities' in Cassese, Antonio, Gaeta, Paola and Jones, John R.W.D (eds), *The Rome Statute of the International Criminal Court* (Oxford: Oxford University Press, 2002), pp. 975–1002.

Gardner, John, *Law as a Leap of Faith* (Oxford: Oxford University Press, 2012).

Gent, Stephen E. and Shannon, Megan, 'The Effectiveness of International Arbitration and Adjudication: Getting Into a Bind', 72 *The Journal of Politics* (2010) 366–380.

Gent, Stephen E. and Shannon, Megan, 'Decision Control and the Pursuit of Binding Conflict Management: Choosing the Ties that Bind', 55 *Journal of Conflict Resolution* (2011) 710–734.

Geny, François, *Méthode d'interprétation et sources en droit privé positif* (2nd edn, Paris: Librairie générale de droit & de jurisprudence, 1954).

George, Alexander L. and Bennett, Andrew, *Case Studies and Theory Development in the Social Sciences* (Cambridge, MA and London: MIT Press, 2005).

Gibson, Clark C., Williams, John T. and Ostrom, Elinor, 'Local Enforcement and Better Forests', 33 *World Development* (2005) 273–284.

Gilligan, Michael J., 'Is Enforcement Necessary for Effectiveness? A Model of the International Criminal Regime', 60 *International Organization* (2006) 935–967.

Gilligan, Michael J. and Sergenti, Ernest, 'Evaluating UN peacekeeping with matching methods to improve causal inference' (unpublished manuscript) Department of Politics, New York University (2006).

Ginsburg, Tom and Shaffer, Gregory, 'How Does International Law Work: What Empirical Research Shows' in Cane, Peter and Kritzer, Herbert (eds), *Oxford Handbook of Empirical Legal Studies* (Oxford: Oxford University Press, 2010), pp. 753–784.

Goertz, Gary and Diehl, Paul F., 'Toward a Theory of International Norms: Some Conceptual and Measurement Issues', 36 *Journal of Conflict Resolution* (1992) 634–664.

Goldsmith, Jack, 'The Self-Defeating International Criminal Court', 70 *University of Chicago Law Review* (2003) 89–104.

Goldstein, Judith L., Kahler, Miles and Keohane, Robert O., 'Introduction: Legalization and World Politics' in Goldstein, Judith L. et al. (eds), *Legalization and World Politics* (Cambridge, MA and London: MIT Press, 2001), pp. 1–15.

Goldstein, Judith L., Rivers, Douglas and Tomz, Michael, 'Institutions in International Relations: Understanding the Effects of the GATT and the WTO on World Trade', 61 *International Organization* (2007) 37–68.

Goodman, Ryan and Jinks, Derek, 'How to Influence States: Socialization and International Human Rights Law', 54 *Duke Law Journal* (2004) 621–703.

Granger, C.W.J., 'Investigating Causal Relations by Econometric Models and Cross-spectral Methods', 37 *Econometrica* (1969) 424–438.

Greig, J. Michael and Diehl, Paul F., 'The Peacekeeping-Peacemaking Dilemma', 49 *International Studies Quarterly* (2005) 621–645.

Gunnarsson, Åsa and Svensson, Eva-Maria, *Genusrättsvetenskap* (Lund: Studentlitteratur, 2009).

Guzman, Andrew, *How International Law Works: A Rational Choice Theory* (New York, NY: Oxford University Press, 2008).

Haas, Mark, 'The United States and the End of the Cold War: Reactions to Shifts in Soviet Power, Policies, or Domestic Politics?', 61 *International Organization* (2007) 145–179.

Hafner-Burton, Emilie M. and Tsutsui, Kiyoteru, 'Human Rights in a Globalizing World: The Paradox of Empty Promises', 110 *American Journal of Sociology* (2005) 1373–1411.

Hafner-Burton, Emilie M., Victor, David G. and Lupu, Yonatan, 'Political Science Research on International Law: The State of the Field', 106 *American Journal of International Law* (2012) 47–97.

Haftel, Yoram Z., 'Designing for Peace: Regional Integration Arrangements, Institutional Variation, and Militarized Interstate Disputes', 61 *International Organization* (2007) 217–237.

Halliday, T. and Osinsky, P., 'Globalization and Law', 32 *Annual Review of Sociology* (2006) 447–470.

Hathaway, Oona A., 'Do Human Rights Treaties Make a Difference?', 111 *Yale Law Journal* (2002) 1935–2042.

Hay, Ellen, 'International Institutions' in Bodansky, Daniel, Brunnée, Jutta and Hey, Ellen (eds), *The Oxford Handbook of International Environmental Law* (Oxford: Oxford University Press, 2007), pp. 749–769.

Heck, Philipp, *Begriffsbildung und Interessenjurisprudenz* (Tübingen: J.C.B. Mohr, 1932).

Helfer, Laurence R. and Slaughter, Anne-Marie, 'Toward a Theory of Effective Supranational Adjudication', 107 *Yale Law Journal* (1997) 273–391.

Henkin, Louis, *How Nations Behave* (2nd edn, New York, NY: Columbia University Press, 1979).

Herz, John, 'Idealist Internationalism and the Security Dilemma', 2 *World Politics* (1950) 157–180.

Higgins, Rosalyn, *Problems and Process: International Law and How We Use It* (Oxford: Oxford University Press, 1994).

Hirsch, Moshe, 'Game Theory, International Law, and Future Environmental Cooperation in the Middle East', 27 *Denver Journal of International Law & Policy* (1998) 75–119.

Holland, Paul, 'Statistics and Causal Inference', 81 *Journal of American Statistical Association* (1986) 945–960.

Hudec, Robert E., *Enforcing International Trade Law: The Evolution of the Modern GATT Legal System* (Salem, NH: Butterworth Legal Publisher, 1993).

Hume, David, *An Enquiry Concerning Human Understanding (1748)* (Oxford: Oxford University Press, 2007).

Hurrell, Andrew, 'International Society and the Study of Regimes: A Reflective Approach' in Rittberger, Volker (ed), *Regime Theory and International Relations* (Oxford: Clarendon, 1993), pp. 49–72.

Husa, Jaakko, 'Farewell to Functionalism or Methodological Tolerance?', 67 *Rabels Zeitschrift für ausländisches und internationales Privatrecht* (2003) 419–447.

Jacobson, Harold K., Reisinger, William M. and Mathers, Todd, 'National Entanglements in International Organizations', 80 *American Political Science Review* (1986) 141–159.

Jervis, Robert, *Perception and Misperception in International Politics* (Princetion, NJ: Princeton University Press, 1976).

Jervis, Robert, 'Cooperation Under the Security Dilemma', 30 *World Politics* (1978) 167–214.

Jervis, Robert, 'Security Regimes' in Krasner, Stephen D. (ed), *International Regimes* (Ithaca, NY and London: Cornell University Press, 1983), pp. 173–194.

Jervis, Robert, 'From Balance to Concert: A Study of International Security Cooperation' in Oye, Kenneth A. (ed), *Cooperation Under Anarchy* (Princeton, NJ: Princeton University Press, 1986), pp. 58–79.

Jhering, Rudolph von, *Der Zweck im Recht* (5th edn (printed 1916), Leipzig: Breitkopf und Härtel, 1877).

Jo, Hyeran and Simmons, Beth A., 'Can the International Criminal Court Deter Atrocity? An Analysis of Violence against Civilians in Civil Wars' (2015, forthcoming).

Johnson, Tana and Urpelainen, Johannes, 'A Strategic Theory of Regime Integration and Separation', 66 *International Organization* (2012) 645–677.

Kennedy, David, 'When Renewal Repeats: Thinking Against the Box', 32 *New York University Journal of International Law and Politics* (2000) 335–500.

Keohane, Robert O., 'The Demand for International Regimes' in Krasner, Stephen D. (ed), *International Regimes* (Ithaca, NY and London: Cornell University Press, 1983), pp. 141–171.

Keohane, Robert O., 'Reciprocity in International Relations', 40 *International Organization* (1986) 1–27.

Keohane, Robert O. and Martin, Lisa L., 'The Promise of Institutionalist Theory', 20 *International Security* (1995) 39–51.

Keohane, Robert O., Moravcsik, Andrew and Slaughter, Anne-Marie, 'Legalized Dispute Resolution: Interstate and Transnational' in Goldstein, Judith L. et al. (eds), *Legalization and World Politics* (Cambridge, MA and London: MIT Press, 2001), pp. 73–104.

Kettler, David, *Domestic Regimes, The Rule of Law, and Democratic Social Change* (Berlin: Galda and Wilch, 2001).

Kim, Hunjoon and Sikkink, Kathryn, 'Explaining the Deterrence Effect of Human Rights Prosecutions for Transitional Countries', 54 *International Studies Quarterly* (2010) 939–963.

Kim, Myeong Hwan, 'Does the WTO Promote Trade? Further Evidence', 19 *The Journal of International Trade & Economic Development* (2010) 421–437.

Klabbers, Jan, 'Redundancy of Soft Law', 65 *Nordic Journal of International Law* (1996) 167–182.

Klabbers, Jan, 'The Relative Autonomy of International Law or the Forgotten Politics of Interdisciplinarity', 1 *Journal of International Law & International Relations* (2004) 35–48.

Klabbers, Jan, 'Compliance Procedures' in Bodansky, Daniel, Brunnée, Jutta and Hey, Ellen (eds), *The Oxford Handbook of International Environmental Law* (Oxford: Oxford University Press, 2007), pp. 995–1009.

Klabbers, Jan, *An Introduction to International Institutional Law* (2nd edn, Cambridge: Cambridge University Press, 2009).

Klamberg, Mark, *Evidence in International Criminal Trials: Confronting Legal Gaps and the Reconstruction of Disputed Events* (Leiden: Martinus Nijhoff Publishers, 2013).

Klami, Hannu Tapani, Alexy, Robert and Bergholtz, Gunnar, 'A Note on Heuristics, Justification and Argument' in Aarnio, Aulis (ed), *Justice, Morality and Society A Tribute to Aleksander Peczenik on the Occasion of his Birthday 16 November 1997* (Lund: Juristförlaget, 1997), pp. 211–220.

Knoops, Geert-Jan Alexander, *Theory and Practice of International and Internationalized Criminal Proceedings* (The Hague: Kluwer Law International, 2005).

Koh, Harold Hongju, 'Why Do Nations Obey International Law?', 106 *The Yale Law Journal* (1997) 2599–2659.

Koremenos, Barbara, 'Contracting Around International Uncertainty', 99 *American Political Science Review* (2005) 549–565.

Koremenos, Barbara, 'If Only Half of International Agreements Have Dispute Resolution Provisions, Which Half Needs Explaining?', 36 *Journal of Legal Studies* (2007) 189–212.

Koskenniemi, Martti, *The Gentle Civilizer of Nations: The Rise and Fall of International Law 1870–1960* (Cambridge: Cambridge University Press, 2001).

Koskenniemi, Martti, 'The Empire(s) of International Law: System Change and Legal Transformation', 8 *Austrian Review of International and European Law* (2003) 61–68.

Koskenniemi, Martti, *From Apology to Utopia: The Structure of International Legal Argument* (reissue, New York, NY: Cambridge University Press, 2005).

Koskenniemi, Martti, 'Hegemonic Regime' in Young, Margaret A. (ed), *Regime Interaction in International Law Facing Fragmentation* (Cambridge University Press, 2012), pp. 305–324.

Krasner, Stephen D., 'Structural Causes and Regime Consequences: Regimes as Intervening Variables' in Krasner, Stephen D. (ed), *International Regimes* (Ithaca, NY and London: Cornell University Press, 1983), pp. 1–21.

Kreß, Claus, 'The International Criminal Court and Immunities under International Law for States Not Party to the Court's Statute' in Bergsmo, Morten and Yan, Ling (eds), *State Sovereignty and International Criminal Law* (Beijing: Torkel Opsahl Academic EPublisher, 2012), pp. 223–265.

Kreß, Claus and Prost, Kimberly, 'Article 87 – Request for Cooperation: General Provisions' in Triffterer, Otto (ed), *Commentary on the Rome Statute of the International Criminal Court* (2nd edn, München, Oxford and Baden-Baden: C.H. Beck/Hart/Nomos, 2008), pp. 1517–1531.

Ku, Julian and Nzelibe, Jide, 'Do International Criminal Tribunals Deter or Exacerbate Humanitarian Atrocities?', 84 *Washington University Law Quarterly* (2006) 777–833.

Kupchan, Charles A. and Kupchan, Clifford A., 'The Promise of Collective Security', 20 *International Security* (1995) 52–61.

Landman, Todd, 'Measuring Human Rights: Principle, Practice, and Policy', 26 *Human Rights Quarterly* (2004) 906–931.

Landman, Todd, 'Social Science Methods and Human Rights' in Coomans, Fons, Grünfeld, Fred, and Kamminga, Menno T. (eds), *Methods of Human Rights Research* (Antwerp and Oxford: Intersentia, 2009), pp. 19–44.

Langlet, David, *Prior Informed Consent and Hazardous Trade: Regulating Trade in Hazardous Goods at the Intersection of Sovereignty, Free Trade and Environmental Protection* (Alphen aan den Rijn: Kluwer Law International, 2009).

Lauterpacht, Hersch, *The Function of Law in the International Community* (originally published Oxford: Clarendon Press, 1933; Clark, NJ: The Lawbook Exchange, 2000).

Lehrberg, Bert, *Praktisk juridisk metod* (Uppsala: I.B.A., 2006).

Lindblom, Anna-Karin, *The Legal Status of Non-Governmental Organizations in International Law* (Uppsala: Uppsala University, 2001).

Little, Richard, 'International regimes' in Baylis, John, Smith, Steve and Owens, Patricia (eds), *The Globalization of World Politics* (5th edn, Oxford: Oxford University Press, 2011), pp. 294–307.

Loibl, Herhard, 'International Economic Law' in Evans, Malcolm D. (ed), *International Law* (3rd edn, Oxford: Oxford University Press, 2010), pp. 722–751.

MacCormick, Neil, *Legal Reasoning and Legal Theory* (Oxford: Clarendon Press, 1978).

Mahmoudi, Said, 'International Use of Force: Quo Vadis?', 15 *Juridisk Tidsskrift* (2003) 341–358.

Mahmoudi, Said, 'Self-Defence and International Terrorism', 48 *Scandinavian Studies in Law* (2006) 203–214.
Malanczuk, Peter, *Akehurst's Modern Introduction to International Law* (7th rev edn, London and New York, NY: Routledge, 1997).
Martines, Francesca, 'Legal Status and Powers of the Court' in Cassese, Antonio, Gaeta, Paola and Jones, John R.W.D (eds), *The Rome Statute of the International Criminal Court* (Oxford: Oxford University Press, 2002), pp. 203–218.
Mathias, Eric and Spencer, J.R., 'The Balance of Power between the Police and the Public Prosecutor' in Delmas-Marty, M. (ed), *European Criminal Procedures* (Cambridge: Cambridge University Press, 2005), pp. 459–487.
Maton, John and Maton, Carolyn, 'Independence under Fire: Extra-Legal Pressures and Coalition Building in WTO Dispute Settlement', 10 *Journal of International Economic Law* (2007) 317–334.
May, Richard and Wierda, Marieke, *International Criminal Evidence* (New York, NY: Transnational Publishers, 2002).
McDougal, Myres, 'International Law, Power, and Policy: A Contemporary Conception', 82 *Collected Courses of the Hague Academy of International Law (Recueil des Cours Académie de Droit International de La Haye)* (1953) 137–259.
Mearsheimer, John J., 'The False Promise of International Institutions', 19 *International Security* (1994) 5–49.
Merry, Sally Engle, 'Transnational Human Rights and Local Activism: Mapping the Middle', 108 *American Anthropologist* (2006) 38–51.
Mitchell, Ronald B., 'Compliance Theory' in Bodansky, Daniel, Brunnée, Jutta and Hey, Ellen (eds), *The Oxford Handbook of International Environmental Law* (Oxford: Oxford University Press, 2007), pp. 893–921.
Mitchell, Ronald B. and Keilbach, Patricia M., 'Situation Structure and Institutional Design: Reciprocity, Coercion, and Exchange', 55 *International Organization* (2001) 891–917.
Morgenthau, Hans J., 'Positivism, Functionalism, and International Law', 34 *American Journal of International Law* (1940) 260–284.
Morgenthau, Hans J., *Politics Among Nations* ((1st edn published 1948) 2nd edn, New York, NY: Alfred A. Knopf, 1954).
Morrow, James D., 'The Institutional Features of Prisoner of War Treaties', 55 *International Organization* (2001) 971–991.
Morrow, James D., 'When Do States Follow the Laws of War?', 101 *American Political Science Review* (2007) 559–572.
Mundis, Daryl, 'Reporting Non-Compliance' in May, Richard et al. (eds), *Essays on ICTY Procedure and Evidence: In Honour of Gabrielle Kirk McDonald* (The Hague: Kluwer Law International, 2001), pp. 421–438.
Mutua, Makau, *Human Rights: A Political and Cultural Critique (Pennsylvania Studies in Human Rights)* (Philadelphia, PA: University of Pennsylvania Press, 2002).
Navari, Cornelia, 'Liberalisms' in Williams, Paul D. (ed), *Security Studies – An Introduction* (2nd edn, London and New York, NY: Routledge, 2013), pp. 32–47.
Niemetz, Martin Daniel, 'Empowering Civil Society: How to Increase the Input of NGOs into Security Council Deliberation', 6 *Journal of Human Rights Practice* (2014) 69–88.
Nikolic-Ristanovic, Vesna, 'Sexual Violence, International Law and Restorative Justice' in Buss, Doris and Manji, Ambreena (eds), *International Law: Modern Feminist Approaches* (Oxford: Hart Publishing, 2005), pp. 273–293.

Oneal, John R. et al., 'The Liberal Peace: Interdependence, Democracy, and International Conflict, 1950–1985', 33 *Journal of Peace Research* (1996) 11–28.

Oneal, John R. and Russett, Bruce, 'The Classical Liberals Were Right: Democracy, Interdependence, and Conflict, 1950–1985', 41 *International Studies Quarterly* (1997) 267–294.

Oneal, John R., Russett, Bruce and Berbaum, Michael L., 'Causes of Peace: Democracy, Interdependence, and International Organizations, 1886–1992', 47 *International Studies Quarterly* (2003) 371–393.

Otto, Dianne, 'Disconserting 'Masculinities': Reinventing the Gendered Subject(s) of International Human Rights Law' in Buss, Doris and Manji, Ambreena (eds), *International Law: Modern Feminist Approaches* (Oxford: Hart Publishing, 2005), pp. 105–129.

Oye, Kenneth A., 'Explaining Cooperation under Anarchy: Hypotheses and Strategies' in Oye, Kenneth A. (ed), *Cooperation Under Anarchy* (Princeton, NJ: Princeton University Press, 1986), pp. 1–24.

Palmer, Vernon Valentine, 'From Lerotholi to Lando: Some Examples of Comparative Law Methodology', 53 *American Journal of Comparative Law* (2005) 261–290.

Pauwelyn, Joost and Elsig, Manfred, 'The Politics of Treaty Interpretation: Variations and Explanations Across International Tribunals' in Dunoff, Jeffrey L. and Pollack, Mark A. (eds), *Interdisciplinary Perspectives on International Law and International Relations: The State of the Art* (Cambridge: Cambridge University Press, 2013), pp. 445–473.

Pevehouse, Jon and Russett, Bruce, 'Democratic International Governmental Organizations Promote Peace', 60 *International Organization* (2006) 969–1000.

Piper, Don C., 'Determining State Adherence to International Law', 12 *Journal of Conflict Resolution* (1968) 398–401.

Piragoff, Donald, 'Evidence' in Lee, Roy S. (ed), *The International Criminal Court – Elements of Crimes and Rules of Procedure and Evidence* (Ardsley, NY: Transnational Publishers, 2001), pp. 349–401.

Posen, Barry, 'European Union Security and Defense Policy: Response to Unipolarity?', 15 *Security Studies* (2006) 149–186.

Posner, Eric A., *The Perils of Global gelaism* (Chicago, IL: The University of Chicago Press, 2009).

Pound, Roscoe, 'Philosophical Theory and International Law', 1 *Bibliotheca Visseriana Dissertationum Ius Internationale Illustrantium* (1923) 71–90.

Pound, Roscoe, *An Introduction to the Philosophy of Law* (rev edn, New Haven, CT and London: Yale University Press, 1954).

Pound, Roscoe, *Jurisprudence* (St Paul, MN: West Publishing, 1959).

Rama-Montaldo, Manuel, 'International Legal Personality and Implied Powers of International Organizations', 44 *British Yearbook of International Law* (1970) 111–156.

Ramirez, Francisco O., Soysal, Yasemin and Shanahan, Suzanne, 'The Changing Logic of Political Citizenship: Cross-National Acquisition of Women's Suffrage Rights, 1890 to 1990', 62 *American Sociological Review* (1997) 735–745.

Rapoport, Anatol and Chammah, Albert M., *Prisoner's Dilemma: A Study in Conflict and Cooperation* (Ann Arbor, MI: University of Michigan Press, 1965).

Ratner, Steven R., 'Business' in Bodansky, Daniel, Brunnée, Jutta and Hey, Ellen (eds), *The Oxford Handbook of International Environmental Law* (Oxford: Oxford University Press, 2007), pp. 807–828.

Redgwell, Catherine, 'International Environmental Law' in Evans, Malcolm D. (ed), *International Law* (3rd edn, Oxford: Oxford University Press, 2010), pp. 657–688.

Regan, Patrick M., 'Third-party Interventions and the Duration of Intrastate Conflicts', 46 *Journal of Conflict Resolution* (2002) 55–73.

Rehbinder, Eckard, 'Obstacles to National Implementation of the Convention on Biological Diversity' in *Fågelperspektiv på rättsordningen: Vänbok till Staffan Westerlund* (Uppsala: Iustus Förlag, 2002), pp. 375–385.

Reisman, Michael W., 'Sovereignty and Human Rights in Contemporary International Law', 84 *American Journal of International Law* (1990) 866–876.

Reus-Smit, Christian, 'International Law' in Baylis, John, Smith, Steve and Owens, Patricia (eds), *The Globalization of World Politics* (5th edn, Oxford: Oxford University Press, 2011), pp. 278–292.

Risse, Thomas and Ropp, Stephen C., 'International Human Rights Norms and Domestic Change: Conclusions' in Risse, Thomas, Ropp, Stephen C. and Sikkink, Kathryn (eds), *The Power of Human Rights International Norms and Domestic Change* (Cambridge: Cambridge University Press, 1999), pp. 234–278.

Risse, Thomas and Sikkink, Kathryn, 'The Socialization of International Human Rights Norms into Domestic Practices: Introduction' in Risse, Thomas, Ropp, Stephen C. and Sikkink, Kathryn (eds), *The Power of Human Rights International Norms and Domestic Change* (Cambridge: Cambridge University Press, 1999), pp. 1–38.

Rochette, Annie, 'Transcending the Conquest of Nature and Women: A Feminist Perspective on International Environmental Law' in Buss, Doris and Manji, Ambreena (eds), *International Law: Modern Feminist Approaches* (Oxford: Hart Publishing, 2005), pp. 203–235.

Rodley, Nigel and Başak, Çali, 'Use of Force in International Law' in Başak, Çali (ed), *International Law for International Relations* (Oxford: Oxford University Press, 2010), pp. 213–233.

Rose, Andrew K., 'Do You Really Know that the WTO Increases Trade?', 94 *American Economic Review* (2004) 98–114.

Rose, Andrew K., 'Do We Really Know That the WTO Increases Trade? Reply', 97 *American Economic Review* (2007) 2019–2025.

Rost, Nicolas and Greig, J. Michael, 'Taking Matters into their Own Hands: An Analysis of the Determinants of State-Conducted Peacekeeping in Civil Wars', 48 *Journal of Peace Research* (2011) 171–184.

Rowlands, Ian H., 'Atmosphere and Outer Space' in Bodansky, Daniel, Brunnée, Jutta and Hey, Ellen (eds), *The Oxford Handbook of International Environmental Law* (Oxford: Oxford University Press, 2007), pp. 315–336.

Ruggie, John Gerard, 'The False Premise of Realism', 20 *International Security* (1995) 62–70.

Ruggie, John Gerard, *Constructing the World Policy: Essays on International Institutionalism* (London and New York, NY: Routledge, 1998).

Russett, Bruce, Oneal, John R. and Davis, David, 'The Third Leg of the Kantian Tripod for Peace: International Organizations and Militarized Disputes, 1950–85', 52 *International Organization* (1998) 441–467.

Safferling, Christoph J.M., *Towards an International Criminal Procedure* (Oxford: Oxford University Press, 2001).

Sarkees, Meredith Reid, Wayman, Frank Whelon and Singer, J. David, 'Inter-State, Intra-State, and Extra-State Wars: A Comprehensive Look at Their Distribution Over Time, 1816–1997', 47 *International Studies Quarterly* (2003) 49–70.

Sarooshi, Danesh, 'The Powers of the United Nations International Criminal Tribunals', 2 *Max Planck Yearbook of United Nations Law* (1998) 141–167.

Schabas, William A., *The International Criminal Court – A Commentary on the Rome Statute* (Oxford: Oxford University Press, 2010).

Scheinin, Martin, 'Improving Fact-Finding in Treaty-Based Human Rights Mechanisms and the Special Procedures of the United Nations Human Rights Council' in Bergsmo, Morten (ed), *Quality Control in Fact-Finding* (Florence: Torkel Opsahl Academic Epublisher, 2013), pp. 54–72.

Scheuerman, William E., 'A Theoretical Missed Opportunity? Hans J. Morgenthau as Critical Realist' in Bell, Duncan (ed), *Political Thought and International Relations: Variations on a Realist Theme* (Oxford: Oxford University Press, 2008).

Schmidt, Markus, 'United Nations' in Moeckli, Daniel, Shah, Sangeeta and Sivakumaran, Sandesh (eds), *International Human Rights Law* (Oxford: Oxford University Press, 2010), pp. 391–432.

Schmitt, Carl, *Political Theology. Four Chapters on the Concept of Sovereignty* (trans. from Politische Theologie: Vier Kapitel zur Lehre von der Souveränität (1922/1934), Cambridge, MA and London: MIT Press, 1922).

Schmitt, Carl, *The Concept of the Political* (trans. from Der Begriff der Politischen (1932), Chicago, IL and London: The University of Chicago Press, 1996).

Schwarzenberger, Georg and Brown, E.D., *A Manual of International Law* (6th edn, Milton: Professional Books, 1976).

Sellers, Patricia Viseur et al., 'Rule 89(C) and (D): At Odds or Overlapping with Rule 96 and Rule 95' in May, Richard (ed), *Essays on ICTY Procedure and Evidence: In Honour of Gabrielle Kirk McDonald* (The Hague: Kluwer Law International, 2001), pp. 275–290.

Sevastik, Per, 'Reflections on the Interpretation of the UN Charter and its Binding Force' in Svanberg-Torpman, Katinka and Amnéus, Diana (ed), *Peace and Security* (Lund: Studentlitteratur, 2004), pp. 23–51.

Shannon, Megan, 'Preventing War and Providing the Peace? International Organizations and the Management of Territorial Disputes', 26 *Conflict Management and Peace Science* (2009) 144–163.

Shannon, Megan, Morey, Daniel and Boehmke, Frederick J., 'The Influence of International Organizations on Militarized Dispute Initiation and Duration', 54 *International Studies Quarterly* (2010) 1123–1141.

Shaw, Malcolm N., *International Law* (6th edn, Cambridge: Cambridge University Press, 2008).

Shelton, Dinah, 'International Law and "Relative Normativity"' in Evans, Malcolm D. (ed), *International Law* (3rd edn, Oxford: Oxford University Press, 2010), pp. 141–171.

Shiping, Tang, 'The Security Dilemma: A Conceptual Analysis', 18 *Security Studies* (2009) 587–623.

Simmons, Beth A, 'Capacity, Commitment, and Compliance: International Institutions and Territorial Disputes', 46 *Journal of Conflict Resolution* (2002) 829–856.

Simmons, Beth A, 'From Ratification to Compliance: Quantitative Evidence on the Spiral Model' in Risse, Thomas, Ropp, Stephen C. and Sikkink, Kathryn (eds), *The Persistent Power of Human Rights: From Commitment to Compliance* (Cambridge: Cambridge University Press, 2013), pp. 43–59.

Simmons, Beth A., *Mobilizing for Human Right: International Law in Domestic Politics* (Cambridge: Cambridge University Press, 2009).

Simmons, Beth A. and Danner, Allison 'Credible Commitments and the International Criminal Court' (unpublished manuscript) (2008).

Sluiter, Göran, *International Criminal Adjudication and the Collection of Evidence: Obligations of States* (Antwerpen, Oxford and New York, NY: Intersentia, 2002).

Sluiter, Göran, 'Appearance of Witnesses and Unavailability of Subpoena Powers for the Court' in Bellelli, Roberto (ed), *International Criminal Justice* (Farnham: Ashgate, 2010), pp. 459–472.

Smits, Jan M., 'Redfining Normative Legal Science; Towards an Argumentative Discipline' in Coomans, Fons, Grünfeld, Fred and Kamminga, Menno T. (eds), *Methods of Human Rights Research* (Antwerp and Oxford: Intersentia, 2009), pp. 45–58.

Snidal, Duncan, 'The Game Theory of International Politics' in Oye, Kenneth A. (ed), *Cooperation Under Anarchy* (Princeton, NJ: Princeton University Press, 1986), pp. 25–57.

Snyder, Jack and Vinjamuri, Leslie, 'Trials and Errors: Principles and Pragmatism in Strategies of International Justice', 28 *International Security* (2003/2004) 5–44.

Song, Yann-huei and Tønnesson, Stein, 'The Impact of the Law of the Sea Convention on Conflict and Conflict Management in the South China Sea', 44 *Ocean Development & International Law* (2013) 235–269.

Spriro, Peter J., 'Non-Governmental Organization and Civil Society' in Bodansky, Daniel, Brunnée, Jutta and Hey, Ellen (eds), *The Oxford Handbook of International Environmental Law* (Oxford: Oxford University Press, 2007), pp. 770–790.

Stahn, Carsten and van den Herik, Larissa, '"Fragmentation", Diversification and "3D" Legal Pluralism: International Criminal Law as Jack-in-the Box?' in van den Herik, Larissa and Stahn, Carsten (eds), *The Diversification and Fragmentation of International Criminal Law* (Leiden and Boston, MA: Martinus Nijhoff Publishers, 2012), pp. 21–89.

Stein, Arthur A., 'Coordination and collaboration: regimes in an anarchic world' in Krasner, Stephen D. (ed), *International Regimes* (Ithaca, NY and London: Cornell University Press, 1983), pp. 115–140.

Stenhammar, Fredrik, *Riktade FN-sanktioner och rule of law i folkrätten* (Stockholm: Jure, 2008).

Strang, David and Chang, Patricia Mei Yin, 'The International Labor Organization and the Welfare State: Institutional Effects on National Welfare Spending, 1960–80', 47 *International Organization* (1993) 235–262.

Tallberg, Jonas, *Making States Comply* (Lund: Studentlitteratur, 1999).

Tallberg, Jonas and McCall Smith, James, 'Dispute Settlement in World Politics: States, Supranational Prosecutors, and Compliance' *European Journal of International Relations* (2012) 1–27.

Teorell, Jan and Svensson, Torsten, *Att fråga och att svara* (Malmö: Liber, 2007).

Thirlway, Hugo, *The Sources of International Law* (Oxford: Oxford University Press, 2014).

Thomas, George M. and Lauderdale, Pat, 'State Authority and National Welfare Programs in the World System Context', 3 *Sociological Forum* (1988) 383–399.

Thompson, Alexander, 'Applying Rational Choice Theory to International Law: The Promise and Pitfalls', 31 *Journal of Legal Studies* (2002) 285–306.

Tickner, Ann L., 'What is Your Research Program? Some Feminist Answers to International Relations Methodological Questions', 49 *International Studies Quarterly* (2005) 1–21.

Tomz, Michael, Goldstein, Judith L. and Rivers, Douglas, 'Do We Really Know That the WTO Increases Trade? Comment', 97 *American Economic Review* (2007) 2005–2018.

Ullman, Richard H., 'Redefining Security', 8 *International Security* (1983) 129–153.

Valentino, Benjamin, Huth, Paul and Croco, Sarah, 'Covenants without the Sword: International Law and the Protection of Civilians in Times of War', 58 *World Politics* (2006) 339–377.

Walt, Stephen M., *The Origins of Alliances* (Ithaca, NY: Cornell University Press, 1987).

Walter, Barbara F., *Committing to peace: the successful settlement of civil wars* (Princeton, NJ: Princeton University Press, 2002).

Waltz, Kenneth N., *Theory of International Politics* (Reading: Addison-Wesley, 1979).

van den Bossche, Peter, *The Law and Policy of the World Trade Organization* (2nd edn, Cambridge: Cambridge University Press, 2008).

van den Bossche, Peter, 'NGO Involvement in the WTO: A Comparative Perspective', 11 *Journal of International Economic Law* (2008) 717–749.

van Evera, Stephen, *Guide to Methods for Students of Political Science* (Ithaca, NY: Cornell University Press, 1997).

Wartanian, Annie, 'The ICC Prosecutor's Battlefield: Combating Atrocities while Fighting for States' Cooperation: Lessons from the U.N. Tribunals Applied to the Case of Uganda', 36 *Georgetown Journal of International Law* (2005) 1289–1316.

Vasiliev, Sergey, 'General Rules and Principles of International Criminal Procedure: Definition, Legal Nature, and Identification' in Sluiter, Göran and Vasiliev, Sergey (eds), *International Criminal Procedure Towards a Coherent Body of Law* (London: Cameron May, 2009), pp. 19–91.

Vasquez, John A., *The War Puzzle* (Cambridge: Cambridge University Press, 1993).

Weil, Prosper, 'Towards Relative Normativity in International Law', 77 *American Journal of International Law* (1983) 413–442.

Wendt, Alexander, 'Anarchy is what States Make of it: The Social Construction of Power Politics', 46 *International Organization* (1992) 391–425.

Wendt, Alexander, 'Constructing International Politics', 20 *International Security* (1995) 71–81.

Werner, Suzann and Yuen, Amy, 'Making and Keeping Peace', 59 *International Organization* (2005) 261–292.

Viljoen, Frans and Abebe, Adem Kassie, 'Amicus Curiae Participation Before Regional Human Rights Bodies in Africa', 58 *Journal of African Law* (2014) 22–44.

Wilkenfeld, Jonathan, *Mediating International Crises* (New York, NY: Routledge, 2005).

Willetts, Peter, 'Transnational Actors and International Organizations in Global Politics' in Baylis, John, Smith, Steve and Owens, Patricia (eds), *The Globalization of World Politics* (5th edn, Oxford: Oxford University Press, 2011), pp. 326–342.

Wilmshurst, Elizabeth, 'Jurisdiction of the Court' in Lee, Roy S. (ed), *The International Criminal Court: the Making of the Rome Statute: Issues, Negotiations and Results* (The Hague: Kluwer Law International, 1999), pp. 127–141.

Wrange, Pål, *Impartial or Uninvolved? The Anatomy of 20th Century Doctrine on the Law of Neutrality* (Visby: Elanders, 2007).

Wrange, Pål, *Aggressionsbrottet och Internationella brottmålsdomstolen* (Stockholm: Totalförsvarets folkrättsråd, Försvarsdepartementet, 2011).

Young, Margaret A., 'Introduction: the Productive Friction between Regimes' in Young, Margaret A. (ed), *Regime Interaction in International Law Facing Fragmentation* (Cambridge: Cambridge University Press, 2012), pp. 1–19.

Young, Margaret A., 'Regime Interaction in Creating, Implementing and Enforcing International Law' in Young, Margaret A. (ed), *Regime Interaction in International Law Facing Fragmentation* (Cambridge: Cambridge University Press, 2012), pp. 85–110.

Young, Oran R. and Levy, Marc A., 'The Effectiveness of International Environmental Regimes' in Young, O.R. (ed), *The Effectiveness of International Environmental Regimes: Causal Connections and Behavioural Mechanisms* (Cambridge, MA: MIT Press, 1999), pp. 1–32.

Zagare, Frank C., 'Game Theory' in Williams, Paul D. (ed), *Security Studies – An Introduction* (2nd edn, London and New York, NY: Routledge, 2013), pp. 45–62.

Zamora, Stephen, 'Is There Customary International Economical Law?', 32 *German Yearbook of International Law* (1989) 9–42.

Zimbardo, Philip G and Leippe, Michael, *The Psychology of Attitude Change and Social Influence* (New York, NY: McGraw-Hill, 1991).

Zweigert, Konrad and Kötz, Hein, *Introduction to Comparative Law* (2nd edn, Oxford: Clarendon Press, 1987).

Åhman, Joachim, *Trade Liberalisation, Health Protection, and the Burden of Proof in WTO Law* (Göteborg: Handelshögskolan vid Göteborgs universitet, 2011).

Index

For Product Safety Concerns and Information please contact our EU representative GPSR@taylorandfrancis.com
Taylor & Francis Verlag GmbH, Kaufingerstraße 24, 80331 München, Germany

www.ingramcontent.com/pod-product-compliance
Ingram Content Group UK Ltd.
Pitfield, Milton Keynes, MK11 3LW, UK
UKHW021720240926
475702UK00029BA/1668
9781138701953